Recent Commonwealth Literature

Eds.
R.K. Dhawan
P. V. Dhamija
A.K. Shrivastava

PRESTIGE

PRESTIGE BOOKS
3/28, EAST PATEL NAGAR
NEW DELHI 110 008

Published by
PRESTIGE BOOKS
3/28, East Patel Nagar, New Delhi 110 008
in association with
Indian Society for Commonwealth Studies
New Delhi

P[illegible]
1989
ISBN 81-85218-09-9
ISBN 81-85218-10-2

Phototypesetting by
data culture
C-15, Amar Colony, Lajpat Nagar IV
New Delhi 110 065

Printed by
Nirman Press
Delhi 110 006

To

Professor C.D. Narasimhaiah

for his excellent work at Dhvanyaloka

Volume I

Contents

Volume I

Contents

Volume II

Contributors

R.G. AGARWAL, Jalna

MULK RAJ ANAND, eminent Indian English novelist

NEENA ARORA, H.P. University, Shimla

SARALA BARNABAS, Ahmednagar

K. CHELLAPPAN, Bharathidasan University, Tiruchi

N. RAMA DEVI, Anantapur

P.V. DHAMIJA, CIEFL, Hyderabad

R.K. DHAWAN, University of Delhi

RADHAMANI GOPALAKRISHNAN, S.V. University

SANGEETA GUPTA, University of Delhi

SHALINI GUPTA, University of Delhi

M.G. HEGDE, Karnataka University

A.D. HOPE, eminent Australian poet

JASBIR JAIN, University of Rajasthan

DAVID KERR, Australia

G.D. KILLAM, University of Guelph, Canada

VINEY KIRPAL, I.I.T., Bombay

VRINDA NABAR, Bombay University

S. PREMA NANDAKUMAR, Tamilnadu

LAL UDAI BHAN PANDEY, Sultanpur

Z.N. PATIL, University of Poona

JOHN OLIVER PERRY, Tufts University

ARTHUR POLLARD, University of Buckingham, U.K.

N.S. PRADHAN, University of Delhi

N. PRATIMA, Andhra University

JAGDISH RAI, University of Delhi

ALUR JANAKI RAM, University of Rajasthan

RATNA RAMAN, University of Delhi

S. RAMASWAMY, Bangalore University

PANDURANGA RAO, Udgir

ARTHUR RAVENSCROFT, University of Leeds

P. BAYAPA REDDY, S.K. University

SURESH C. SAXENA, Rewari

SUSHILA SINGH, B.H.U., Varanasi

A.K. SHRIVASTAVA, Lucknow University

SHASHI TALWAR, University of Delhi

SHRIKANT R. TAMBE, Aurangabad

S.K. TIKOO, Manipur University

K. VENKATACHARI, A.P. Open University

C. VIJAYASREE, Osmania University

WILLIAM WALSH, U.K.

Commonwealth Literatures

R.K. DHAWAN, P.V.DHAMIJA, A.K.SHRIVASTAVA

The term 'Commonwealth' has a long history. It was first used by Oliver Cromwell, after establishing the Republican government in England, in 1649. Literally it implied common good or public good; a body-politic in which power rests with the people. It came into disuse as a form of government for nearly three hundred years, till it was resurrected in the Statute of Westminster 1931, when with the creation of the Dominions, the British Empire was re-christened as the British Commonwealth of Nations.

Though Commonwealth concept came into practice in the mid-twentieth century, there are various factors that were responsible for its growth in the nineteenth century. The concept began to evolve in the aftermath of the American War of Independence which had convinced the British statesmen that they should formulate a new approach towards the emerging nationalism in the colonies which were destined to become independent states in due course. In order to forestall a violent break-up of the Empire, in the pattern of what happened to its thirteen colonies in America, Britain thought it imperative to follow a path of concessions and reforms, and develop self-governing institutions in the colonies. The Durham Report of 1839 was a concrete expression of this new approach; it envisaged that the colonies could govern themselves, and yet remain colonies. The colonies could be self-governing in all respects but external affairs. As a natural corollary to this development, Canada, Australia, New Zealand and South Africa attained the self-governing status in 1867, 1900, 1907 and 1909 respectively. These four self-governing colonies, together with Britain, formed the founder members of the Commonwealth.

The distinctive feature of this new grouping was that they all were colonies of settlement, with close ethnic connections with Britain and had adopted the British pattern of political institutions.

However, the Balfour Declaration of 1926 had concretized the Commonwealth concept further and made it the group of self-governing communities composed of Great Britain and Dominions. This institutional framework remained unchanged until independence was granted to India in 1947 and until India decided to stay in the Commonwealth after becoming a Republic in 1950. With the entry of India, the modern Commonwealth acquired a new complexion and character and demonstrated its potential for evolution and growth. The association became multi-racial; and it was declared as a free association of independent nations where equality of status was fully recognized. The Commonwealth is the British Empire in reverse. It is the flowering of independent entities out of the bondage of colonial dependency.

Ideas, beliefs, notions, prejudices, presuppositions mould man's social behaviour. Sometimes nations of vast differences in flora and fauna, and in climate have shown amazing similarity in outlook, temperament or attitude. Though rich in diversity, in the sense that it is composed of black, brown and white, rich and poor, democracies and dictatorships, aligned and non-aligned, the great similarities among the Commonwealth countries overwhelm the diversity in the association. These similarities encompass their similar background, working methods, and institutional traditions in several important traditions in several important fields of operation, and the use of English language. The homogeneity of British cultural dominance in the Empire gave way to an English-speaking national culture. The characteristics, problems, themes and context of each literature has an applicability to the writing of other nations. Beginning with the dissolution of the British Empire, the emergence of Commonwealth Literature is primarily a twentieth century phenomenon. The growth of literatures in English began at almost the same time, followed similar courses of evolution and reflected somewhat similar human experience.

Significantly, English language represents a significant point of convergence in the multi-racial, multi-cultural, multi-regional Commonwealth. In terms of historical impact, the English language is perhaps the most useful legacy left over by the British Empire. It is a matter of gratification that the language of the rulers never dies with the rulers. It lives a new life in the life of the erstwhile ruled, by becoming part of their free existence. This has been true of Greek and Latin in the ancient West, Arabic and Persian in the medieval East, and now of English and French in the modern world. English has been a powerful vehicle of protest in the past and has become the most important medium of communication in the international spheres. Its terminology, its concepts have greatly enriched the languages of the people in Commonwealth countries. The English-speaking world has now come to realise that English literature is a creative endeavour of many countries and cultures including some of the older civilisations of Asia and Africa and newly-formed nations such as Australia, New Zealand and Canada.

In Australia, New Zealand and Canada on one hand, and in Asia, Africa and the West Indies on the other, the English language--whether as an inherited or an acquired language--has been employed as the medium of creative expression in diverse cultural contexts, thereby achieving a texture and resonance not usually found in the purely Anglo-Saxon idiom and usage. While writing in English, the Indians, the Africans and the West Indians are writing in the language of the colonizer, in a language that in a number of ways carries with it a distinctly English culture and ethos.

Literary works coming from bilingual cultures demonstrate how the tension or interaction between different language systems can be utilized for narrative, dramatic, analytical ends. The appearance of fiction as a literary form following Western models is in itself a cross-cultural phenomenon. It is the emergence of a new genre of writing resulting from the meeting of two cultures. A literary genre that belongs to a particular culture is often the form in which the values of that culture find expression. Hence we witness, in the culture contact, two sets of values coming into conflict with each other, each struggling for supremacy over the other. The genre introduced from outside has to adapt itself to the new milieu, and in so doing, it undergoes some change both in form as well as in content. Chinua Achebe, Wole Soyinka, George Lamming and V.S. Naipaul, for instance, reinforce their stylistic resources by drawing upon the native speech.

New experiments in form and technique also come more readily to the writers from the developing cultures, since they are open to free forms, to new amalgamations of experience and expression. A newness comes from the re-discovery of the old, from the shocks of recognition that reveal the amazing modernity of the residual traditions. Patrick White, Wilson Harris and Raja Rao achieve this kind of intensity and power in their writing. V.S. Naipaul has shown how one can be new remaining sternly old, pressing the old into the service of the new both in form and style.

Commonwealth Literature thus refers to the literature, or literatures, written in English in the Commonwealth countries. The name has now come to stay, and Commonwealth Literature forms part of the graduate curricula in several universities in the Commonwealth countries. The emphasis in such courses is generally on the common denominator of the literatures written in these countries. There is, of course, a measure of similarity in the broad outlines of the literatures written in English in these countries, and it may be attributed largely to a similar colonial experience and a similar impulse on the part of these countries to engage vigorously in post-colonial reorganization and reconstruction. But, the crucial reason for this similarity is not so much the common political experience and common social aspirations as the common language in which these literatures are written, namely, English. English could thus be taken, in a way, as the raison d'etre of the term 'Commonwealth Literature,' which therefore includes the literatures written only in English in these countries, and excludes the literatures written in their native languages even though these latter literatures may quite often be much richer and much more authentic than the literatures in English.

This being the case, one can understand some critics's special interest in the manner English is exploited in Commonwealth Literature and in investigating the extent to which the literature in any one of these countries differs from that written in any other chiefly on account of a different use of English

Commonwealth Literature can be usefully studied under two different categories: (1) the literature written in those Commonwealth countries where English is practically a native language, for example, in Australia, New Zealand, and Canada; (2) the literature written in those countries where English is used as a second language (or even as a foreign language), for example, in India, Commonwealth countries in Africa (Kenya, Nigeria,

Tanzania, Uganda, Zambia, Zimbabwe), the West Indies, Sri Lanka, and Bangla Desh.

The use of English in literature written in the first group of countries is radically different from that in the second group. Language is an inseparable part of its matrix culture, and English likewise is an inseparable part of the British culture. In a similar cultural ambience, the use of English in creative writing will not be very different in general terms, of course, apart from certain individual and idiosyncratic variations. But in an entirely different cultural setting, for instance, in India, Sri Lanka, Philippines, or Africa, the use of English cannot but be widely different. Whatever cultural assumptions already inhere in its denotative and connotative repertoire, it should now be under great pressure to orient itself to new tasks and challenges. It must expand its expressive mechanisms to the utmost to conceptualize, to analogize, and to mythologize experience in an entirely new way.

This is precisely what English has done in the countries in the second group. Its *essential* grammatical structure remains intact, and so does its *essential* semantic structure. But beyond this point, it appears to be a 'new' language. The same words now carry new meanings and new concepts; in a new cultural environment, the same English words are referential in a different way in that they refer to new items of human experience and new categories of an 'alien' culture; the same words have expanded, and are expanding, to express ideas and feelings which they have never done before. The grammatical structure also has been progressively under tension. The structures and rhythms of the native languages have influenced English in a substantial way. As English took on the new role of expressing alien experience, it borrowed from the native languages certain morphological and syntactic elements, and also certain rhythmic structures. A new native urgency, a new response to a new experience, a new perception of reality could not have been expressed in the traditional English (or American) way. A different national sensibility needed a different idiom for expression. Raja Rao's *Kanthapura* (1938) is, for instance, a specifically Indian experience, and the idiom used to convey it is anything but the traditional English idiom. R.K. Narayan's use of English is beautifully and adequately adapted to communicate a characteristically Indian sensibility. Chinua Achebe's *Arrow of God* (1964) has created an absolutely African world and found the right idiom--very diferent from any other English idiom--to do so. The Nobel Laureate Wole Soyinka's treatment of the theme of time in his plays, especially in his *Dance of the Forests* (1965), is one of the best examples of the creation of a suitable new idiom to serve a new theme. The language is successfully modulated to serve the exigencies of the mood and the moment. At one end of the scale, there is a pidginized English to capture the raucous simplicity of West African life; at the other end, there is a sophisticated rhetoric to communicate the convoluted complexity of this life.

Just one example from West Indian literature may show how English is 'stretched' to subserve the local needs. Victor S. Reid's *New Day* (1949) is built on the reminiscences of an old man. Its language, composed from a number of dialects, gives the impression of an artificially constructed medium, but it unmistakably testifies to the amazing potential of the English developed in the West Indies to cope with the intransigence of new themes and environments.

The essays that form part of this collection are representative in two ways. First, they represent critical evaluations of the different genres of literature written in the Commonwealth; secondly, they represent critical commentaries written in as many different countries as possible. They have been both selected and arranged from this point of view.

Is There a Shared Tradition in Commonwealth Literature ?
Variety of Ways

MULK RAJ ANAND

If autobiographical reminiscence be forgiven, may I tell you of the small beginnings from which Commonwealth literature has grown.

Already in the twenties some of the British intellectuals and creative men and women had accepted the young hopefuls among the writers from the colonies as equals without patronage.

Apart from the respect paid to the doyen Tagore, the Bloomsbury group, specially Leonard Woolf, Lawrence Binyon, E.M.Forster, T.S. Eliot, Arthur Waley (and his wife Beryl de Zoete) and the Stracheys sponsored young authors from India, Ceylon, Africa and the Caribbean. In Soho Nancy Cunard sang the praises of the American Negro poets. And soon Paul Robeson was to be the rage of London, when Maurice Browne presented him in the role of *Othello*.

In the thirties Bonamy Dobree became Professor of English literature at Leeds University. And, by sheer coincidence some Indian, Australian and African students began to hear his lectures and a few researched under him. Not only was he a teacher with a style, but he was casual, unbuttoned and hospitable, in the manner of the Egyptians with whom he had spent long winters in Cairo and Alexandria.

It was not strange, therefore, that, later, Professor Norman Jaeffers should have taken the initiative to urge the formation of the Commonwealth Association of Writers. The minds and hearts opened by Bonamy Dobree were to accept the once suppressed voices, of even those who had launched out on unknown seas.

Luckily, F.R.. Leavis had been offering friendship to students from the colonies in Cambridge. As he had championed the cause of 'bottom dogs' like D.H. Lawrence, so he took up the fight on behalf of the 'untouchables' of the Empire. (I shall never forget the way he boosted my own low morale after several rejections of my first novel, by saying: 'Anand, you wait--truth will win through ! I have written to Edgell Rickward to welcome a new rebel !)

And the coincidence of the world-wide thirties movement, sponsored by the liberals, radicals, and communists, against Fascism, brought pioneers like Gorky, Gide, Malraux, John Strachey, C. Day Lewis, Stephen Spender, Ernest Toller, Hemingway, Dos Passos and many other western intellectuals on the same platform of life against death, as Paul Robeson, Mulk Raj Anand, Peter Abrahams, Lengston Hughes, Pablo Neruda and Shelley Wang.

The defence of the Spanish Republic against the dictators rallied the advance guard intelligentsia of the whole world.

And the gruelling years of the second world war united, under the leadership of George Orwell, in the *Voice* magazine of B.B.C., men and women of letters like E.M. Forster, T.S. Eliot, Herbert Read, Strom Jameson, Naomi Mitchinson, Mulk Raj Anand, Stephen Spender, Dylan Thomas, Narayana Menon, Louis Macniece, Arthur Koestler, J.B.S. Haldane, Balraj Sahni and Zulfikar Bukhari.

I have referred to the friendships, in spite of the differences of opinion, of the various pre-war writers, as I wished to emphasise the fact that the western intelligentsia had accepted the concept of a variety of ways of life and expression, in the spirit of the 'Atlantic Charter,' in spite of the snobs. The stresses of the common struggle for decencies against world reaction, through the prolonged seven year bloodbath, brought even the most whimsical individualists together.

And, with the coming of the political freedom for almost all the colonies of the various empires (the chain effect having been started by Gandhian India), the acceptance of a more congenial, egalitarian and mutually helpful attitude for pooling the resources of the commonwealth, has become a happy augury for the future growth of solidarities.

The thing which unites us is the English language, which will come to be recognised as the one positive residuum of the erstwhile British Empire, as a link language among vast people.

Curiously, however, the English language which we Indians inherited from the British-Indian universities, has changed in the hands of our creative writers and become Indian-English.

Only a very few of the new generation of writers use what is called the 'Queen's English,' whatever that may mean in the polyglot that is current in the United Kingdom. Like the Irish, the Scotch, the Welsh, the Americans, the Australians, the Newzealanders, the West Indians, the Nigerians, the Kenyans, the Ugandans, the new young of India often seem to echo either the intonation, or the rhythm or the atmosphere of the mother-tongue. Specially is this so, in the writing of fiction, where dialogue is involved. Almost all Indian writers in English have given up the 'thee' and 'thou' used as a convention by the British writers about India.

And it is no longer possible for even the most blatant denigrators of Indian-English writings, to dub the style as 'Babu English.' The truth is that most Indian writers in English have a fair command of English grammar and know what is cliche and what is clap-trap in the English language, as it is being written in various countries, where English is the mother-tongue.

Consciously or unconsciously, they have also seized on the fact, that the 19th and 20th century narrative prose of English and American literatures, has changed from the twelve to seventeen word sentence to a seven to eleven word sentence. And many new words from all parts of the world have entered the 'Queen's English.'

The Indian-English writers (and this may be true of most of the Commonwealth writers), have thus found themselves giving up the old closed *literary* language of the coteries of London and New York. They have, sometimes deliberately, and often from the need to reproduce local characters, introduced vibrations, sounds, and words from their mother-tongues, as also sometimes coined synthetic words, to introduce new metaphors and imagery into the Commonwealth literature.

This phenomena has sometimes disturbed the literati of the cosmopolises. Also, the 'little critics,' in the pockets of reaction with the ex-colonies (now free countries), have been throwing jibes at the various new expressions of our talents for seeking to express themselves in free, expressionist, vital words, even if they should seem odd to the ears of the remaining 'Brown Sahibs.'

The fact that the African, Australian and Caribbean writers in English have also been writing in a spontaneously mixed speech, or in the peculiarly expressive English dialect of their own peoples, in their novels and short stories, adds force to my argument that 'Pigeon-Indian' (by which I mean the Indian-English which coos messages of love) is the right name to use for the new Indian-English rather then 'Pidgin-English.'

All the emergent styles of the different Commonwealth countries reinforce Professor Dobree's hunch that there are a 'variety of ways' in life as in literature.

I suggest that we make 'variety of ways' a motto of our organization.

It is too early, to say, at this juncture, which writers, of what country, will succeed in creating more authentic expressions of the genius of their people, of their joys and pains and of their imperceptible feelings.

Some of us feel that it is necessary to keep an open mind and allow the flood of creative expression to fertilise the consciousness of these vast peoples, who could not enter literature during the prolonged era of one-man rule. Criticism can, at best, only interpret an emergent style: it should not be used to inhibit innovation, experiment and genuine utterance.

I would like to recall here the way in which Irish-English came into being under the patronage of W.B. Yeats, A.E. (George Russell) and Lady Gregory, through the recognition of the brave initiatives of the pioneer Irish writers like William Allingham, Samuel Ferguson, Maria Edgeworth, Charles Lever, Standish O'Grady, Douglas Hyde, Synge, Sean O'Casey, Frank O'Connor, Paeder O'Denniel, Elizabeth Bowen, Francis Stuart and others.

At the end of the 19th century Yeats and his colleagues realised that, before them Irish writers had not dared to bring in their native genius, as well as their inheritance of old Gaelic myths, but had approximated to the English heroic ideals, influenced by the Graeco-Roman tradition.

This had made their verse into 'literary poetry' and their prose into the prolonged cadences of Richardson and Smollett and the architectonics of Thomas Hardy. The Irish exuberance, which was to come into the new novels and stories from the love of the folk, and Ireland itself, arose from the deliberate introduction of the folk dialectic particularly by Synge, Lady Gregory and Sean O'Casey.

This style of Irish-English, which Lady Gregory humorously called 'Kiltartan' (as I call Indian-English 'pigeon-Indian'), was defined by Yeats in the following words:

> The Anglo-Irish idiom is a form of English, modified by Gaelic habits of thought, speech, imagery and syntax: the words and meanings are English, but the word corresponds to the word order of Gaelic. [1]

Later on he insisted:

> The English idiom of the Irish speaking people of the west, is the only good English, spoken by any large numbered Irish people today. And we must, found good literature on a living speech ! [2]

The admiration which Yeats had for Synge, particularly, was the renunciation literariness of its hollow images and for treating of characters, like the fisherfolk of the west coast, in all their heroism against the sea, face to face with their poverty, their sense of humour, their passion for life, against all the odds.

In fact the naked truth came into Irish-English writing. All the embroidery and decorativeness was discarded. The later writers even dissolved the 'Celtic Twilight,' taking from it only the emotions, moods and physical realities of Irish legends into their humanist framework, uplifted their works into the world of imagination. In turning to life, away from sentimental sadness of 'the country of shadows' and upturning the earth of fresh fields, they gathered harvest in every season.

All the writers of the Commonwealth countries, I feel, will find themselves in similar situations.

They are bound to recreate the authentic lilts of speech of their peoples. They will find themselves confronting the realities of the fundamental situations of their own landscapes. They will realise that no language is inheritantly more poetical than another. And they will realise that if they resort more to the rhythms of their own ballads, they will be far more allied to the consciousnesses of their own people. The distinctive idiom of their characters, when transcreated into English, will bring new metaphors and imagery into their writings.

And it is these fresh flavours exuding from the expression of the new hearts, the new minds and the different imaginations, which the world is looking for, beyond the classics in the changing situations of the contemporary world. This does not mean that we have to accept from the late Henry Ford, the dictum that 'history is bunk !' No. We will still read Palgrave's *Golden Treasury*. The students will open the old books in the libraries. But we may want to adventure out on our different quests, in our journeys to the interior as well as the open spaces of our lands, with light hearts and as little luggage as possible.

We have to go and meet millions of those peoples in our countries, who have come newly from one man rule into the pool of the world democracy. We have to recognise the human dignity of each of these individuals. We have to concern ourselves with the well being of each one of them. And we have to help bring them into the first and last freedoms.

Thus we have to worship the new consciousnesses of our people as part of our love of man himself--urged by the exigencies of a tragic age, where we all stand on crossroads of possible death through the enormous armaments piled up and of abounding life in co-existence. Our beloved friend, leader and guide, Jawaharlal Nehru, often reminded us that it is co-existence or co-death.

May I add to this magic word co-existence--co-discovery.

This will involve exchange, and mutual aid as well as solidarity or friendship.

I consider literature as a means of communication which connects, and this connection is the extension of love. Because it is not possible anymore to be an island, on one's own, in this world.

Paradoxically, the same forces which divide the world today through rigid frontiers, have united the world, even against their will, by faster means of communication.

And we are already ushered, on several planes, into a one world culture.

This means that we are likely to meet each other, to visit different countries frequently. And we will have to find out the inner patterns of the lives of our brethren, to appreciate the variety of ways of life, and to taste different cultures,. Indeed, we have to pursue co-discovery.

I suggest that the English language which connects us has already become one of the most important mediums of co-existence and co-discovery. Our books are in the libraries of different universities of the world.

And currently, we are unconsciously in the process of 'connect.'

I think writing arises from the deepest urges for communication.

And communication ends our loneliness and fosters friendship, intimacy, and brings love.

If someone asks me why I have written so many books, I find myself answering that: I love.

NOTES

1. *Synge and the Irish Drama*, p. 38
2. *Plays and Controversies*, p. 28

Standard English: Whose Standard

A.D. HOPE

It was C.D. Narasimhaiah, in an essay 'Indian Writing in English,' who first drew my attention to the nature of Indian English and to its growing extent and importance, but it was only during my first visit to India in 1977 that I realised the wide use and variety of English in that country, and that it is not only a literary language but a vernacular which has really taken root there with an idiom and accent that is peculiarly its own. It was so much taken for granted that I met no overt discussion of the subject. But in a subsequent visit to Pakistan, on the occasion of my talking to a group of postgraduate students and teachers of English in Lahore, the question of the status of the local brand of English was raised. It was raised, I thought, rather defensively becuase I had frequently to ask my questioners to repeat what they had said and they took this to be a reflection on their pronunciation. After I had explained that it was largely due to my deafness, I expressed some surprise that there should be a feeling that Pakistani English should have any lower status than the so-called Standard English.

In my own country, Australia,' I said, 'we have developed our own pronunciation of English, our own recognisable idiom and vocabulary and even some syntax peculiar to ourselves. For over a hundred years this Australian English was despised as an inferior, uneducated form of the language. This was in part due to the colonial status of Australia in the first hundred years. The English attitude to us was very similar to that towards the population of the British Raj in this country: the attitude of the rulers towards the ruled. India, at least had a great literature and an ancient civilisation. It was secure in having a number of languages in its own right. But the language of the Australians, like their civilisation, was simply a derivative and therefore an inferior form of the English exemplar. Now Australia stands socially and politically on its own feet and we hear little criticism of its form of English. In fact that form of English is now the subject of scholarly interest, recording and exploration and there are at least two respectable dictionaries of Australian English in course of production. Anyone in Pakistan,' I concluded, 'who does not regard his country's brand of English as an asset, something to be treasured, studied and promoted, is labouring under an ancient delusion: the delusion that what was labelled *Standard English* at the end of the nineteenth century, has prior rights, top status and indisputable authority among the various forms of English now current in the world.'

I don't know how much my listeners took in of my brand of pronunciation of English, but after this we seemed to get on a much easier footing.

Although my early training was in the field of comparative philology, it was still in an era in which another form of the standard Language still cast a shadow over language studies, the form in which the classical tongues of Rome and Greece were assumed to be superior to and a model for assessment of others. And, because of the prestige of classical civilisations, the states of those languages were themselves supposed to be a *floreat* from a more primitive era from which they later declined. A kind of almost unconscious scholarly snobbery helped to promote and prolong this attitude of mind which had nothing to do with scientific theories of language. For science a language is a language, neither better nor worse than any other and all dialects of a language have equal status as forms of the language, no matter what their social or political standing may be.

There are of course aesthetic considerations, but these are always apt to be confused with what is socially accepted. To my mind the most beautiful form of English spoken today is that employed in Jamaica and with some differences in the Barbados. The most repulsive sub-dialect I recall is the so-called Oxford Accent of forty years ago, the high, rather consciously sneering quack-quack of the twenties and thirties and both popularised and parodied by stage and film. But these are personal prejudices. Value judgements about language are limited to questions of efficiency of structure and this is a murky subject since the only real test of relative efficiency is what native speakers can contrive to do with their own language.

In the period in which I grew up, I took it for granted, Australian though I was, that what was called Standard English was the standard against which all other forms of the language must be compared and judged. Shakespeare was an Englishman. It never occurred to me that, coming from Stratford, Shakespeare probably spoke an English dialect. At the period I write of, English dialects were studied for their historical interest but the English educational system systematically discouraged them in favour of the ruling Standard, which at that time really meant an artificial dialect favoured by the B.B.C. King George the Fifth, to his credit, talked to the nation and the empire in ordinary London English without a trace of the fashionable quack-quack.

I do not mean to indulge in what is perhaps the most unrewarding form of controversy, but to draw attention to the fact that we live today in a new world in which such controversy is out-of-date and irrelevant in view of the actual situation.

That actual situation is that English is now the main language, or an important alternative language, of about forty countries and of more than four hundred million people. It is bound to be different in those different regions, each with its own culture, and literary and social background. Each establishes its own right to be language *sui generis*. Technically speaking, each is a 'dialect' of English but there is no longer a norm against which they can be appraised. In the last half century the language of educated people in the south of England (Standard English) has lost its commanding position; it is now no more than one of the accepted forms or 'dialects' of English and it is 'accepted' only for its own region. Even there it has lost much of its prestige. Scottish, Welsh, and Irish English have finally established their long-standing claim to independent status as valid forms of educated and literary English. When I was a student in England fifty years ago it was unthinkable that one should hear announcers on the B.B.C. speaking with regional accents. Now it is a commonplace.

The revolution was due for the most part to the success of American English in establishing recognition as a form of English in its own right, though in the nineteenth and early twentieth centuries English writers and public alike tended to treat it as an inferior and debased variant of their accepted standard. The collapse of the claims of Standard was probably hastened by the fact that it was the dialect of a class rather than of a region or a people. But in any case, once educated American was recognised throughout the world, the way was open for educated Canadian, Australian, New Zealand, South African, Indian, Sri Lankan, Pakistani and other forms of English to establish the same claim and in due course for the whole regional or rational form of the language to be accepted as a single entity 'educated' or not.

Does this mean, as some have taken it to mean, that English, like Latin in the early middle ages, has reached a point where it is beginning to break up into a number of separate languages, just as Latin gave way to Italian, French, Provencal, Catalan, Spanish, and Roumanian ? This is a possibility if the different regions where English is spoken should ever become isolated from one another. But as things are it seems improbable; general education and literacy, improved and rapid world-wide means of communication and the fact that English is one of the great international commercial languages, seem to ensure its cohesion. Whatever differences of pronunciation and colloquial idiom its various forms may show, the written language is still perfectly viable and will probably continue to be a strong binding force between the various regional or national groups that use it. On the other hand we may look for a great enrichment of literature when so many cultures sue a common language each form of which is coloured and instinct with its particular setting. The great writers of each country will be available to all as they are today.

One question of course must inevitably arise: should we not find a new name for a language which no longer belongs to England any more than to Scotland or India or Australia or the United States ? The name itself is perhaps the last operative link with the now defunct notion of Standard English.

Third-World Literature: Purpose or Indulgence ?

ARTHUR RAVENSCROFT

Most scholars and critics working in the area designated 'Commonwealth Literature' have arrived there from initial training and practice in 'English Literature.' I certainly have. It has seemed a very natural extension of one's professional journeying, for, after all, one is still working with literature in the English language or regional variants of it. No doubt the original navigational equipment is still pretty serviceable when used in exploring Australian, Canadian, New Zealand, and some South African writing in English, if augmented with such additional historical and cultural instruments as are necessary for those areas. Nevertheless, with every allowance made for local terrain, there remains a certain, quite comfortable, sense in which writers of these countries show an awareness of belonging to 'western,' North Atlantic literary traditions, or at least adapting these traditions, even when they most vigorously assert their unbelongingness. Though in different ways and to different degrees, the gamut of British and American literary traditions (both of primary creation and of criticism) is 'European' in the sense that at the heart of all of them is accorded a profound, post-Renaissance, and often post-Reformation, respect for the centrality of individuality in artistic and intellectual discourse.

An eminent twentieth-century North Atlantic poet and critic could see English literature as an organic part of European literature, 'the several members of which cannot flourish if the same blood-stream (Latin and Greek) does not circulate throughout the whole body.'[1] To observe that Eliot made this critical pronouncement while much physical as distinct from metaphorical blood was flowing throughout Europe, is not to deny the importance of such long-sighted avowals being uttered when the material circumstances of the moment seem inauspicious. Nevertheless, it was an ironical enactment of the 'still point of the turning world,' and it does point to the kind of questioning I hope to raise in this paper. The literatures of those Commonwealth countries that can conveniently be regarded as belonging to the Third World are either very much concerned with 'the turning world,' as in Africa and the Caribbean, or look back to great cultural phenomena unrelated to Europe's Renaissance, as in India--despite Raja Rao's interest in the Albigensian heresy in *The Serpent and the Rope*. The really interesting literature in English of India begins with Mulk Raj Anand's *Untouchable* and R.K. Narayan's *Swami and Friends* in 1935, of Black Africa with Sol Plaatje's *Muhdi* in 1930 and Amos Tutuola's *The Palm-Wine Drinkard* in 1952, of the Caribbean with Claude McKay's *Home to Harlem* in 1928, or alternatively with C.L.R. James's *Minty Alley* in 1936. There were earlier writings in verse and prose, but these titles are markers of the rising tide which proclaim that the Third-world Commonwealth literatures truly begin in the second quarter of the twentieth century, at least a decade after the end of the first of Europe's two holocausts. The high moral sentences that accompanied Allied gunfire in both of Europe's wars were taken seriously by the subject peoples of Europe's overseas empires, as was much of the political creed that toppled the Tzar of all the Russians.

It would be futile to pretend that most of the writings that constitute the Third-world literatures in English are not concerned with political issues, even if often, indirectly, with cultural situations brought about by colonial political history. Political concerns, then, and their relation to community life, from the literary material handled by most Third-world writers (frequently in over ways), whereas most western writers concentrate, when they turn to political themes, upon the relation to individuality--most often in conflict with community. Perhaps it is generally true that in the west, literature that is primarily about political concepts, about how political events act upon the lives of ordinary people, tends to be treated with suspicion, or at least reserve, and seems to have to pass the non-propagandist test more stringently than writings on other themes. What made Chinua Achebe's anti-colonialist novel, *Things Fall Apart*, eminently acceptable in the west was his having projected the tragedy of the destruction of a valuable pre-colonial African culture, but made it measurable through the personal tragedy of a hero who embodied most, but, very importantly, not all of his society's cultural characteristics. Similarly, it is often overlooked that, though V.S. Naipaul's *A House for Mr. Biswas* seems pre-eminently a novel about individual struggle in the classic tradition of western fiction, the struggle itself enacts colonial man's physical and psychic dispossession and his twentieth-century attempt to heave himself out of a nullity thrust upon him by the history of European colonization and colonialism.

Before these generalizations take complete control, it is necessary to return to my opening remark about the western critical equipment which many of us have brought to the literatures of the Commonwealth countries. Not that there is a single western critical outlook, or at most just a few critical positions (as some Third-world critics assert), though Matthew Arnold's 'common pursuit of true judgement' does imply a degree of disinterestedness and simplicity that actual critical practice keeps denying. That F.R. Leavis's greatness in Arnold's pursuit was so often castigated by lesser, reputedly eminent, minds at least underscores the ideal nature of the Arnoldian goal. Its aim is to arrive at the determination of literary excellence. And this term, 'literary excellence' is the particular part of my English literary luggage that has most often raised misgivings about the total suitability of my equipment for the literatures in English of Africa, India, and the Caribbean. I would not be understood to be going neatly as far as Dr. Robin W. Winks, Professor of History at Yale, who once said that he ran what his students called a 'Bad Books Course' of literary works, the criterion for inclusion being not literary excellence but serviceability to historians. Instead, and with no claim to originality, I am merely uttering private doubts about the old problem of the relationship between Life and Art, doubts stimulated by some exposure to Third-world literatures that deal with problems of life in a century which has seen the obscenities of six million Jews done to death by Hitler and twenty million Russians dying under Stalin. Is there any point in trying to differentiate morally between two such appalling tallies ? Is it meaningful to ask which was the *greater* atrocity, implying, therefore, that the other was *lesser*, in motivation rather than quantity ?

In *Middlemarch* (Book II, Chapter 21) George Eliot allows Dorothea Casaubon to ask questions unccmfortably related to such a moral conundrum, while she is speaking to Will Ladislaw during her honeymoon in Rome:

> In Rome it seems as if there were so many things which are more wanted in the world than pictures.

And, again to Will, in the next chapter:

> I should like to make life beautiful--I mean everybody's life. And then all this immense expense of art, that seems somehow to lie outside life and make it no better for the world paints one. It spoils my enjoyment of anything when I am made to think that most people are shut out from it.

Certainly no endorsement here of art for art's sake. This wondering about how important great art can possibly be in a world full of abject poverty and its attendant human miseries, to the point that 'art' almost seems to spell 'selfishness'--is it George Eliot measuring an intellectual *naivete* in Dorothea ? Or does it (also ?) indicate that such a subversive question about creativity and the life of the mind wasn't very far below the surface in the consciousness of one of the great English novelists ? I used to think the former only, but that I now believe the second possibility indeed valid is the result of reading Third-world literature from *Kanthapura*, via *Things Fall Apart*, to *Petals of Blood*. What really disturbs is the relationship, or lack of it, between art and scholarship on the one hand, and ordinary, everyday humanity on the other. I mean their comparative lack of meaningful relationship in twentieth-century western literature, for the literatures of Africa, the Caribbean, and India do on the whole comprehend individuality within community, with community including ordinary people. Nor is it sufficient answer that the two kinds of literature are drawing upon different kinds of reality, that they are at different stages of development on a uniform time scale, that the enthronement of individuality is the tacitly accepted universal gold standard to which art and intellectual discourse aim. I suspect that the more specialized and in-turned intellectual life becomes, the less qualified it is to pronounce upon life, upon that large proportion of humanity whom Matthew Arnold contemptuously (and unworthily of himself) dismisses as surnamed Wragg.[2] A.K. Ramanujan and Edward Brathwaite are certainly intensely aware that there is a meaningful relationship between their writing of poetry and the Wraggs of the Third World.

If T.S. Eliot revitalized English poetry in 1917 and after, he also, from the very nature of western culture then, and from the very nature of what he was trying to do, turned the subsequent mainstreams of poetry in English into largely esoteric art. The judgement given in the case of Regina versus *Lady Chatterley's Lover* in 1960 was a wise and liberating decision, but hasn't it also made possible a vast industry in Britain in what are euphemistically called 'girlie' magazines and other crude commercial exploitations of sex that are a gaping hellmouth away from Lawrence's vision of sexual frankness and healthful, humane relationships ? Though opposed in principle to censorship, I have great sympathy for President Nyerere's banning from Tanzania some of the novels in a new semi-pornographic, 'popular' species of writing that began to flourish in Kenya about 1975. Such an admission might suggest a lack of faith in the beneficent function of one's own trade in humane letters, though I would counter that it merely acknowledges the truth of the economic adage that debased coin must drive out sterling,[3] and admits that vast social and educational problems in some parts of the world have an urgency that requires measures generally regarded elsewhere as undesirable. Does not the western respect for 'freedom' often disguise mere indifference, or even fear of disturbing the prevailing political dispensation ?

Literature is art in the use of words. If it were universally agreed that brilliance in the use of words should be to some more than merely evanescent or crepitant end (as it is more so, say, in *Love's Labour Lost*), then it might be felt that attaching Oscar Wilde's sort of importance to being earnest falls short of what was being looked for. What, indeed, should be necessarily involved in the brilliant use of words ? It is here that every literary critic must be on his mettle. To distinguish between meaning and technique is itself to distort, for words both mean and are arranged to mean, and out of the interaction of the magnetic fields of these two modes of meaning is generated what is recognized as great literature. Yet the distinction is a useful piece of temporary scaffolding. It is most useful when one is dealing not so much with 'the best that is known and thought in the world' (the tacit gold standard ?), as with works belonging to a second order of literary excellence where the interaction between the two modes of meaning is not quite complete.

It is here that the reading of Third-world literature in English has increasingly undermined some of my former certainties about the response to literature. There would be little disagreement about placing in the first rank of writers in English in our time, the poet Derek Walcott, or the dramatist Wole Soyinka, or the novelists Chinua Achebe, Raja Rao, and Wilson Harris. No real problem there, but I do include in my African literature course at Leeds at least two novelists of secondary quality who I would not have thought, twenty years ago, merited attention. Poorly constructed, unintentionally episodic novels, with much spurious feeling conveyed in language that is often in turn banal, sensational, clichaic. Yet I know I am right to include them, for the South African writer Peter Abrahams and the Nigerian novelist Cyprian Ekwensi are important writers for *what* they say and try to say. What they say has required considerable moral courage, because they have reported things that undermine what their works make clear they regard as cherished ideals. And none of their technically abler fellows has ventured into such territory. Moreover, what they say constitutes extremely important interpretation of experience in the Third World, even though the execution is indifferent. Perhaps one of these days better novelists will do these jobs with brilliance, and then I can strike Ekwensi and Abrahams off my list. But I think not; they are still there despite the publication of Ngugi's *Petals of Blood* in 1977. What they say could not have been said without extraordinarily sympathetic and acute insight into things as in themselves they really are, yet insight inextricably mixed up with the most ordinary and banal observations too. Their work, I would argue, is the outcome of a largeness of understanding that implies an act of the creative imagination, even though that understanding also is mingled with what any lightly imaginative person would have grasped. Is there a parallel here to reading foreign works in translation ? How much of Dostoevsky do we lose in even the best available English translation and *what* exactly is it that we lose ? Or, rather, what 'o'erjumps' language and affects us profoundly--imagination as distinct from language, since we are not reading the author's original words ? Another difficult example: Does the moral impact of Juggut Singh's sacrifice of his own life for the sake of another at the end of Khushwant Singh's *Train to Pakistan* derive entirely from the novelist's artistry in words, or does it owe a great deal to the moral nature of such a sacrificial act (conceived, of course, by the novelist) ?

In his novel, *People of the City* (1954) Ekwensi deals with the unhappiness, rootlessness, inner confusion, yet excitement of young rural people (especially young women) first experiencing urbanization, as they flock to Lagos in the hope of striking it rich. His purpose is clearly to trace out the corrosive moral effects of city life, with its tinselled delights, on a code of conduct quite oblivious to the immense pressures upon it exerted by a city. It is Ekwensi's identifying of these pressures, his showing them working upon and within the characters, which is important and authentic, the more so (*ironically*, from the reader's point of view) because Ekwensi is part of his material, is himself fascinated by the very pressures he is presenting in the fiction; and his own moral ambivalence argues a serious lack of fictive sophistication. The author's ambivalence, or uncertainty, is not unlike Defoe's in *Moll Flanders*, and indeed Ekwensi's novel *Jagua Nana* (1961), about a Lagos prostitute trying to win respectable security before her pneumatic charms start sagging, is a much more coherent and skilful rendering of the new West African urban experience than the earlier novel. In 1966 Ekwensi published *Iska*, a novel based again on a young woman's sufferings in the city, but important because it makes Ekwensi the only Nigerian novelist before the Civil War of 1967-70 who dared to grapple with tribalism and inter-tribal conflict, instead of hoping that silence on the subject would give the still pale plant of Nigerian nationality an opportunity to put down roots. One must not, however, forget Ekwensi's origin as a popular Onitsha market writer in the 1940s. (He still calls himself a teller of stories, not a novelist.) His Onitsha market origin accounts, on the one hand, for the romantic treatment of love, for the mild sexual titillation, for the direct moralizing, and, on the other hand, for a sure grasp of ordinary people's anxieties and hopes in a period of rapid social change. When one has catalogued all his weaknesses as a writer of fiction, one has to acknowledge that he is an articulate recorder of importrant areas of experience in his time, who uses the outward shape of the novel genre for his recordings.

In 1956 Peter Abrahams published *A Wreath for Udomo*, about a charismatic West African politician (with distinct resemblances to the early Nkrumah), who leads his country to independence, and then discovers that political independence means little without economic independence. He believes the answer lies in rapid industrialization, which is impossible without technical co-operation from a neighbouring, South-Africa-like state. The latter refuses to complete the negotiations unless Udomo reveals how a black guerrilla leader, who is also Udomo's close friend from his London days, gets into the neighbouring territory. For the sake of his own country's industrial development, Udomo betrays his friend and the technical-assistance treaty is signed. Abrahams seems incapable resolving this discrepancy between Udomo the dedicated national leader and Udomo the private individual. Much of the writing, including the semi-ritual killing of Udomo at the end, is journalistic and melodramatic, but the analysis of political realities (made when political independence for Britain's African colonies was just beginning) is remarkably clear-sighted, unsentimental, and sober.

This Island Now (1966) turns fully to neocolonialism. The novel is set on a Caribbean island when the first independent president (a Kenyatta-style 'Father of the Nation') dies and is succeeded by President Josiah. Very much a novel of political themes, its characters are in the main representative rather than individualized--deliberately pared down to serve the political themes efficiently. Josiah, however, is a development of Udomo, and this time Abrahams presents much more persuasively the political leader who sacrifices his peace of mind and the luxury of a private conscience to his political determination to slash a way for his black islanders through creole and neo-colonialist economic fetters that deny them their full humanity. As President Josiah curbs the profit margins of local capitalism and of foreign economic power operating on the island, then (to help achieve that purpose) the freedom of the press and even the independence of the judiciary, he sees each step as a ruthlessly unhappy, but inescapable, means of achieving his people's legitimate freedom. Each act leaves him, personally, more lonely than before, none more so than when he has to use force against the people themselves for a mild form of directed labour, and two hundred are killed in clashes with the police. For a moment Josiah has doubts, but they pass and he says: 'If this way is wrong then there is no way out for the people of the so-called underdeveloped world.'

Unlike Soyinka's Kongi,[4] Abrahams's Josiah is no monster or clown. The portrait is sympathetic. Though the novel begins and ends with a scene in which a young idealist gets Josiah in the telescopic sights of a rifle, the would-be assassin doesn't press the trigger. What do we have then ? That bursting out of neo-colonialism (which means international capitalism) is essential if the peoples of the Third World are to be themselves and assume their full humanity, but that the realization is impossible without a trampling upon individual freedoms ? The denial of certain freedoms for the sake of freedom, killing two hundred ordinary people for the good of most people, enforced vasectomies to help arrest famine, the imprisonment of saintly politicians ? By what standards do we judge as insensitive and morally obtuse the writers who would appear to endorse such actions ? We seem to be back at my conundrum about the six million Jews and the twenty million Russians.

Artificial colonial frontiers that declare Igbo, Yoruba, and Hausa to belong to one Nigeria, that, conversely, bisect one tribal heartland and cast the two parts into different national boundaries; vast economic clientship; external pressures to industrialize economies unsuited to industrialization. Such ills require strong, centralized government. Thus one-party states, control of the press *and* of individual behaviour as surgical instruments to deal with the economic and political and cultural malignancies inherited by former colonies. Such things are anathema to liberal humanism, itself a western ethos, which isn't much given to distinguishing between an Amin and a Nyerere, between a Boukassa and a Mrs Gandhi. What Ekwensi and Abrahams pointed to in the 1960s were becoming commonplaces in the Third World, even as they were writing. And a writer of the first rank, Wole Soyinka, in his second novel, *Season of Anomy* (1973), drawing upon the same massacres that inspired Ekwensi's *Iska*, distinguishes between the obscenity of tribal or racial slaughter and the necessity of the social surgery carried out by the character whom he calls The Dentist, in the service of a peace-loving, almost utopian community. It must be added, though, that one is thinking in these terms only of those very few newly independent countries where the rulers are not drawn from a colonial elite who saw independence merely as the chance for private capital gains by a small group. Ngugi's *Petals of Blood* richly demonstrates that the Kenyan leadership has been of this elitist kind. In other words, different kinds of authoritarian government are distinguished in Third-world literature reporting Third-world realities.

I've taken a long time and relied on illustrations from two novelists not of the first rank in order to try to explain why I come increasingly to give paramountcy to meaning at the apparent expense of form and technique in literature. But, in the Third World, writers of the full range of abilities undoubtedly see their writing, more than western writers tend to, as an act of interpretation of complex experience that digs home hard into the ribs of ordinary people. There does seem to be a relationship between literary artists and common people that hasn't existed in the west since the nineteenth century and before that the early seventeenth. It is no accident that East Africa's foremost novelist should have engaged fully *as a writer* (not simply as a citizen) in a communal cultural enterprise among largely illiterate villagers and that for his share in a play performed there Ngugi was held in political detention for a year.

To have arrived at a view which emphasizes the role of literature as social, as what Senghor characterizes African literature as being, that is, 'functional and collective' is a very uncomfortable position to find oneself in, after years of dogmatic belief in the sanctity of the individual conscience. Moreover, a functional and collective' view of literature must radically affect one's view of literary criticism and at least question that illustrious pronouncement that the business of criticism is

> Simply to know the best that is known and thought in the world, and by in its turn making this known, to create a current of true and fresh ideas. Its business is to do this with inflexible honesty, with due ability; but its business is to do not more, and to leave alone all questions of practical consequences and applications.[5]

My question mark certainly doesn't hover over the honesty and ability bit, but it does over the practical consequences part, which implies a variation upon the beguiling theme of 'knowledge for its own sake,' itself a moral cognate of 'art for art's sake.' I'm very content to have been spared the anguish of being one of the physicists who were pursuers of knowledge for its own sake when atomic fission led to Hiroshima, and latterly to lethal waste deposited in the deep-delved earth. It would have been an act of the sublimest imagination *not* 'to leave alone all questions of practical consequences.'

Chinua Achebe has declared of his own practice as a novelist:

> Perhaps what I write is applied art as distinct from pure. But who cares ? Art is important but so is education of the kind I have in mind. And I don't see that the two need be mutually exclusive.[6]

In the same essay he indicates that the kind of education he had in mind wasn't so much a refining of individual sensibilities (though his novels also work at that level) but a practical attempt to help his fellow-Africans to a recovery of their diminished African identity, to greater understanding of what in themselves they are, and can be. To conceive of literature as having such a broadly practical, social, educative function is hardly ignoble, and certainly need not deny the affective role of literature in opening men's minds and hearts to one another. In response to all the urgencies pressing upon the peoples of the Third World, the writers have indeed been attempting such tasks. Far from laying down a prescription for writers anywhere (which would be futile anyway), I would suggest that critics might well be more descriptive and interpretative in their discussion of writers who undertake 'applied art.' To do so would at least call in question any belief that the true accents of literary excellence are to be heard only when they convey the navel-gazing preoccupations of the individual identity, the individual talent, the Very Self. It is an old lesson that the west could learn afresh from the Third World: Sir Philip Sidney would have understood what Senghor meant by literature being 'functional and collective'; so would Dr. Johnson.

The over-riding problems of the Third World constitute a reality of the west's creation. If elitism in economic power, social structure, and educational system is a left-over piece of colonialism, its matrix still flourishes in the west. Behind it lies the, in some ways, attractive social spectre of the cultivated gentleman. Nevertheless, it has a confining appetency, a shrinking into the individualism of mere self, which is but a hair's breadth from egotism--from what I am tempted to call personal fascism. It encourages the worship of the abstractions Art and Culture, so chillingly delineated by Henry James, in its extreme form, in the character of Gilbert Osmond. There are not three worlds. There is only one world, and it is everything to do with real, breathing human beings whose needs do need to be reasoned. The individual objects from which our concepts of Culture, Art, Literature are abstracted are artefacts of the human creative imagination, and it is illogical to grant them a wholly independent status higher than that of objects created and used by man for his delight and instruction. If what literature says, or does, or performs, or enacts doesn't affect our own lives and attitudes, and even behaviour, if it has no practical outcome, then what is its worth ?

There is probably more rhetoric than substance, more 'old hat' than new thought in this paper, but it has been whipped up by a sharper consciousness, stimulated by Third-world literature, of how draughty our century is. And perhaps there is some simple prudence in reaching again for a discarded old hat when tufts of thatch are being torn out of the communal roof by rising gales. The search for new concepts of community is as much needed in the west as in the Third World, where writers do address themselves to it. Wilson Harris has put it admirably:

We . . . need to re-think our biases if our concern is with the creation of the future as a capacity to sustain contrasting elements and talents in community.[7]

NOTES

1. T.S. Eliot, *What is a Classic ?* (London, 1945), p. 31.

2.Matthew Arnold, "The Function of Criticism at the Present Time," *Essays in Criticism* (London, 1884), pp. 23-24.

3. Norman Angell, *The Press and the Organisation of Society* (Cambridge, 1933 rev.ed.), p. 17

4. Wole Soyinka, *Kongi's Harvest* (London, 1967).

5.Matthew Arnold, pp. 18-19.

6.Chinua Achebe, "The Novelist as Teacher," *Commonwealth Literature*, ed. John Press (London, 1965), p. 205.

7. Wilson Harris, "The Native Phenomenon," *Common Wealth* , ed. Anna Rutherford (Aarhus, 1972), p. 144.

The English Reader and the Commonwealth Writer

ARTHUR POLLARD

I had been teaching Commonwealth Literature for a year or two when I first met C. D. Narasimhaiah in 1969 and mentioned that I had not hitherto dared to include anything from India because of what seemed to be the insuperable problems involved. Australia, Canada, New Zealand--they were all right, for their roots lay in metropolitan British culture: and, as I thought at this time (and I was far from alone in this), Africa and the Caribbean, their authors already publishing through British outlets, could be fairly easily managed. We have learnt better since. But India was different. How could one come to terms with a civilisation at once so multifarious and so complex ? CDN's reply to my comment was, "But English is the only language in which we are all able to speak to one another." It gave me courage then and it provides my text for this paper.

Perhaps because some of us were, and may be even still are, too confident, I feel that I detect too often for my comfort and too often, I believe, for the truth a repeated note of hostility among non-metropolitan writers and critics about the position of the Englishman in the understanding of Commonwealth literature. There is indeed the movement to reject the very name 'Commonwealth Literature,' and though the phrase 'New World Literature' does this successfully, it fails to include the old dominions and at the same time carries with it all the overtones of novelty and immaturity that the word 'new' suggests. We British can no more help our situation in the imperial relationship than the African, West Indian, Indian or Australian can help his.

Indeed, the position of the Australian may well be more complex than that of the others by virtue of their apparently closer relationship to the metropolitan civilization. A.A. Phillips coined a now-famous phrase when he spoke of the "cultural cringe." John

Docker has written: "In colonial and neocolonial historical situations, a hierarchy of cultural importance and value is imposed by the colonising power, both on the conquered indigenous societies and on the white agents of colonial oppression themselves."[1] One can see how that has a ready application, say, to the Empire Day episodes of Lamming's *In the Castle of My Skin*, but who would guess that it follows this sentence: "The argument of this paper is that there is a ruling anglocentric assumption in university teaching of English, an assumption derived from the total experience of colonialism and neocolonialism in Australia." As my reference to Lamming makes clear, I find it easier to understand the note of colonial rebellion in Caribbean writing and even in African. What is interesting in this context is that I do not find it in Indian writing in English. The Indian writer may apologise to his fellow-nationals for using English as his medium, but there is the hint neither of cultural inferiority nor of cultural rebellion in his work. It may have something to do with the infinite riches of his own background, or, as, for instance, Desani makes so hilariously clear in *All About H. Hatterr* and the jacket-comment on Raja Rao's *The Cat and Shakespeare* puts it, it may be a case of "the unaffected universality of Shakespeare whom India has wisely made her own." Even in literary-cultural matters, there is wisdom in not throwing out the baby with the bath-water. Though there may be much that some of us dislike, English, after all, is only the language in which we speak to each other, and, like it or not, for many of us the metropolitan culture will remain the basis of our own.

Lest you should think that this paper is turning into a kind of Pollard's Last Stand or, in the title of a recent film, "The Empire Strikes Back," I would bid you notice the change of reference in the first person plural I have just used. I speak there, as I want mainly to speak throughout this paper, not as a partial Englishman but simply as any English reader, whatever his nationality, reading Commonwealth literature. The problems that face us are literally of global dimensions and are different in kind and extent from those that confront scholars who work in most other literatures. The student of any modern European literature works within the framework of a common heritage and regular contacts with the classics, the Renaissance and modern parallel developments to aid him. The reader of more obscure literatures, whether East or West, is likely to be confined within well-recognised limits both of language and culture. For us, English unites and at the same time it displays our difference.

It may therefore be pertinent to consider the question: Why English in the first place ? For some, of course, there is no choice, but that does not mean that for us their readers there is no difficulty. Lamming is right when in *The Pleasures of Exile*, speaking of West Indian novels, he says: "The language in which these books are written is English--which I must repeat--is a West Indian language." (p. 44) He goes on: "And in spite of the unfamiliarity of its rhythms it remains accessible to the readers of English anywhere in the world." He is right there also, but there are degrees of accessibility. Vocabulary, rhythm, intonation, to mention no more. Louise Bennett reciting Jamaica labrish is an unforgettable experience, but, for me at least, intellectual apprehension did not play a great part in it. This is one of the difficulties we have to face. We cannot alter it , nor should we wish to do so.

English is a West Indian language. It is *the* Australian language, and yet there is plenty of room for lexical confusion on both sides. 'Keeping a poddy in a dunny' does not readily suggest to most of us 'rearing a calf in an outside lavatory,' and I know more than one Australian who has been embarrassed to find on asking for 'durex' in an English stationery shop that his request for cellotape has been misinterpreted as an attempt to purchase contraceptives.

What, however, of those who could choose whether to write in English or in another language ? I have mentioned the defensive attitude of certain Indian writers, and Africans too have been under attack. Replying to one such onslaught, Chinua Achebe is well worth quoting:

> (Colonialism) did bring together many peoples that had hitherto gone their several ways. And it gave them a language with which to talk to one another. If it failed to give them a song, it at least gave them a tongue, for sighing. There are not many countries of Africa where you could abolish the language of the erstwhile colonial powers and still retain the facility of mutual communication. Therefore those African writers who

have chosen to write in English or French are not unpatriotic smart alecs with an eye on the main chance--outside their own countries. They are by-products of the same process that made new nation states of Africa.[2]

It was not a matter of choice, Achebe is saying, but of conditioning factors. In a somewhat different way Raja Rao is saying the same thing:

> One has to convey in a language which is not one's own the spirit that is one's own. One has to convey the various shades and omissions of a certain thought-movement that looks maltreated in an alien language. I use the word "alien," yet English is not really an alien language to us. It is the language of our intellectual make-up--like Sanskrit or Persian was before--but not of our emotional make-up. We are all instinctively bilingual, many of us writing in our own language and in English. We cannot write like the English. We should not. We cannot write only as Indians. We have grown to look at the large world as part of us. Our method of expression therefore has to be a dialect which will some day prove to be as distinctive and colourful as the Irish or the American. Time alone will justify it.[3]

That last sentence is an interesting one. "Time alone will justify it." Here are two statements--one from a writer in a new nation, the other from a writer in an old one, one from a country that effectively knew British rule for a mere fifty or sixty years, the other that experienced it for nigh on two centuries. The Indian statement is suffused with what time has already justified, and what for Achebe is principally an external and political problem is for Raja Rao an internal and psychological one. Indeed, in him we see the paradox of a divided consciousness and a determined purpose side by side. He is reminding us also, as George Lamming was, that there is not just English but several varieties of it. He is telling us that the writer cannot just provide what any reader wants, only express himself as he can, and perhaps for those he may be able to identify as his potential audience.

This paper has a two-fold intention. It is at once an attempt to indicate the problems of understanding in the sense of apprehending and the need for understanding in the sense of appreciating and making allowances. In this latter regard we are all, from whatever part of the Commonwealth, the products of our history, as this comment of Raja Rao on the English language and its development in India makes clear. We are all the products of our history and none of us can alter that by the proverbial jot or tittle, but we can try to understand in the sense of appreciating and making allowances. In this sense one can understand--and enjoy--Lamming's unrestrained condemning comedy of the farce of Empire Day in a Barbadian school. Likewise, one can appreciate Ngugi's passionate identification with those who mounted the Mau-Mau campaigns and recognise his own recognition of the divisive influences of Christianity in the African situation. One can do all this, but one is in the end left wondering about two things, whether a non-indigenous reader can ever apprehend the immediacy, the poignant immediacy, of it all to the author and whether, on the other hand, the author himself apprehended the sincerity of motive inspiring those he opposed.

A failure to sympathise with the British in their imperial role is not surprising at this particular Roman stage in the history of colonial independence in Africa and the Caribbean. The political passions are still too high for the impartial perspective to have yet developed. Again it is a curiosity in the comparative study of Commonwealth literature that, generally speaking, this anti-British betterness is both less widespread and less virulent in Indian than in other Third World literature. I can suggest only two possible reasons for this. They rest in language and history. As it seems to me (and I confess my comparative ignorance of the African linguistic situation), the Indian *writer* is faced, linguistically, with the need for a more deliberate choice between his own language and English; and historically he is more conscious of his country and his nation than the African writer. By contrast, the Caribbean writer has no choice in either language or history: he is even removed from his ethnic origins in Africa. If I am right, the Indian writer is in a both more complex and more sophisticated situation. As G.P.Sarma has put it in the foreword to his *Nationalism in Indo-Anglian Fiction*, "many of the ideas of the new world--of secular humanism, political self-determination, social justice, etc.--came to us through English. It may therefore appear that English came to India as a historical necessity and that it is bound up with our national destiny." This is an apt quotation (and incidentally, not unlike Achebe's which I cited above), for it points to what is so characteristic in the Indian fictional treatment of nationalism, the stress on the positive pursuit of such things as political self-determination and social justice, the exaltation therefore of indigenous proponents of such ideals rather than the militant condemnation of the expatriate oppressor. What, however, is interesting--and what one must add--is that whereas the African and Caribbean writer has been quick to spot that new indigenous politician and bureaucrat is not only old expatriate writ large but also writ crooked, the Indian novelist has but rarely found this theme. Again it may be that one part of sophistication is the permanent presence of corruption. The zemindar and the bunniah have a long history in the Indian economy.

I would sum up this part of my case thus--first, that the novel of protest and condemnation is understandable; and, secondly, that the novel of celebration is always welcome. In this respect I find myself constantly delighted with the tone of V.S.Reid's *New Day* for the way in which it makes suffering heroic, distinguishes dedication and glories in ultimate success.

There are two forms of greater subtlety, however, which the novel of colonial independence requires and which, in pleading for historical understanding, I must accept that only time will bring. Both of them involve humility, both require detachment. One of these is the capacity for self-criticism, the other is for that understanding of what I have called "the sincerity of motive inspiring those the writer opposed." I can illustrate my first point best by invoking Naipaul. By self-criticism I mean the ability to criticise the society from which the writer himself has originated. I have mentioned the examples of novels where there is some criticism of the writer's own society, where new indigenous politician and bureaucrat is not only old expatriate writ large but also writ crooked. These, however, are but variations on the us-and-them conflict. It is in this respect that Naipaul stands alone in more senses than one. He has cultivated a detachment which, *pace* Lamming and his jibes about castrated satire, has enabled him to view Caribbean society in a perspective that provides his novels with a universal rather than a local and insular significance. Of course, here is another difficulty for some sorts of English reader. Is Naipaul a traitor to his heritage ? Or, is he right in saying that there is nothing to inherit ? I should like to think that these are not alternatives and that "No" is the correct answer in both cases. It is certainly the answer that the proper humility I am advocating would dictate.

My second form of needful greater subtlety requires an act of historical understanding and sympathy, to recognise the sincerity of motive inspiring those the writer may find antipathetic. That sincerity of motive may have been no more than doing their duty, themselves trapped in a situation they did nothing to create and could do little to alter. It is, in fact, an appeal for the generous heart that, to take a different but relatable historical situation of victim and apparent oppressor, distinguishes, say Mrs Gaskell in her treatment of the situation of employer and workman in the *laissez-faire* economy of the mid-nineteenth-century cotton industry from the crude, monotonous, insistent, repetitive and partial diatribe of Robert Tressell in his portrayal of exploited workmen in *The Ragged-Trousered Philanthropists*. One does not deny the power of Tressell as one does not deny the power of that equally one-sided account of the convict-system that Marcus Clarke provides in *For the Term of His Natural Life*, but for my money Thomas Keneally's *Bring Larks and Heroes* is more varied, more balanced and ultimately more moving. We have, of course, to remind ourselves again that none of us can escape our history. It may indeed catch up with us after long periods of desuetude. Keneally again, in *The Chant of Jimmy Blacksmith*, records the belated guilt-consciousness that the Australians have recently developed about their aborigines, itself perhaps a tangential effect of the current world-wide increase in racial sensitivity.

I have referred to those trapped in a historical situation they did nothing to create and could do little to alter. It is my contention that, though the creative artist must lament and may condemn the crimes of history, it is precisely he who can help to break the barriers of misunderstanding and precisely he who can help to break the barriers of misunderstanding and prejudice by the sensitivity he possesses to enter into the historical situation, to portray its many-sidedness and at the same time not ignore error or excuse crime. This is the other form of subtlety to which I referred. It is sometimes said that to understand is to forgive. I do not think that is always so or should be so, but in my mind it is the highest function of literature to help us to understand. In the context in which I am now speaking I know nothing better than R.D. Fitzgerald's poem, "The Wind at Your Door," to illustrate my point. We are back to the Australian guilt-consciousness about the convicts in their past. Fitzgerald's ancestor, Michael Mason, was a doctor whose work required his attendance at judicial floggings. One of the convicts to be flogged was named Fitzgerald. I can quote only briefly, though even that must be at some length:

> There was a high wind blowing on that day,
> for one who would not watch, but looked aside,
> said that when twice he turned it blew his way
> splashes of blood and strips of human hide
> shaken out from the lashes that were plied
> by one right-handed, one left-handed tough,
> sweating at this paid task, and skilled enough.
>
> That wind blows to your door down all these years.
> Have you not known it when some breath you drew
> tasted of blood ? Your comfort is in arrears
> of just thanks to a savagery tamed in you
> only as subtler fears may serve in lieu
> of thong and noose--old savagery which has built
> your world and laws out of the lives it spilt.
>
> For what was jailyard widens and takes in
> my country. Fifty paces of stamped earth
> stretch; and grey walls retreat and grow so thin
> that towns show through and clearings--new raw birth
> which burst from handcuffs--and free hands go forth
> to win tomorrow's harvest from a vast

ploughland--the fifty paces of that past.

Then a passage on the inescapable link with Mason, the doctor:

This man had Hunter's confidence, King's praise:
and settlers on the starving Hawkesbury banks
recalled through twilight drifting across their days
the doctor's fee of little more than thanks
so often; and how sent by their squeezed ranks
he put their case in London. I find I lack
the hateful paint to daub him wholly black.

Perhaps my life replies to his too much
through veiling generations dropped between.
My weakness here, resentments there, may touch
old motives and explain them, till I lean
to the forgiveness I must hope may clean
my own shortcomings; since no man can live
in his own sight if it will not forgive.

Certainly I must own him whether or not
it be my will. I was made to understand
this much when once, marking a freehold lot,
my papers suddenly told me it was land
granted to Martin Mason. I felt his hand
heavily on my shoulder, and knew what coil
binds life to life through bodies, and soul to soil.

And finally, the end of the poem, Fitzgerald desiring a link with his convict-namesake; and his final understanding or rather acceptance of his inability to understand or say what he would have done in Mason's place:

It would be well if I could find, removed
through generations back--who knows how far ?--
more than a surname's thickness as a proved
bridge with that man's foundations. I need some star
of courage from his firmament, a bar

against surrenders: faith. All trials are less
that rain-blacked wind tells of that old distress.

Yet I can live with Mason. What is told
and what my heart knows of his heart, can sort
much truth from falsehood, much there that I hold
good clearly or good clouded by report;
and for things bad, ill grows where ills resort;
they were bad times. None know what in his place
they might have done. I've my own faults to face.

Let us return from understanding as sympathy to understanding as intellectual apprehension, whilst recognising, of course, that in literary appreciation the two cannot ultimately be separated. So far I have been concerned principally with the problems created by language and history. My references to the continuing influence of the past upon the present in Australian fiction serve to remind us of other problems of understanding. What I have called the Australian guilt-consciousness is in some ways the converse of, say, the Caribbean victim-consciousness, and what the Australians feel about their convicts is parallelled by what some English writers feel about colonialism, Forster's *A Passage to India* being but one of the earliest and best examples.

In its quintessential form only the Australian himself can really experience that feeling about the convicts as only the West Indian can fully enter into his heritage of enslavement. For the rest of us the gulf is probably unbridgeable, but yet the attempt must be made with both more effort and more determination than in Forster's novel. The non-native needs help with the simplest facts about the environment and locale in which much Commonwealth writing is set. There used to be a condescending joke about the African coming to Britain who, familiar with Wordsworth's poem, confused the dandelion with the daffodil because both were "golden". But could we be sure of recognising the frangipani or the wattle, to name nothing more exotic than these ? And my beautiful colour illustrations of Australian flowers and scenery convey all too inadequate an impression of the original. Even in our world of wonderful television documentaries it is hard to gain a sufficient idea of the bush, the prairie and the jungle. And yet the landscape has played so large a part in the making of the nations and the consciousness of the people. Who else but a West Indian like Walcott could have written of "the doomed lushness of a green mind" ? Or who but an Australian like Judith Wright could express the ageless antiquity of her young country in the image of "The Cycads" and the way it affects the poet ?

> Their smooth dark flames flicker at time's own root. . . .
>
> Only the antique cycads sullenly
> keep the old bargain life has long since broken;
> and, cursed by age, through each chill century
> they watch the shrunken moon, but never die,
>
> for time forgets the promise he once made,
> and change forgets that they are left alone. . . .
>
> Take their cold seed and set it in the mind,
> and its slow root will lengthen deep and deep
> till, following, you cling on the last ledge
> over the unthinkable, unfathomed edge
> beyond which man remembers only sleep.

Even more fundamentally in the rural societies of Africa physical nature dictates the very livelihood and survival of man; and hence the sensitivity to sun and rain, forest and river, mountain and plain, and the association of folklore, myth and religion with each and all of these.

If, on the one hand, we must heed what the landscape speaks of aeons, on the other, we must regard what history tells of social organisation and its effects. To take Australia again, there is the concept of mateship. In a country where a little over a century ago the sexual ratio was of the order of 38 men to 1 woman it is easy to understand the attraction of a man and his mate. Convict confinement on the one hand, and the lonely conditions of shepherding in the outback, on the other, render that understanding still easier. Out of it there come, as T. Inglis Moore in what is a model for very necessary similar studies, *Social Patterns in Australian Literature*, has remarked, the recognition of "valuable spiritual truths: the virtue of a selfless loyalty standing firm in a world of chaos, a loyalty which can reach the supreme heights of self-sacrifice; the democratic equality of all men, with its corollary of human worth and dignity; and an inclusive belief in the brotherhood of men. These are values of the spirit which can be as potent and significant for us today as they were in the days of Lawson and Furphy, O'Dowd and Mary Gilmore." (p. 237) The title of the book speaks of "social patterns"; this quotation refers to "values of the spirit." Literature deals with both, finding spiritual significance embedded in social organisation. That is why we need to know the "social patterns."

Another book that for me illuminatingly works in a similar direction is Emmanuel Obiechina's *Culture, Tradition and Society in the West African Novel*. Like Moore, Obiechina is the indigenous commentator--and it is only he who can ultimately help in this context. Thus Obiechina places Achebe's Okonkwo with brilliant discrimination:

> Okonkwo's life-history illustrates the working of the traditional system because he is a fully realized traditional character. This is not to say that Okonkwo is a representative of the Igbo race in particular or that his life is an illustration of the values which Igbo people admire (the view held by G.D. Killam, which I believe to be in error). All one can justifiably say is that Okonkwo is a fully realized traditional character who also has, as human beings must have, distinctly individual traits. Indeed he is atypical in some respects, and his extreme idiosyncrasies draw him into conflict with traditional practices. His friend Obierika, who is a flexible, pragmatic Igbo titled elder, is nearer the traditional ideal. But for all his personal weaknesses Okonkwo is a full-blooded traditional character and can be used to examine the relation between the individual and society under the traditional system. (p. 204)

If this is to emphasise the right reading of the individual character, another section of Obiechina's consideration concentrates attention on traditional society and its demands to explain "the apparent inhumanity of the destruction of twins and killing of Ikemefuna, and all other situations in which the balanced and peaceful relationship between man and god, the living and the dead, and the living among themselves is subverted and threatened." (p. 214)

Obiechina's treatment of tradition and the individual character also reminds us of certain literary dimensions. Why are African individual characters different ? Why do we not get the psychological development so familiar in the Western novel ? Why is there so much of what he calls the "parabolic approach" ? He suggests two reasons: "First, the moral determination of parabolic charaterisation suits West African novels with their overwhelming preoc+cupation with social morality. . . . In the second place, one must see this as a "back accretion," or reversion, to the method of characterisation familiar in traditional narrative." (p. 107) And *there* is a whole new area we need to learn about--"traditional narrative" !

In reminding us of the relationship of society and the supernatural Obiechina brings us into that most multifarious areas of cómprehension within the whole field of Commonwealth literature, at least as it regards the so-called Third World countries--religion. I am sure that there is so much that we still need to learn about African religion that we do not know how ignorant we are. The varieties of Christian and sub-Christian revivalism, Pocomania, Rastáfarianism and what else struggle for expression in the Caribbean consciousness, but my own ignorance prevents more than mention. And India remains tantalising and elusive. Thus we can only contemplate, never understand, caste; and yet this social phenomenon has its roots in religious belief.

Balachandra Rajan entitled his novel *Too Long in the West* and some little time ago Ruth Prawer Jhabvala decided that she had been too long in the East. That encounter of Oriental and Occidental is at the centre of Raja Rao's *The Serpent and the Rope* and it is expressed climatically in religious terms:

> 'What is it separated us, Rama ?'
> 'India.'
> 'India ? But I am a Buddhist.'
> 'That is why Buddhism left India. India is impitoyable.'

'But one can become a Buddhist ?'
'Yes, and a Christian and Muslim as well.'
'Then ?'
'One can never be converted to Hinduism.'
'You mean one can only be born a Brahmin ?'
'That is--an Indian,' I added, as an explanation of India.

The dialogue continues:

'This is too mystical even for me.'
'Would you understand if I were to say, "Love is not a feeling, it is, you might say, a stateless state, the whole condition of one-self"?'
'I don't. But suppose I did ?'
'Can you understand that all things merge, all thoughts and perceptions, in knowledge. It is in knowledge that you know a thing, not in seeing or hearing.'

Surely this meditation on transcendental realities is applicable, and bleakly so, to the lesser preoccupations of this paper. In the English countryside of *Howards End* Forster's plea was "Only connect"; under the pitiless sun of the Indian landscape he heard a chorus of "a hundred voices, 'No, not yet,' and the sky said, 'No, not there.' " And yet I do not think that we need surrender quite so hopelessly. Narasimhaiah himself has thrown considerable light on Raja Rao's puzzling novel. John Docker has accused Australian academics of "always striving to become what they cannot be, metropolitans serene and confident in the knowledge of being metropolitans." (p. 30) He is right, and just as the 'colonial' cannot become a metropolitan, neither can the metropolitan, however much he or others may desire it, become a 'colonial.' We can only appreciate each other's differentness.

This paper has pleaded for two sorts of understanding, for apprehension and sympathy, for the understandings of the intelligence and the heart. Thereby, whatever our differentness, we may discover that common humanity and those overriding values that transcend our singularities. Penultimately, and with due reverence, I interpolate from St. Paul that I speak "not as though I had already attained . . . I could not myself to have apprehended"; and I conclude with some of the last words of the dialogue in *The Serpent and the Rope* from which I have been quoting: "History, if anything, is the acceptance of human sincerity. But truth transcends sincerity." If that ultimate truth evade us, I at least shall be content with the lesser goal--'history,' all that life has made us, the understanding of the intelligence; and 'the acceptance of human sincerity,' all that we are in ourselves, the understanding of the heart. English, after all, is the only language in which we are all able to speak to one another.

NOTES

1. John Docker, "The Neocolonial Assumption in University Teaching of English," *South Pacific Images*, ed. C. Tiffin (Brisbane, 1978), p. 26.

2. Chinua Achebe, "The African Writer and the English Language," *Morning Yet on Creation Day* (1975), p. 57.

3. Raja Rao, Foreword to *Kanthapura* (1938).

Commonwealth Literary Criticism: Past, Present and Future Prospects

G.D. KILLAM

Perhaps in a few days we will be able to say, or perhaps I should say I hope it will not be said of us, or perhaps I should say I hope we will not say of ourselves as Moth said of Holofernes and Sebastian: "They have been at a great feast of languages, and stolen the scraps." For we are a new discipline striving after a definition of ourselves and until we can define what we are it makes criticism of what we are difficult. The problems of definition can perhaps be inferred from a series of quotations by Canadian figures and an analogy may be found by other colleagues here in the problems they experience in adducing a definition of Commonwealth literature from the various parts which go to make up the whole.

The statemets are as follows. From Goldwin Smith:

> Canada is a political expression. This must be borne in mind when we speak of Canadian Literature.

From W.L. MacKenzie King, the model of political longevity among Canada's Prime Ministers:

> If some countries have too much history, we have too much geography.

And there are two quotations from Stephen Leacock:

> I myself talk Ontario English; I don't admire it, but it's all I can do; anything is better than affectation.

In Canada we have enough to do keeping up with two spoken languages without trying to invent slang, so we just go ahead and use English for literature, Scottish for sermons and American for conversation.

The languages and literatures which feast at the high table of this gathering are those with relatively clearly defined literary traditions--France, Germany, Britain and more recently, the United States of America. Our discipline on the other hand is a new one busy trying to establish itself. Moreover, we are a new discipline in a language which already possesses powerful scholarly critical traditions in which there are certain expectations as to how the literary activity ought to shape and conduct itself. As well, the pace at which the literatures which make up Commonwealth literature have developed puts each of them in a different stage of continuity within these literatures is largely futile. The diversity in the literature is something to celebrate because it adds much to the richness of literature in English. The movement of Commonwealth literature from the periphery of English literary studies toward the centre is made the more difficult by the fact that the formal teaching of Commonwealth literature is itself peripheral. A rough canvas of the number of courses in Commonwealth literature which are taught in the literature departments or the English departments of universities reveals literatures or even, for that matter, on national literatures. The University Department of Literature at Nairobi is an exception and may well be a model. Not that local literatures or national literatures should supersede the literature of the world available for contemplation and illumination but that the main organizing conception of the department is local literature with the international brought in to sustain the local. Finally, few, if any universities offer an undergraduate degree in any of the literatures which go to make up what we called Commonwealth literature. I do not mean to argue that this is right or wrong but merely suggest it accounts in some measure for the difficulty of the discipline to establish itself.

An analogy to this difficulty may be found in the difficulty of sustaining periodical publications devoted to the scrutiny of Commonwealth literature. No journal which deals with

Commonwealth literature can compete in terms of subscriptions with journals covering more orthodox areas of English and American studies which are obviously not only well established but thriving and therefore insistent in demanding shrinking library funds. The more we consolidate and see funds shrink further, the greater the problem of survival for journals of Commonwealth literature, whether of the international kind, such as the *JCL, Kunapipi, World Literature Written in English* and *CRNLRE* or regional journals such as *Joliso, Mana*, and *Islands* to name but a few.

But this brief paper is meant to be devoted to Commonwealth literature criticism, past, present and future prospects and having identified the difficulty of defining the subject matter it is nevertheless necessary to press forward to suggest the ways in which the literature may be scrutinized and the various critical systems which may be apposite to its scrutiny. I think it is important, as well, to enter this caveat:

> Commonwealth literature studies in an important sense supersede considerations of the Commonwealth itself. For even if the Commonwealth as a British-sponsored connection were to disappear, Commonwealth literature would remain, its literary and linguistic material existing independently of organizational definitions and the study and the contemplation of their inter-national comparisons would continue to be valid and the subject would cohere at an international rather than a national level even if the political links were broken. The fact that we include--or can include--such places as the Phillipines, Cameroons and Mauritius in our discipline testifies to this.

I suspect that Professor Molly Mahood is correct when she asserts that:

> I should be happy (if my juxtaposition did something) to persuade the guardians of the pure English tradition of fiction that we do not need to change our criteria in approaching Third World Novels.

This does not mean as Connor Cruse O'Brien suggests in his critique of Professor Mahood's book that all of the New World literatures in English are extensions of English literature: they are not: they are Nigerian, Canadian or whatever else. But they spring from the same stock as English literature and therefore are in this sense deeply traditional in the way that Joyce or Eliot are deeply traditional, however innovative they at first seem to be. The degree to which this is so in our inquiry can be discerned from a glance at the poetry of Christopher Okigbo:

> Bright
> With the armpit dazzle of a lioness
> she answers
> wearing white light about her;
> and the waves escort her,
> my lioness,
> crowned with moonlight.

This is where the links remain strong with England: because the writing has beginnings in the English literary tradition and represents a modification of that tradition, so criticism of the literature has its beginnings there and in like fashion will represent modifications to traditional English literary critical method.

Nevertheless, because of the ubiquitous nature of our subject matter we as practitioners of Commonwealth literature teaching and criticism are perhaps more open to certain dangers inherent in literary evaluations and systems proposed for its evaluation than are critics who address themselves to one body of literature--by which I mean the literature of one nation or country or autonomous segment of a country. Again, one encounters problems of definition comparable or analogous to defining Commonwealth literature itself. It has been noted in more than one place that a good deal of discussion has gone into considering the best sort of criticism which will serve African literature and we may use African literature as an analogy to the problem as a whole. There are those critics of African literature who tie their critical apparatus to theoretical standards of the main tradition of English literature and judgements are reached by their application. At the other extreme, there are critics like

Grant Kamenju, who maintain the need to define African aesthetics (read: Indian or Caribbean or Australian or Canadian aesthetics) which modifies the critical standards of the parent tradition and makes it subservient to the newer national ones. In the middle are those critics who seek to account for the uniquely African (sic: others) qualities in a work of art but who, in the end, judge the work by its capacity to meet some standard of universality.

It has been noted more than once, as well, that the questions of appropriate criticism revolve not around standards *per se* but around methodology. The methods of the formalists, the structuralists, the Marxists, have been and doubtless will continue to be applied to the scrutiny of Commonwealth literature, each advocate defending the method he adopts as asking of a text what none of the others ask. The Marxist, for example, argues that the work of literature cannot be freed of the conditioning placed on it by history; the formalist takes the opposite stand. We see and shall doubtless continue to see existing side by side different and potentially antagonistic critical positions adopted; the application of pluralistic standards of criticism applied to a pluralistic body of literature; possibly even the abuse of the application of certain methodologies by exponents of an alternative critical approach because deriving from the hints or statements made by the authors themselves who are under scrutiny. I think, for example, of the clues which Ngugi provides about the purposes he has as an author and the implicit invitation to judge the works along fairly rigorous and clearly demarked lines.

What presumably will continue to happen in Commonwealth criticism as elsewhere (but of special interest becuase of the wider bounds than the merely national which are set on it by the adoption and acceptance of the term Commonwealth literature--or Third World Literature in English, or New World Literature in English) is the adoption and adaption of the various critical methodologies, the traditional and the modern and ultra-modern, the formalists, Marxists and myth critics; the structuralists, mythopoeic critics and Hermeneutic critics. What will provide a fascination in this critical activity is not only the kind of method which is chosen in one part of the Commonwealth or another, since criticism is like literature responsive to different social forces (in the broadest sense), but also the pace at which it will develop and its longevity in the various parts of the Commonwealth or the English-speaking world. One thinks here, as an example, of the claim made now ten years ago by Dr. Izevbaye that the heavy social or political reference of Nigerian or African writing and the response of critics in attending to this bias in the writing will in time disappear as the social and political conditions which account for the production of that type of literature are altered and the work of art as art is thus freed to emerge. We may note in passing a recent review by the Nigerian teacher and critic, Niyi Osundare of the current state of Nigerian drama in West Africa magazine under the title "Social Message of a Nigerian Dramatist":

> The Nigerian Writer today is under considerable pressure to choose between his vision and his purse, between the rich patronage that comes from being in the good books of the establishment and the hunger and benign hostility that greet the voice of sustained dissent. Everywhere there is greed and graft, cheating and profiteering bordering on cannibalism: paupers transmogrify into millionaires overnight, and money, easy-come naira, has deified itself in the psyche of almost every Nigerian.
>
> The Nigerian's level of political, social, economic and cultural awareness is abysmally low, the typical Nigerian being hidebound, parochial, and stifled by narrow tribal loyalties. In addition to these contemporary ills, the Nigerian mind is tortured by the dual monster of history and myth, it shrinks from challenging realities, seeking infantile refuge in metaphysical alibis, like religion, baseless myths, and superstitions.
>
> How does the writer react to such hydra-headed problems ? Does he, like the proverbial ostrich, bury his head in the sand and pretend not to hear the sound and fury of the monstrous footsteps on our shores ? Does he, like the Elizabethan social climber, close his eyes to the rot and sing the eulogy of the powers-that-be who, apart from doing nothing to eliminate the ills, have contributed their own potent quota to them ? Or does he, like Bertolt Brecht or Pablo

Neruda, pitch his tent on Justice's dwindling but abiding side and challenge a monstrous, cannibalistic system that teaches its victims to feed upon one another by eating them up first ?

Nevertheless, there are certain basic matters which the critic needs to attend to when scrutinizing Commonwealth literature no matter what methodology he adopts. And here, too, we find another respect in which the critic of Commonwealth literature or whatever designation we choose to apply to it is in an unique position. This is with respect to the way in which this role as critic is defined for his work embodies two kinds of critical activity: that usually associated with academic critic and that associated with the reviewer. Ideally, he must, like the reviewer of current books--and much of the writing which concerns us is current, or at least, new--focus his comment in such a way as to lead up to a judgement, to make a firm statement on whether he thinks the book worth reading and possibly studying. Like the academic critic, he is concerned with the scholarly organization of literature and his activity as a critic is not evaluative because the book or body of literature he scrutinizes has been accepted already as a valid subject for scholarly study. We think of the classics of Commonwealth literature--Achebe or Patrick White or Edward Braithwaite.

We are concerned as critics then with making informed judgements--in taking all the usual risks--about the value of recent literatures and we have also to ask the usual questions of the work that criticism asks: our primary question is "What does the text say ?" And, if because our texts are generally always modern we avoid a principal problem with the academic critic who must consider what the text says in the language of its own time. Nevertheless, we must replace this problem with an even greater one: although we consider a body of literature in the same chosen tongue, it is a tongue much modified by local demand and use. Moreover, it says things about culture and society about which the critic often has but the dimmest perception. And it is in this regard that it seems to me the best criticism of Commonwealth literature ultimately will be collaborative criticism.

Like the traditional academic critic we must attempt to relate the literature to the assumptions of the society and to the age which produced it. The problem of coming to an understanding for the contemporary critic of Commonwealth literature in, for example, the poetry of Christopher Okigbo is as complicated now as it will be for the Nigerian critic of Okigbo's poems in the twenty-third century. The problem of relating the material to the age remains constant; the stance of the critic accounts for the degree of difficulty in appraising it.

Commonwealth literary criticism divides the functions of the critic between the critic who from whatever culture as general reader comes upon the work and contemplates it because it is there for him to consult, and the specialist critic, the only one who can verify the authenticity of the use of certain materials in the work and suggest their appropriateness to the work as a whole.

Another and last function of criticism, judging from comment made and resolutions passed at various conferences devoted to the discussion of Commonwealth literature, seems to be a need to widen the boundaries of our inquiry, to lower the boundary between literary and non-literary forms. Professor Lloyd Fernando points a way when, in writing his essay on "The Social Imagination and the Functions of Criticism in Asia" says:

> Of course, one must be concerned with all levels from the popular to the 'literary.' In the popular field we will need to maintain close scrutiny over the quality of newspapers, magazines, and journals if we are to avoid in due time publication and readership habits we do not desire. The cinema and television, too, have flooded Asian countries with the artistic sewage of the West. The rapid spread of educational opportunities in Asian societies makes a complex problem of literacy. Literacy inevitably alters aesthetic tastes drastically, even throws the newly-educated into confusion about aesthetic criteria. When old habits are attenuated, new and usually shoddy ones replace them effortlessly. A generation of gullible newspaper readers and television watchers can emerge overnight. Their very credulousness in the face of media technology accustoms them to accept poor standards of presentation and production. Resurgent national languages, put to intensive use under pressure from the new

consumers, undergo startling changes of vocabulary, idiom, and flexibility. The ways in which the exigencies of the present either develop or retard the expressive powers of language users will be as much a pointer to the state of the culture in a given society as the attitudes adopted towards serious modern literature and towards the literature of the past.

As multiple literary traditions are jostled into close contact with each other in a world of instant communication and increasingly intermingling social organizations, it is clear that the literatures of certain large areas of the world have been badly neglected. One underlying principle of this essay has been that the literatures of Asian nations have a great deal to contribute to extending our knowledge of human culture; another, that genuine interest in them will naturally enjoin, upon all learners of culture, participation in practical recovery programmes as well as more academic kinds of study. The production, dissemination, and study of the literary arts involve everyone, not (as of old) in the clearly demarcated roles of practitioner, or student, or critic, but in more challenging combinations of the three.

Such a notion finds support in many places. Anthony Burgess, writing recently in the *London Observer* about the new Krio-English Dictionary notes the dual responsibility of literary scholars, one we have mentioned to date. "We ought" he says, "to know what has happened to English outside of England. . . ." We have "a kind of ancestral responsibility for the spread of the language." In time we must attend to "the great linguistic things which are happening all over the world." Having just returned from a trip to South-East Asia, Burgess writes:

> Languages once thought fit only for rice-planters and fisherfolk are modernising themselves and facing the semantic problems raised by an age of electronics and cybernetics. These languages are also looking at themselves, drawing on the descriptive techniques made available by men and women in the linguistics departments of Western, and now Eastern and African, universities. This is far more important than what

the politicians say and the terrorists do, but it never makes the headlines.

We have, then, in my view special commitment and responsibility through our criticism and discussion of literary works to achieve what Northrop Frye advocates when he writes "Some view of the place of literature in civilization as a whole." Our inquiry will take us from the local to the national and from the national to the global and the modes of criticism will continue to be as various as the local conditions which produce a literature of infinite variety and complexity.

The Child Archetype in the Commonwealth Short Stories:

Katherine Mansfield, Janet Frame, and Mulk Raj Anand

K. CHELLAPPAN

The Commonwealth, though in the words of K.R. Srinivasa Iyengar, "an accident of history"[1] is no longer a symbol of an old bondage,but a new bond of common values and traditions binding a rich diversity of nations and cultures into a significant partnership of equals in the international area. The colonial wounds have healed and what is left is a federation of free nations and free minds of distinct identities but with a common cultural heritage. If colonialism was the common fate shared by these countries at a certain point, they have also become symbols of a new hope to humanity--and that is why the Commonwealth has been called, "a cross between a memory and a hope."[2] A significant point to note now is that the English language which was a witness of this tryst with destiny has itself undergone and absorbed the agonies of this process and gained new depths and a richer human content and idiom by catalysing and responding to the birth of freedom itself. In brief, the English language which was a binding force of the erstwhile Empire has itself become a symbol of this new association of hope. By a strange irony which is almost Sophoclean, the erstwhile instrument of the conquest has now become a vehicle of the creative urges of this large chunk of humanity, and the consequence is the extension of the horizons of English literature into "a new commonwealth."

If Comparative Literature is a study of "physically separate, but originally related areas of human creativeness,"[3] the Commonwealth Literature in general, and the Commonwealth short story as a sub-genre in particular is potentially a very rich field of investigation for the comparatist, because in it we see a transnational literary phenomenon beyond geographical, cultural, ethnic and even linguistic boundaries. In this particular form, which is both old and new, we find a convergence of their old traditions and a new nationhood, of colonial pain and the birth-pang of freedom and in most cases at the formal level too we find a synthesis of fable and realism, of myth and the modern consciousness and the singleness and suddenness of perception characterising the short story--which is normally a slice or ripple of reality, has acquired a richer human voice and content having absorbed the contemporary agonies of the socio-economic problems of the erstwhile colonies and their age-old traditions and their new aspirations. The purpose of this paper is to study the child archetype which is one of the most recurrent themes in some of the important short story writers in the Commonwealth.

The child became a dominant image significantly in the 19th century British Romantic literature--the era which elevated the individual and glorified the Imagination as God. When Wordsworth saw the child with the milk of paradise at the Heavenly gate, he found it as an alien in this strange step-motherly universe and the dream-children of Charles Lamb symbolise the pathos of the loneliness of the souls waiting to be born in the womb of time. Even though when Wordsworth refers to the shades of the prisonhouse closing in upon the freedom of the child, it is only in Charles Dickens we find the child becoming a fullfledged symbol of exploitation. The Wordsworthian image of immortality and the alien in a corrupt world, becomes a symbol of exploitation in history--in the social and economic areas. Significantly it is these twin dimensions of the symbol of the child that are exploited in the short stories of the Commonwealth writers, of course with a colonial colouring, in different ways and degrees. And for methodological reasons we would like to confine our comparison to two New Zealand writers, and one Indian writer in English. In Katherine Mansfield's short stories, the child stands for a lost world of innocence--the primal worlds of the Edenic New Zealand as well as childhood and the child's consciousness, is the pivot around which the world of experience revolves. The experiences of Katherine Mansfield who is yearning for a lost childhood at the personal level are inseparable from the racial longings for the primordial relationship with New Zealand as well as an archetypal longing for the home or the heaven. The child-artist she lost due to her separation from roots is recovered by the artist-child, Katherine

Mansfield while she is recreating the world of helpless but sensitive children in her stories, who are at home with the universe, though not with the society. The sense of homelessness even at home is counterpoised by the sense of a larger brotherhood with other children as well as a kinship with the cosmos is clearly brought in most of the Commonwealth stories and this could be due to their colonial experience, besides other reasons.

The sense of being an exile is an archetypal experience of the human soul, of which the child is the primal image. A writer like Katherine Mansfield combines this with her personal and racial experience, but as we said earlier, there is no bitterness either at the personal or at the racial level, and that is why her stories have become the prose poems that they are. The child symbolising the oneness of humanity--of the soul transcending social and economic distinctions is the major concern of the writer, and in the freshness of the child's perception, we can see the dews of paradise. "The Doll's House" can be considered as a representative piece in this sense. Here we find the poetry of the commonplace and the concern for the details which is the essence of the child's vision. There is also the juxtaposition of the two worlds--the joyous world of the children and the adult world with distinctions, and even the School reflected it.

> It was the only school for miles. And the consequence was all the children of the neighbourhood, the Judge's little girls, the doctor's daughters, the store-keeper's children, the milkman's, were forced to mix together. Not to speak of there being an equal number of rude, rough little boys as well. But the line had to be drawn somewhere. It was drawn at the Kelveys."[4] (p. 385)

Katherine Mansfield was acutely conscious of the deep divisions in the colonial set up and the child's consciousness serves as the touchstone for these contradictions. The doll's house is a symbol of this contradiction--it can be opened in the ways the God opens houses at the dead of night when He is taking a quiet turn with an angel. It is a micro-world, like the child or its world, and yet so different. Even though the social differences are there in any society and the child is indifferent to them, the situation is aggravated in a colonial set-up. So the doll's house can be said to symbolise the human predicament as intensified in the colonial set-up and the lamp within the doll's house, is a metaphor for the lingering child's vision, in the prison-house of the world. It is ironic that the doll's house itself whose door has a magical touch is shut to certain children. But Kezia's desire to show the doll's house to the Kelveys shows the desire of the human soul to transcend the class consciousness.

> "Mother," said Kezia, "can't I ask the Kelveys just once ?"
> "Certainly not, Kezia." (p. 387)

But in spite of that she manages to show it to Lil, though Aunt Beryl interrupts it violently. But in Lil's heart nothing remained, but a sense of fulfilment.

> She put out a finger and stroked her sister's quill; she smiled her rare smile.
> "I seen the little lamp," she said softly.
> Then both were silent once more. (p. 391)

This typical Mansfield story brings out the clash of classes in a colonial society, and the clash consciousness like the tyranny of the male ego in Kamala Das's poetry is itself part of a large conflict--not only between races, but between the possessive instinct on the one hand and a primal sense of oneness and sharing on the other.

Janet Frame, another New Zealand writer, also uses the short story to create a form in which fantasy and reality are interwoven with the dumb thoughts of a child at its threshold of adulthood. As Donald Hannah points out, "taking as its starting from Longfellow's works from his poem, "My lost youth," 'a boy's will is the wind's will, and the thoughts of youth are long, long thoughts,'- the style itself develops the theme."[5] (p. 149) Janet Frame is recording the boy's unspoken thoughts to himself. The story traces the flow of the boy's consciousness in which fantasy and day-dream continually mingle together with memories of the past and with immediate experience like coloured patterns in a kaleidoscope."(p. 149) But the style is significant only in so far as it provides a correlative to the consciousness of the child feeling alienated from the adult's world. And his struggle is to preserve his fifteenth year for himself. But the agony of growth is seen in his identification with the homelessness of his aunt. Above all, he doesn't want to accept the values of his mother's world: "to the great dismay of the adults, he suddenly found clouds more interesting than words. Clouds, light, heat." (p. 159) He didn't particularly like the other adults trying to live his life for him or his elder brother Paul thinking that he acts like a kid. When he thought of making kites he also remembered the warning of the parents against flying them in forbidden places like the streets where entanglement in the wires would cause electrocution and death. But his mind would not allow him to associate his box kite with death.

> It was a box kite, that anything so beautiful could help to destroy. It was a box kite, blue and white, as light as a bird's wing on bamboo-stick bones. None of the other boys in the street would make a box kite; theirs would be the usual kind, flat, a skeleton cross of sticks fleshed with brown paper or plastic with a sharp nose and tail and though it would fly the flight would be a plunging swooping movement as if it were not at home in the sky and longed to descend to earth whereas the box kite, Peter knew, would float and drift without panic or restlessness, like a cloud." (pp. 161-62)

The imagery in the story is significant. The other kite is an objective correlative to the life urge which forces on the child a descent to earth. Again the description of the clouds that flow can be linked with the child himself: "In a mysterious way they seemed to contain promises of a wall or a window opening beyond into the light." (p. 162) This linking of the child with heaven and the home is reminiscent of Wordsworth. As last he chooses to fly it alone in the playground:

> He could almost feel that he might be standing in the sky, sailing through it, steering his path on a voyage of discovery. (p. 163)

When he actually flew it, his feet and legs soaked in the long wet grass and "he felt the kitestring as if, tied to himself, it were a part of his own body. He knew a pleasurable feeling at once of lightness and of anchorage, as if his fast-running legs were tangled for ever in the twisted stems of grass while another part of himself were floating lightly up near the shredded white clouds." (p. 164) This is quite symbolic of the child struggling between two worlds, the world of vision and the world of fact, and very soon the vision dissolved when the kite fell when a stronger gust of wind came buffeting. More than the loss of the kite was his fear about the adult world's attitude to 'that boy.' But as Anna Rutherford and Hannah say he also ultimately finds a truth. (p. 149)

> He saw his mother with a stone in her eyes and a bone in her throat. Stone and bone were his future and she could never remove them nor perhaps would he want her to. He did not want her to grow old, or go to an institution and have her treasure snatched from her." (p. 165)

And then when he looks at the flying sheets and lavels slapping at her face she is said to have felt "a surge inside him as if he still anchored the blue and white kite and the kite itself flew on towards the hidden sun." (p. 165) The vision is pessimistic, and it shows the crumbling of the paradise of the childhood, but still the child refuses to accept defeat.

There are significant parallels between the vision of childhood in the two New Zealand writers and that of Mulk Raj Anand. Eventhough Anand's fiction also uses the child archetype to show the process of alienation in the modern world in terms of socio-economic factors, we would confine this study to his vision in "Three prose poems." "The Lost Child" is almost Blakean and also in the tradition of Indian devotional poetry where the lost child is a symbol of the soul separated from God and even though it strays from the parental love of God while it is involved in the Vanity Fair, once it begins to be conscious of itself in the true sense, it seeks union with that primal source. Whereas in Blake, God takes the shape of the Father to restore the child to the Mother-God, Anand is content to leave with the human cry: "I want my mother, I want my father." ' (p. 74)

"The Eternal Why" is also a metaphoric story--where again there is a fruitful ambiguity, since the eternal why can be seen as symbolic of the Eternal quest of man or the quest of Eternity itself for man. The symbols are archetypal--the boat, the mother, the imperceptibly moving water signifying the world of process, and the reflection of the child in the water, which may be taken as the Platonic idea of the soul's image in the world, or the springs of self-consciousness in relation to the child's first awareness of life. To the child the few heads in the floating water seem to be perplexingly unreal and indistinct. The river ultimately makes him think of its source: "He could see its vast sheet of rippling power converge into an ever smaller chasm of silver light till it lost itself in the dim vaults of steep precipices," (p. 78) and thus it became an objective correlative to his own sense of a source of the soul beyond himself. "Deep, deep in him, deep in his little soul, he knew there was something beyond the river, some dark force, some mysterious source from which it came." (p. 78) When the mother refers to the sea as the source, the child struggles "to fit the mountains, the snow, the clouds, the sea into his dark pre-natal feeling for order." (p. 79)

Again with the conviction of the supporting love of the mother he stares into the stream again. Now he sees a whirlpool which does not seem to move. This could be seen as time in its static dimension. The process of becoming is also the way to the source itself, as the river and the sea are the same, though they appear to be separated. The story is quite reminiscent of Wordsworth's lines in "Ode on Intimations of Immortality":

> Though inland far we be,
> Our souls have sight of the immortal sea
> Which brought us hither.
> in a moment travel thither.

The moment of vision for the child finds its correlative in "a smile of endless light lingering in the eyes of the day" which again is like Wordsworth's technique of bringing out the perceiver's attitude in relation to what is perceived in "The Immortality Ode."

The third story in this group also links the rays of the sun with the child's tender heart and appetite for life. Here again there is the archetypal loneliness of the child, as other children refuse to let him join them, but the child would not yield. Unconscious of himself as of his goal he runs desperately and he stumbles across a stone-Shiva as he had lost the dodging sense and he lay looking at the turquoise sky above him and the hazel earth about, the dreary sense of failure deserts him. While the boys at the foot of the hill stood broken, the child surveys the conic peak whose shapely form reminded him of something he had seen before. With this Platonic recollection of the Paradisal vision, the child runs towards the foot of the hill, strangely enough aided by the small, mounds, themselves. If the grown-up boys (like the boys in *Lord of the Flies*) shout "go back," the child is true to its vision, and (like Simon in *Lord of the Flies*) runs up the hill.

It is interesting to see that all the three Commonwealth writers attribute more or less same characteristics to the child--its heavenward gaze, its unconquerable spirit and above all its isolation. But the isolation in the New Zealand writers is brought out at the social level whereas Anand seems to be portraying it at a more metaphysical level. In all the stories, the child is both attracted by and resists the charms of the world and even the parents do not understand it, though in Anand there is a greater understanding between them. The child is seen to be different from even boys. And in that sense, as in *Lord of the Flies*, the child's world is a micro universe, and it preacts all the processes of life in its own little kingdom, and the very resistance to life makes it accept life, though not fully.

Even at the formal level there are significant similarities--all the stories use a metaphoric structure as opposed to the metonymic mode and become prose poems. The child's moods are brought out in relation to objects pertaining to the sky or light, and they are the metaphors for the vision of the child, whereas the child itself is a metaphor for the soul at one level, and the adult world at another. "Child is the Father of Man" in the Commonwealth stories not only in the sense that it has a better sense of the divine, but also because in its consciousness there is an intense enactment of the adult's problems too. But there is a difference among these writers in the intensity in which this alienation is brought out.

NOTES

1. K.R. Srinivasa Iyengar, "The Colonial and Neocolonial Encounter in Commonwealth Literature," *The Colonial and Neocolonial Encounter in Commonwealth Literature*, ed. H.H. Anniah Gowda (Mysore, 1983), p. 9.

2. *Ibid.*

3. Henry H.H. Remak, "Comparative Literature: Its Definition and Function," *Comparative Literature: Method and Perspective*, ed. Newton P. Stallnecht and D. Horst Frenz (Carbondale and Edwardswill: Southern Illinois Press, 1971), p. 22.

4. Katherine Mansfield, *The Collected Short Stories* (U.K.: Penguin Books, 1982).

5. Anna Rutherford and Donald Hannah, ed., *Commonwealth Short Stories* (Macmillan Intercollege Edition, 1979).

6. Mulk Raj Anand, *The Barber's Trade Union and Other Stories* (Arnold Heinemann, 1944, rep. 1977).

Hugh MacLennan's *The Watch That Ends The Night*: An Inter-disciplinary Approach

S. RAMASWAMY

I

Hugh MacLennan begins his novel with the sentence, "There are some stories into which the reader should be led gently and I think this may be one of them." (p. 3) He ends the novel with an 'Epilogue' which begins with the sentence, "I could end here because my story is told. But if this has been a story into which the reader was led gently, I think it may also be one out of which he should be led factually." (p. 370) In both these objectives the author has succeeded completely and the story itself that has been told is such a delicate web woven from the lives of three highly sensitive souls living through a difficult time in history--the 30's and the Depression years. Montreal is the 'mise en scene' for the most part. Halifax, Ottawa, Toronto also do figure in the story. So do Spain, Russia and Germany to define the atmosphere against which the human drama unfolds itself. But it is Montreal itself that has been described with such loving care that the novel may even be taken as the story of this great city. Just one reference out of more than three dozen references to Montreal:

> It is a curious city, Montreal, and in this story I keep returning to the fact that it is. Strangers never understand its inner nature, and immigrant families, even from other parts of Canada, can live here two generations without coming to know it in their bones. I am absolutely certain that Montreal is the subtlest and most intricate city in North America. With her history she could not have been otherwise and survived, for here the French, the Scotch and the English, over two centuries, have been divided on issues which ruin nations and civilizations, yet have contrived to live in outward harmony.

> This is no accident. They understand certain rules in their bones. (p. 255)

It is in this 'subtlest and most intricate city' that three of the 'subtlest and most intricate' characters in modern literature are described, psycho-analysed and philosophised upon. The novel is best comprehended in an inter-disciplinary approach--in terms of the political, the psychological and the philosophical levels. *The Watch That Ends The Night* is the voyage of self-exploration of three people--George who is the narrator of the story, Catherine and Jerome. There are several well-conceived minor characters like Norah Blackwell, Caroline, Sally etc. but in the interests of focus from the inter-disciplinary approach, the three main characters are examined here briefly in terms of politics, psychology and philosophy.

II

The Watch That Ends The Night can be read as a 'Political Novel' about the 30's. Spain figures so largely in the novel that Jerome's obsession about Spain, Fascism, Franco, Communism, etc., forms the very crux of the matter in the novel. The crisis in the relationship between Catherine and Jerome, the breakdown of their relationship, Norah Blackwell's affair with Jerome and her desperate bid to establish a meaningful relationship with Jerome has partly to do with the political ideology which she shares with him. The novel's 'reality' is firmly grounded in the political turmoil of the Thirties as is so obvious:

> I tell you, there are few people who passed through the Thirties who even dare or can recall what that time was really like or what it did to human beings. . . . There were times when, being young, I allowed myself the luxury of hope. But there was poison in the air then, and I think it spread from the rotting corpses of the first war. The Thirties lie behind us like the memory of guilt and shame. (p. 123)

George, the narrator of the story is himself a political commentator for the CBC with 'a voice a little like Roosevelt's,' (p. 278) and is immensely popular for his politically astute views. At one point in the novel the 'names and phrases of the time' (p. 142) are given--Laski, Keyenes, Marx, Selassie, Lenin, Ras Desta, Trotsky, Hitler, Mussolini, Goebbels, Baldwin, Chamberlain, Lansbury, Franco, Roosevelt, Dos Passos, Hemingway, etc., and is followed by the wry comment:

> The 1930's was the last time in which college professors could believe themselves capable of planning the future of humanity. (p. 142)

It is interesting that the author of the novel MacLennan himself is a Professor and in many ways *The Watch That Ends The Night* is a very 'academic' novel--dealing as it does with human life at various levels lending itself for an inter-disciplinary approach.

III

The Watch That Ends The Night can certainly be read as a 'Psychological novel' as the characters in the novel are analysed with clinical precision and the motivation behind every choice and 'action' of Jerome can be discussed in terms of clinical psychology. Jerome himself is an excellent surgeon and his prowess as a healer extends beyond the operation table. He healed the patients by understanding their minds and he is aware of his own neurosis too. His mind is constantly and incessantly in conflict and so are his loyalties. His own illegitimate birth and his extremely religious upbringing by his foster parents, especially Mr. Martell the clergyman--these come into sharp conflict with his rejection of middle class morality and indeed, he resigns his job as a surgeon at the height of his professional success to follow his political ideology in Spain and he breaks away from a perfect marital relationship with a beautiful woman Catherine, and defends and teams up with another man's wife. Indeed, throughout the novel Hugh MacLennan bestows a great deal of space to expatiate upon this psychological enigma of an extraordinary man--Jerome Martell. In order to illustrate the 'psychological' dimension of the novel, just one illustration--the dialogue between Sally, the daughter of Jerome and Catherine, and George the narrator.

> "Why does everybody stand up for him ?" she said
> "Everybody doesn't."
> "But you do. I think there is something neurotic in your whole attitude. It's all mixed up with how you feel about mummy. She loved him and you want to kid yourself you love him, too. You want to share him with her the same way you share me."
> I shook my head. . . .
> "You are talking like a child." I said. "Do you think my generation invented neuroses ? Do you think things in the Thirties were the same as now ? Mistakes ? For God's sake of course, we made them ! But let me tell you something Sally. You haven't earned the right to despise your father. You may HAVE that right, but by God, you have not earned it."
>
> Our eyes met and she looked away, still headstrong, considerably upset, resentful and guilty because she was. Truly I thought this girl felt guilty whenever she detected a trace of neurosis in herself and this made me smile grimly. Was neurosis the new word for sin ? (p. 47)

Indeed, throughout the novel, the three main characters, George Jerome and Catherine are not only 'psychoanalysing' each other but they seem to be expert psychiatrists analysing themselves--their actions and their reactions--absolutely honestly and even ruthlessly ! The question "Was neurosis the new word for sin ?" leads to the third dimension of the novel--the philosophical dimension, which according to the present writer is the most significant one in the inter-disciplinary approach to the novel.

IV

To the present writer, the novel *The Watch That Ends The Night* is much more than merely a good novel because of its spiritual dimension. In the case of all the three characters, who are immensely intelligent, hyper-sensitive and intensely self-critical, the thread that unites as well as separates them is their spiritual quest. The old Socratic injunction 'Know Thyself' is at the root of the quest of all these three characters--George the narrator, always in love with Catherine, Jerome, who is married to Catherine but is moved by strange longings, Catherine herself, one of the most intelligent and sensitive portrayals of women characters in the whole range of English fiction--all the three are going through a voyage of self-discovery in the novel. "Who am I really ?" is the self-inquiry in which all three engage themselves in the novel. George thinks at the beginning of the novel that "he had come to terms with myself." (p. 4) Sally, the daughter of Jerome, is interested in finding out who she really is as she dislikes Jerome but likes George--"Underneath her banter, she had been disturbed lately and in one way or another she had been asking me questions about the 1930's. I had not realised that her motive had been to lead me on to talk of Jerome. "Who am I ? Whence come I ?" (p. 22) *The* character in the novel who is most spiritually inclined is Catherine. Indeed, the novel by MacLennan is his 'Portrait of a Lady'--the portrait of Catherine who is an extremely extraordinary lady. Her physical condition of a heart patient, her psychological maturity in the understanding of human strength and weakness, her spiritual strength of selfless acceptance of others--all these are highlighted by the author throughout the novel. To give an illustration:

> Her fate was that rheumatic heart of hers. Her strength, her essence, her mystery in which occasionally I had almost drowned--this I can only call her spirit, and I don't use the word in a sentimental sense. Far from it. For to me this has become the ultimate reality, so much so that I think of this story not as one conditioned by character as the dramatists understand it, but by the spirit. A conflict, if you like, between the spirit and the human condition. (p. 25)

Catherine's spiritual maturity, her philosophical outlook and detachment, her utterly selfless appreciation of others, these qualities make her one of the most endearing portraits ever created in English fiction. No wonder George feels--"she was my rock, she was my salvation." (p. 26) Right at the end of the novel, Catherine's face is described in these terms by George:

> It had become so transparent one almost felt one looked at a spirit. Light was in it. Light came out of it. Light came from her constantly into me. (p. 371)

This is a remark which sums up the George-Catherine relationship which is the main theme of the novel because she was his 'rock,' his 'salvation.' Instances can be multiplied to emphasize the spiritual dimension of the novel but the third dimension--the philosophical one--has been illustrated to emphasize the multi-dimensional approach that can be made to this complex Canadian novel.

V

What has been sought to be indicated in this brief analysis of Hugh MacLennan's *The Watch That Ends The Night* is the fact that it is a great novel which is complex enough and profound enough to be analysed from a multi-dimensional, inter-disciplinary approach and the three levels of the novel, the realistic political level, the psychological level, the philosophical level, are all complementary to each other. In the present cursory analysis, while it is pointed out that at the political level, George is important, at the psychological level, Jerome is important and at the philosophical level, it is Catherine that is important, all these three characters, because of the proverbial 'menage a trois' situation and their interaction with each other form an inseparable aspect of the exploration of the human condition. The spiritual, philosophical aspect of the novel is best expressed in the words: "A man must belong to something larger than himself. He must surrender to it." (p. 270) This is reiterated at the end of the novel:

> All our lives we had wanted to belong to something larger than ourselves. Whatever the spirit might be, I did not know, but I knew it was there. Life was a gift; I knew that now. (p. 372)

The total meaning and achievement of Hugh MacLennan's *The Watch That Ends The Night* can be comprehended only through an inter-disciplinary approach.

NOTES

1. Hugh MacLennan, *The Watch That Ends The Night* (Macmillan of Canada, Toronto, 1958).

Language and Responsibility: Two Versions of Psychological Reality in the Anti-War Writings of Roger Pulvers and John Romeril

DAVID KERR

Despite considerable differences in tone and method, Roger Pulvers and John Romeril reach similar conclusions on the process by which racial prejudice inserts itself into the rhetoric of a people and achieves, for them, the status of objective fact. Each writer was stimulated by a specific set of circumstances, the common thread being an interest in the impact of cultural difference on value judgements, especially in the context of warfare.

Roger Pulvers explained his three works on the Second World War in terms of his recollections of Macarthyism and his revulsion at racist attitudes. In an interview with the author ("Writing in the Eighties") he said:

> The anti-Japanese feeling in America and here before the war was astounding. . . . Americans were lulled into the idea the Japanese couldn't fight. Racism permeated military strategy, and had disgusting effects on the way people treated each other.

In particular, *Yamashita* was triggered by a picture he saw in the Nagasaki peace museum showing fliers posed in front of one of the planes that A-bombed Nagasaki. Of it he says "That photograph was the most horrible thing I remember about my visit to the museum."[1]

Romeril, on the other hand, initially felt drawn to a study of the clash of cultures under the stress of war. Speaking of the genesis of *The Floating World*, he said:

> I began work in 1969, a thing about New Guinea . . . during the Second World War. [I was going] to develop a cultural clash--I had been reading on Kabuki and the Japanese theatre. . . . I thought of it as highly evolved, ornate and delicate, and I was interested in stacking that up against Australian cultural mores. The show took a peculiar turn in 1972 when I had to stow away to get home from Singapore. This ship became the ship on which lots of *The Floating World* is based. The rituals of shipboard life, talent night, the comic, fancy dress, crossing the equator. . . . On the same trip I met a friend who told me the Les Harding story. (Interview with the author: "Writing in the Eighties")

Racism and psychological stress, therefore, provide the impetus to the work of both writers. However, while both work through dramatic structures that owe a great deal to the experimental "rough" theatre of the Pram Factory and the Playbox theatre in Melbourne in the early seventies, their tone and impact differs markedly. Romeril's comedy is shot through with the stench of rotting corpses, the recollection of excrement, swollen bodies, of desperate gambles with one's sanity in order to survive. Further, Romeril uses the ship-board rituals to explore the relationships between language and thought, in particular through getting into the tortured, often surreal wanderings of Les Harding's mind. Pulvers, also deeply interested in language and meaning, treats both character and action more schematically and with less earthy gusto than Romeril does. Both set their works in "the present" and rediscover the past through present action. However, in *Yamashita* the impulse to move back in time is determined by the structure and method of the play, not through psychological pressure, as happens with Les Harding. The narrator of *The Death of Urashima Taro* is admittedly driven to final self-sacrifice by a generalized guilt but Les Harding's guilt is his own, and it overwhelms him.

Pulvers, moved by the absurdity of sacrifice for "something higher"--whether that be an Emperor, or an ideology, wants his audience to *see* the absurdity first, then feel it.

Romeril is equally moved by the implications of sacrifice. In his play Les Harding's destruction traces to his failure in self-sacrifice as demanded by the creed of mateship. "Humankind cannot bear very much reality," a line from the last page of Romeril's play, is offered in part explanation of Les Harding's psychological collapse.

For Pulvers (and most of mankind) the atomic bombing of Hiroshima and Nagasaki on August 6th and August 9th, 1945 is the most unbearable reality in human history. The climax of both*Yamashita* and *The Death of Urashima Taro* is built around images of and responses to the bombing. In the play the climax acts to underscore the gross, bullying presumptuousness of racism, while in the novel it focuses on questions of power and responsibility.

These two works illuminate each other in a number of ways despite the obvious differences between them. Issues of subjectivity and objectivity, central issues in the novel, are implied in the play's action, which is concerned with prejudice in the guise of objective "definition," in turn offered as substantial grounds for sweeping moral judgements of one person by another.

The power in language to express and confirm cultural and political hegemony is central to the play. First, the settings illustrate how societies transmit values and codes through institutional frameworks by giving a particular colour to language. Second, Pulvers confronts the assumption that this process is just and equitable, by showing it being actively subverted, as the connection between language and reality becomes distorted by human wishes and illusions.

For example, Chow points out to the perpetually silent Yamashita that:

> Morality is as incorruptible as language. . . . Justice and morality must be approached with a mind to structure and propriety. (p. 39)

As Chow explains, language and personal relationships convey the same thing--the categories and divisions of experience. Consequently, if language is distorted, so are relationships between people.

As the play progresses, Chow and the janitor, where their interests are concerned, allow meanings to slide. Chow, for example, writes the words "dirty" and "clean" on the blackboard and rubs them out, remarking that "some things require only a superficial dusting."[2] (p. 39)

The janitor takes this process to its extreme, transferring the idea of "dusting" onto the bombing of Hiroshima and Nagasaki, by implying that the "two little nuggets like the sun" will wipe out distinctions, thereby "cleaning up" an Asian plague spot. (p. 45) The Japanese will be taught a lesson, defined as inferior culturally, intellectually, morally, politically and physically---thereby retaliating for the humiliation of Pearl Harbour.

His aggressive paternalism becomes ugly and vindictive:

> We're gonna over-expose 'em. Until they look like naked shadows on a negative. Until there's nothing' lef' a' Nip but a yella scum spread on the groun,' like melted butter. (p. 46)

In essence, *Yamashita* is a parodic analogy, in its form and structure, of the way the United States of America has interfered, through forms of cultural imperialism in the post-war period, in Japan and East Asia. America's claim to moral superiority is shown to be absurd as, in a series of metamorphoses, the classroom becomes a courtroom, the school janitor becomes a hanging judge of the Old West, the Hawaiian (Chow) becomes the prosecuting attorney, and the Japanese student, Yamashita, becomes the general of the same name, executed in 1946 by a military court for "crimes against civilization."

The play raises, through its ironic method, two issues--what was the real "crime against civilization" in the Second World War, and who bears the responsibility for that crime ? What degree of responsibility should be felt (this is a question that Pulvers approaches again, with subtler emphasis in the novel) by someone who was not "there" at the time the crime was committed ? In the mock trial the janitor/judge acquits Yamashita of sexual depravity on those grounds, but later finds him guilty of the attack on Pearl Harbour, because "innocence applies to someone who fought against the Japs. Not even the Japanese will argue that one."(p. 37)

A further link between play and novel is mankind's need to feel at the centre of things. This feeling, which confers a delusive sense of absolute knowledge, of Godlike wisdom, is thematically linked via the concept of *kokoro* to the sun on the one hand, and the nuclear bomb on the other. In the novel the interconnections are explored ironically through Ron's mental delusions, whereas in the play, as I have noted, emphasis is placed on the parallel identity of the bomb and the sun.

Despite these delusions, mankind cannot escape responsibility. In fact, Pulvers casts the net wider than most of us are prepared, in the interests of self-preservation, to do. As he points out in the novel, if being "there" is not in itself significant, the use of atomic weapons against the Japanese profoundly implicates the whole of Western society, then and now. Those who approved that act, or failed to oppose it at the time, or in retrospect support it, or fail to oppose it now are, in Pulvers's terms, responsible. When I interviewed him Pulvers claimed to feel responsible for events in human history that occurred long before he was born.

The structure of *The Death of Urashima Taro* is designed to give substance to this view. Ron, a film producer for the A.B.C., is in Japan to arrange a co-produced documentary on the Cowra prisoner-of-war escape. He senses a mystery surrounding a series of murders and a suicide that, he eventually concludes, were committed to prevent the Emperor's complicity in the A-bombing of Hiroshima and Nagasaki being publicly revealed. For Ron the investigation becomes obsessive. Any act that might contribute to solving the mystery seems justified.

As the narrative develops, Ron shows progressive signs of instability. His meticulous chronology, which serves to order reality for him, lapses, and he loses two weeks of his life. He spends long periods in bed. He is troubled by childhood memories, especially of his father. In order to make sense of what he calls his subjective account of events he attempts to re-order his memory of them objectively. In the process, some events are transformed to their opposite, others are elaborated, others fade from view. His memory, in effect, responds to his need.

In the interview Pulvers argued that there is no difference between the subjective and objective way of seeing the world. All seeing is interpretative, and what changes when we claim objectivity is our attitude of being at the centre of events.

Being at, or seeing into, the centre of things, is the unifying image of the novel. It is Ron's habit of mind to probe--not merely the mystery of the Cowra war graves and its connection with the Emperor, but more fundamentally, the mystery of man's place in the universe. Ron's quest parallels the scientific quest to unlock the secrets of nature.

To the traditional Japanese, *kokoro*, or the heart of things, may be contemplated but neither analysed nor communicated, for to attempt either is destructive. In defiance of this view Ron pursues his quest, disregarding the consequences that become increasingly threatening. In the end he murders a man to gain access to a television tape that might contain one more piece to the jig-saw he is assembling. Finally his frenetic search takes him to the Imperial household where he is shot as a possible terrorist, thereby completing a martyrdom he has unconsciously prefigured for himself.

His death has been carefully prepared in other ways. Through the incorporation of the Urashima Taro legend into the narrative, Pulvers is able, by a circuitous route, to integrate his narrator's psychological collapse into his symbolic evocation of the power of nuclear weapons, thereby suggesting a redefinition of reality to the reader.

Pulvers summarises the legend early in the novel:

> Urashima Taro rode a turtle's back down to the bottom of the sea, He spent three years there in ecstatic delight. Every piece of his imagination was given vent, every fold in his brain was given the warm thick liquid until his eyes could hardly see though they were opened in awe and amazement at everything before them. Everything he did there came through sound and touch and smell. There was no picture, no image to see. When he came back from the bottom of the sea he carried a box, given to him, a kind of gift. Then, back on land, he opened his eyes for the first time. But he could recognise nothing at all there. No person was the same person. No place was the same place. He was left with nothing to do. He opened the box. Smoke came out of it and from the smoke a very old, old man who was himself. The old man had his eyes open all the time,

> but he had heard no sound nor felt a thing since the time when Urashima Taro went down to the bottom of the sea.[2]

Urashima Taro, a name given to an unidentified Japanese soldier in a Cowra war grave, represents all the Japanese soldiers who died in the war, and the narrator himself. The legend, which hints at the elasticity of time, experience and memory, implies that knowledge cannot be transmitted from one world--that of the imagination--to the so-called real world without destroying its bearer. The box Taro brings back, therefore--analogous to the one Ron opens in the final scene of the novel--causes, when opened, man's collective amnesia in the face of overwhelming knowledge.

Pulvers is seeking to establish the state of collective consciousness in a nuclear age. The hints are numerous and diverse. His narrator, for example, born in 1945, entered a world where atomic weapons had been used in warfare for the first time. In addition, Ron's efforts to solve the riddle of the Cowra war graves is paralleled by an image which reflects mankind's drive to probe the mechanism of nature. Pulvers uses the image of the detective story to make his point.

> A certain writer has written: "The people in a detective story are, inevitably, only cogs in a larger mechanism, the artificially manufactured story itself. They are people, and at the same time, *not* people. No matter how many murders are committed, no matter how cruel is the method of elimination, the victims are victims only in a game of 'crime on paper' that these people are playing. . . .I am totally outside the mechanism watching the man who is manufacturing it, as if my life depended on it. (p. 17)

Ron's position outside the mechanism of the puzzle he is trying to solve, is similar to that adopted by those who dispose of the lives of others for a "cause." In looking back at such atrocities they too easily become "a crime on paper" where the victims, as a generalised concept, seem stripped of humanity. The persistence of such thinking creates the conditions for people accepting genocide as something which, though not desirable, may sometimes be inescapable. The victims at best are treated as imaginary. At worst they become animals, less than human. When Ron finally commits murder to achieve ends that he is convinced are important (he is mad at the time, but feels objectively in control), he shares in the mentality of those still capable of endorsing the bombing of Hiroshima or Nagasaki--or genocide against any race or nationality.

Ron's sacrificial martyrdom represents a subconscious fulfilling of his destiny. He sees himself as made for sacrifice, *exactly* like his father. (p. 120) Like Christ, he wishes to take responsibility for mankind's transgressions. In doing so, he becomes part of the series of ritual sacrifices designed to suppress knowledge of the emperor's complicity in the bombing of Hiroshima and Nagasaki. As the novelist says, taking over Ron's narrative for a moment:

> They had done it as sacrifice, never for themselves. Sacrifice for something else, something higher, is another form of murder. (p. 119)

The last scene of the novel brings a number of thematic strands into a relationship: madness, sacrifice, problems of perception, the twin illusions of power and knowledge, are inextricably bound together. The focus is on the mysterious "box" that contains an awesome secret. Ron, sliding towards death, watches as the guards open it:

> They were treating the box with care, as if it were a bomb, a bomb meant to be put at the very centre of things. That's why I carried it like that, in both my hands, above my head. Because it was sacred. To them it was a bomb.
>
> My head moved back and forth, as if swimming on the smooth liquid surface of the floor. There was no-one around. The two guards carefully unwrapped the box now. I didn't have time to see what was inside it. And there was no other person in my mind any more to think about who would be imagining me there, or anywhere. (p. 120)

Pulvers's conclusion to the novel suggests the slender hold that contemporary man has on reality. Like Ron, we tend to construct a

God and claim to be exactly like him, as Ron does. Our worship of power and of knowledge are combined in the image of the nuclear weapon, which is the product of understanding some of the central secrets of creation. While sliding out of control into oblivion, we can still convince ourselves that we are governed by a rational morality based on objective criteria.

Ron represents that part of mankind that, like Faust, seeks to probe secrets and control destinies. However, Pulvers's fiction illustrates the unreality of the subjective/objective dichotomy, as it is not possible to obtain a position not subject to the relativity that comes from being part of the system. It is a moral fable illustrating the consequences of not accepting the limitations of being human, and to a degree fettered by the limitations of time, space and perspective.

John Romeril's *The Floating World*, approaches the dominant responses to war--madness, alienation, sacrifice and racism--more directly than Pulvers does. His main character, Les Harding, comes to us more fully fleshed out than the shadowy Ron, who seems to be the vehicle for an idea rather than a person. Harding represents men who knew the war first-hand. Therefore, whereas Pulvers has no occasion to include gross physical details in his narrative, Romeril wades right in. He responds to a challenge to make something resembling poetry from the gross, physically disgusting material.

It is this which gives a particular quality to Harding's mental state, where the casual obscenities of the soldiers are shown to be an inadequate defence against the real horrors they are, as prisoners-of-war, forced to go through. As Irene naively remarks, foreshadowing her husband's collapse, "Course we'll be unrecognisable when we get back."[3] The process by which Ron becomes unrecognisable is merely sketched in, whereas Romeril immerses his audience in Les Harding's interior drama, creating not only what has been locked away in his mind for thirty years, but the dynamics of the process that will shake memory loose.

In keeping with the metaphor that governs the play--the floating world--as Les Harding approaches Japan he moves from expressing old resentments against the British to hallucinating, and projecting fragments of his interior drama onto those around him, so that the dialogue develops a fugue-like pattern of interweaving strands.

The recurrent question that nags him is--how could he visit as a tourist a country that caused immeasurable suffering to his mates ? "I never split on a mate" (p. 28) is Harding's creed. Ironically, the play is about betrayal, in particular self-betrayal. It emerges that Harding feels guilty because he is alive while so many others are dead, and he kept hold of life--it is the lesser admission--by eating the rations of dead men. It is not until the final scene of the play, when Les is well gone in madness, that he relives his deepest shame--that he owes his life to a pack of vitamin B tablets that he stole from a Japanese officer, and did not share. His plaintive "I was well again" which concludes the play is one of the most moving ironies in contemporary Australian drama.

The play reaches wider than Les Harding in its delineation of human suffering. Through the "floating world" metaphor Romeril explores the suffering caused by the forced connection, or false connection between one circumstance or object or state and another. In his floating world the latrine and the kitchen become near neighbours, boats go on roads, people diagnose problems without seeing them (or from someone else's description, like the Pakistani doctor of Irene's imagination), and the unknown is romantic and desirable because it is unknown. Reality is not confronted because, as already noted, mankind cannot bear too much reality.

In effect, it is the rupture of something Les Harding feels should be unbreakable--his fidelity to his mates--that pitches his mind into the random succession of "states" that, in his case, characterises madness. Nothing belongs with anything else in this state. The world is a drifting chaos. Les Harding's mind symbolises the twentieth century mind plagued with a sense of the falsity of its cherished ideas, and with nothing to take their place.

Romeril and Pulvers, in their differing ways, are deeply conscious of the way language becomes perverted in the political process. But, whereas Pulvers insists on the primacy of subjective reality and our shared humanity, Romeril shows that, in attempting to hold on to ideas and prejudices that have lost their force we place ourselves, and the world, at risk. After reading their works it should be more difficult to ever again feel comfortable with the idea of going to war.

NOTES

1. Roger Pulvers, *Yamashita* (Currency Press, Sydney, 1981), p.7

2. Roger Pulvers, *The Death of Urashima Taro* (Angus and Robertson, Sydney, 1981), p.31.

3. John Romeril, *The Floating World* (Currency Press, Sydney, 1982), p. 54.

The Christ Figure in the Plays of Soyinka

RADHAMANI GOPALAKRISHNAN

Bringing about a perfect synthesis between the regional and the universal elements in his plays, Wole Soyinka has, with ease, bridged what he calls "the artificial gap between the theatre in Yoruba and the theatre in English." Adrian Roscoe points out how "a modern grafting has been performed on a vigorous traditional plant."[1] A highly complex and compactly worked out system of symbols employed by Soyinka serves very effectively in bringing about the synthesis of several layers of meaning. The corpus of Soyinka's plays, quite modest in the quantitative sense, forms a small universe of its own. The original uniqueness, faithful to the native soil, is assiduously preserved, to the minute details, but new elements are being absorbed into the mainstream all along.

The Ifa religion,"the Africanised Ageless Wisdom," is still prevalent in West Africa after the advent and progress of Christianity. Fela Sowlande observes: "Ifa will not die, Ifa cannot die. It cannot die, because it is the Africanised Ageless Wisdom, and like the Phoenix, it will always arise from its own ashes, fresh, young, invigorated, dynamic, instinct with new life and new vitality, to run another course."[2]

The Yoruba gods have proved to be fertile sources of ideas for Soyinka. Flexible as they are in the symbolic values associated with them, the deities on the Ifa pantheon have provided the playwright with the key figures in building up the symbolic superstructrues. Adrian Roscoe comments on the flexibility of the gods:

> Such is its flexibility that Sango, the god of thunder and lightning has, with perfect ease, become also the god of electricity. Ogun, a god of prodigious power and responsibility, the deity associated with iron and metals, generally with war, explorations, artisans and creativity, is now also the god of the

road and the god of workers. He would preside as naturally over Ibadan's Department of Metallurgy as Jeremy Bentham over the London school of Economics.[3]

Ogun, with all the symbolic associations, is at the very core of Soyinka's art which is irretrievably linked with several facets of the deity who represents sheer driving energy, creative in general, but destructive at times. The Ogun myth is explored to the very depth in his poem *Idanre*, where the concept is elevated to the heights of universality. Erinle, the animal god, Eshu, the god of fate, Oro, the god of punishment and death and Oya, the wife of Sango, are among the gods frequently appearing in his plays.

Native rituals like Agemo, Egungun, and Oro appealed to Soyinka in being rich with symbolic significance. Agemo was the cult of the dead, or a religious cult of flesh dissolution. "Agemo, the mere phrase, includes the passage of transition from the human to the divine essence." Oro is the cult of sacrifice, more specifically it refers to an individual's sacrifice for the benefit of the community, voluntary or otherwise. Soyinka has drawn very heavily upon the meanings associated with these rituals, and has made them the richer, adding several new aspects of interpretation leading to universal significance.

Soyinka uses yet another group of symbols, including deformed or disabled characters like the Blind Beggar, the Hunchback and the One-Legged Imp to represent abstractions and additions in human nature. They bear close similarity to those symbols used by Yeats in his Blind Man, Lame Man, Hunchback, and the Fool

Another very conspicuous presence felt frequently is that of the Christ figure. Aloof and isolated in the physical sense, these figures represent the negation of self, their very existence being for the sake of the community. The Blind Beggar in *The Swamp Dwellers*, and Emman in *The Strong Breed* are representative Christ figures. The same theme, clearer than in these two plays, is introduced, as a specimen of bold innovation, in Soyinka's version of the *Bacchae* of Euripides.

In *The Swamp Dwellers*, located in a simple hut among the swamps suggestive of the Niger Delta, the aged father and mother are awaiting the return of their younger son Igwezu. It is getting dark, and Makuri and Alu have their own fears, having already lost the elder son who went away to the city, never to return. The three visitors who arrive in succession illuminate the entire theme. Drought and flood, scarcity and surfeit, impatience and humility, the polar opposites are brought together under the same roof, represented by the village priest, the Kadiye and the Blind Beggar who arrives from the land of droughts and locusts. The corpulent, over-fed Kadiye, the chief priest of the "serpent of the Swamps" is the universally familiar voice of religious hyprocisy and exploitation, injecting venom into the blood stream of the entire population of the area. Pitted against him quite appropriately, as the original Jesus Christ was against the pharisees during His days, is the Blind Beggar, arriving from nowhere, bringing message of hope, peace, and love. He belongs to the soil, and enjoys the feel of loose mud between his fingers. The wet earth sends a thrill through his entire being. He is the master of the situation himself when he succeeds in consoling Igwezu who has lost the entire harvest of the year. Yet, he prefers the role of the slave and calls Igwezu his master, and promises to stay to 'render account' to him whenever he returns from the city. He is positive in every word of his; wants nothing for himself, and is capable of bringing solace to men who need it. He wins where the Kadiye fails, because the latter stands for exploitation. The Blind Beggar gives himself away in service. This humility makes him the master who prefers remaining the slave.

The Beggar here is a Christ figure, though drawn in rather dim outlines. Wandering about, all alone, taking little for himself, he can give himself completely away. Soyinka has superimposed yet another meaning here when he introduces the Blind Beggar unmistakably as a Mohamedan. The best in Islam and the best in humanity come together in his art, as such instances are seen with clear frames in *The Strong Breed* and *Bacchae*. He stands for the negation of self for the benefit of the community, represented in this context by Igwezu who loses everything including his faith in the soil. The sacrifice element is absent in *The Swamp Dwellers*, the emphasis being placed on the positive benevolence of Christ. The Master, preferring to treat Himself as the Slave, He revives human faith in life. The overtones of Islam add to Soyinka's assertion that the basis of all religions is the same in the positive sense--affirmation of one's faith in the benevolence of mother Earth representing the Creative Power.

The Strong Breed is a tragedy based on the Yoruba ritual of Oro Sacrifice, usually observed on New Year's eve. A man, considered to be the 'carrier' of all the evils of the village for the past one year, is tortured to death and hanged at midnight heralding the new year, thus warding off all the evils for the future. The play deals with the theme in all its crude details, the ritual gaining universal significance from the symbolic values attributed to it by the playwright. Animal scapegoats were used frequently in the ritual, but human sacrifices were not infrequent.

Introducing the central figure, Eman, Soyinka dramatizes the need for sacrifice which is the only sure means of expiation or retribution even to one's own self. The Yoruba, the classical, and the Christian elements are blended together in the tragedy of Eman. The play opens in an atmosphere of tension and foreboding. The town is preparing for the celebration of the New Year. Eman, a stranger who has come to the town as a dispenser, is being hurried away by Sunma. Eman is reluctant to leave, and fails to understand for some time why she sounds so nervous and desperate. Sunma is exasperated when he is adamant, but continues to be evasive when he asks for explanation. She offers to go with him anywhere, provided he would hurry up and board the last lorry that is about to leave. It dawns on him that the towns-people believe in catching hold of a stranger and making him the sacrificial scapegoat for the New Year's eve. Sunma, who loves him deeply, would like to save him. Ifada, the crippled idiot boy, is with them, and Sunma knows he has already been chosen for the purpose. Yet, one cannot say. A stranger is safer away from the town on such occasions. Eman remains stubborn as if he is persuaded by some unseen power to stay on. A sinister drama is being enacted simultaneously outside the hut. A girl enters dragging a cloth effigy, 'a carrier' by a string. She has been ill, and according to the local belief, the carrier, properly beaten up and finally tied to a tree and burnt off, would carry off the last traces of her illness. The girl, herself breathing evil, wants Ifada to join her in beating up her cloth carrier. The scene for the enactment of a similar drama in larger dimension, is set. The last lorry moves off. Eman will face whatever might befall him. Sunma knows their fates are linked, yet she does not understand the true meaning of his reluctance to leave the scene, even though he has understood the gravity of the situation. It is clear that he wants to expiate for some sin in the past, far beyond Sunma's comprehension. Eman reiterates his strong conviction that he has been seeking something all along, and that he can fulfill himself only if he stays on and spends himself. He has to continue playing the role of the stranger. He cannot define anything in clearer words. But his words have the finality.

Two men drag Ifada away and the girl runs off, scared, leaving her cloth doll on Eman's doorstep. Eman stoops to pick it up. Sunma makes a last desperate bid to prevent him from encountering the blow of fate. Ifada manages to flee from his torturers and seeks shelter with Sunma. She knows the outcome only too well, and hesitates. Eman pushes her away and offers to protect the idiot boy, shuddering in panic. What Sunma wanted to prevent has happened. A group of men, led by her father Jaguna, arrives in search of the missing scapegoat, only to find a stranger, more admirably suited to be their sacrificial carrier. Eman's destiny is taking its grim shape, despite Sunma's efforts to forestall it. Eman takes the place of the crippled boy. What follows is a series of brief unlocalized scenes, gradually leading towards the climax. These scenes re-enact how Eman's father was once playing the hereditary role as the 'carrier' of his village who had to ride a dwarf boat, representing the sins of the community. It was only seldom that such dwarf boats returned safe, bringing the surviving carrier back. Eman refused to take over the hereditary role from his father. He runs away deserting his role, deserting his father, and deserting his wife Omae who stays on with his father, and dies in bearing Eman's child. His father's words reverberate in his ears:

> Son, it is not the mouth of the boaster that says he belongs to the strong breed. It is the tongue that is red with pain and black with sorrow.[3]

Eman reappears, crossing the stage in pain and thirst, still trying to escape in spite of the soul's will to sacrifice himself. It is over.

Eman's sacrifice ends the play, but Soyinka would like to point out how ironical the reaction of the village turned out to be. Sunma lapses into loneliness. But, instead of looking up at the dead carrier hanging from the tree and pronouncing curses on him, "One and all they looked up at the man and words died in their throats." Even earlier there was a faint suggestion that the people caught a glimpse of a strange 'something' in the victim's face as he was about to face death.

Eman's path has been a lonely one from the beginning. He thinks, he suffers, he errs, and thinks again. He grabs the opportunity for expiation which leads to fulfilment. Yet, there are a few momentary glimpses of his suffering as a human being, and the agony of the flesh that longs to escape. The soul asserts itself.

Eman's sacrifice is reminiscent of Christ's Passion, and the subsequent crucifixion. The parallel is subtly worked out. He too is a teacher and a healer. Eman's conscious sacrifice for those who are unable to understand or appreciate him is another point of similarity. Eldred D. Jones works out these points of similarity: "Towards the climax of the physical sacrifice, his body flinches, and he needs water. Eman's pathetic appeal to the girl who betrays him parallels Christ's agonized cry 'I thirst.' Eman's death, like Christ's, stuns the people in whose name it had been demanded, and leaves a remarkable impression on some unlikely minds."[5]

Eldred Jones evaluates the role of Eman: "He represents a moral force which transcends social boundaries. His is the broad humanity which the world both needs and rejects at the same time, while individuals and individual societies relentlessly pursue their particular concerns. . . . He cannot escape this role because he is of the strong Breed."[6]

Gerald Moore examines the significance of the sacrificer and disapproves of the intention that Soyinka was rejecting traditional religious ideas. "Soyinka implies that the tradition of the willing carrier which is Eman's inheritance is one working of respect, in that it dignifies both the suffering of the hero and the witness of the spectators. His rejection of such character as the gross Kadiye and the hateful Jaguna does not, as some critics have supposed, amount to a rejection of traditional religious ideas. On the contrary, it is the best of these ideas, together with the ritual and mythology which embody them, that have provided his richest store of metaphor and dramatic symbol; but they call out for reinterpretation in terms of ever-changing values and conditions."[7]

The Yoruba myth and the Christ figure come together in Soyinka's plays. Soyinka himself finds all these essentially the same:

> It is true that to understand, to understand profoundly, is to be unnerved of the will to act. For is not human reality dwarfed by the awe and wonder, the *inevitability* of the cosmic gulf ? Suffering, the truly overwhelming suffering of Sango, of Lear, of Oedipus, this suffering hones the psyche to a finely self-annihilating perceptiveness and renders further action futile and above all, lacking dignity.[8]

This is the essence of tragedy, the suffering of Christ, and the agony of carriers like Eman. Andrew Gurr explains how Soyinka, the committed social critic, finds Yoruba tragedy a meaningful concept. In an attempt " to return to our own sources," in his words, Soyinka seeks out new meanings in the traditional rituals. He finds the finest expression in *The Strong Breed*, dealing with the Oro Sacrifice. Andrew Gurr observes "Quietest wisdom, resignation, and acceptance of one's fate are close to being the same thing in this context. They are all close to determinism."[9]

Eman, the lone figure, bears strong resemblance to the figure of "The Dreamer" in one of Soyinka's poems, unmistakably the Christ figure.

> Higher than trees a cryptic crown
> Lord of the rebel three
> Thorns lay on a sleep of down
> And myrrh; a mesh
> of nails, of flesh
> And words that flowered free.

The influence of the martyred figure leads to growth and rejuvenation, images of growth follow. The seed falls to the earth and 'dies,' only to germinate. These images are suggestive of the church organization and the wide spread of religion.

The theme of retributive sacrifice leading to expiation and rejuvenation has been introduced by Soyinka in his version of the *Bacchae* of Euripides. Remaining faithful to the main outline of the original, that of Dionysos's revenge on the Theban King Pentheus who refuses to acknowledge his godhead and worship him, Soyinka has made certain additions of his own, adding a new dimension to the great classical tragedy. The deviations, adding new significance to the roles of the Blind seer Tiersias and of King Pentheus are introduced in an attempt to superimpose his theory of the 'carrier' sacrifice theme on the classical theme, thus proving that the essence of tragedy is the same whether in a Greek drama or in a primitive Yoruba ritual. In addition, the Greek and the Yoruba themes dovetail into each other so perfectly that the Christ theme also finds itself fitting into the Dionysian pattern rendering a new significance to the well-known plot.

Soyinka's emphasis in the play is on expiation through sacrifice, and Pentheus's gruesome death at the hands of his mother Agave assumes wider connotations in his version. The deviations introduced by him in his stage adaptation of the play make it less Euripidean in essence, but Soyinka has managed to bring about a rare synthesis between Greek, Yoruba, and Christian concepts.

In Soyinka's version, the prophet, blind Tiersias, is being chased and flogged by a number of people, obviously as he has been chosen as their 'carrier' for the new year. He should be flogged to death for cleansing the entire country. Tiersias accepts the role willingly or so it seems. Dionysos appears dressed as a stranger, and is easily recognized by the seer, though blind. He explains the meaning of the sacrificial ritual. The Old Kind Kadmos arrives. Both the old men have already turned votaries of the new God Dionysos, or Bromius as he is being called. Dressed in fawn-skin, and carrying the ivy-wand, they proceed to the mountains to watch the excited rites of the Maenads's Dionysian worship. Kind Pentheus appears, infuriated by the attitude of the royal women who have turned the votaries of the god whom he refuses to acknowledge. Dionysos gradually wins over him, casts a spell, and leads him on to the mountain, dressed as a Maenad himself. Pentheus, completely hypnotized by the god whom he fails to recognize, submits himself to the plan. Dionysos sets Pentheus on the top of a tall pine tree at his request so that he would get a proper view of the intoxicated women's activities. Dionysos disappears. Pentheus is spotted out by the women who are already hysterical with excitement, almost to a point of blindness. They stone him till he falls from the tree, and kill him, wrenching him apart, limb by limb. The irony is that it is his mother Agave who takes the lead. Proudly hoisting his head aloft on a staff, Agave returns to the palace, followed by others, ready to celebrate their triumph. It is the sad plight of Oro Kadmos, Agave's father, to tell her the truth and bring her back to the sad world of reality. She realizes what she has done. With regal dignity, both in the original and in Soyinka's version, she accepts the responsibility and is prepared to face it. In the original, Dionysos decrees that both Kadmos and his daughter have to leave Thebes and wander about from country to country to expiate for the crime of the royal house. In Soyinka's version, Tiersias reappears at this stage, reintroducing the 'carrier' theme. It is Pentheus, and not he, who should sacrifice for the sins of the entire country, voluntarily or otherwise. In atonement for his own personal sin against god the sacrifice becomes inevitable.

The closing part of the play is Soyinka's crowning achievement. Pentheus's severed head is taken up to be kept along with the rest of his mortal remains for cremation. Suddenly blood starts gushing out in powerful jets from all the orifices in the dead skull. Kadmos and the others present shudder at the very sight, shaking at the thought of Dionysos's renewed wrath. But Tiersias goes forward, allowing the stream to fall on his face. He smells it, tastes it, and screams in excitement, "It is not 'blood'. It is wine !"

The God of wine has won ! And, he is pleased. He has forgiven the Theban royal family and the country. He bathes the country in wine. The play ends them, bathing the entire tragedy in purity and on a note of fruition. Pentheus's sacrifice has had its desired effect. God has accepted it. Thebes will become the land of prosperity.

The rejuvenation theme, coupled with the theme of sacrifice, has thus been superimposed on "the finest extant drama of the social coming-unto-being of a semi-European deity." It ends not on the note of Catharsis alone, but goes far beyond, on the promise of fruition.

NOTES

1. Adrian Roscoe, "Soyinka as Poet," *Readings in Commonwealth Literature*, ed. William Walsh (Clarendon Press, Oxford, 1973), p. 166

2. Quoted by Adrian Roscoe, p. 167.

3. *Ibid*, p. 167.

4. Wole Soyinka, *The Strong Breed*, *Collected Plays of Wole Soyinka* (Osmania University Press, 1973), I, p. 133.

5. Eldred Jones, *The Writing of Wole Soyinka* (W. Heinemann, London, 1973), p. 49.

6. *Ibid.*, p. 54.

7. Gerald Moore, *Wole Soyinka* (Africana Publishing Corporation, New York, 1971), p.56.

8. Wole Soyinka, "The Fourth Stage," *The Morality of Art: Essays Presented to G. Wilson Knight by His Colleagues and Friends*, ed. D.W. Jefferson (Routledge, 1969), p. 129.

9. Andrew Gurr, "Third-World Drama: Soyinka and Tragedy," *The Journal of Commonwealth Literature*, X, 3 (April 1976), p. 51.

John Masters's India

N.S. PRADHAN

Soon after India became independent John Masters who had been a British Officer in the Indian army began to write about the Raj, in retrospect. His eight novels on India and two works of autobiography were written in quick succession between 1951 and 1962. Masters had witnessed the folding up of the British rule in India and the loss of the Empire and like most Englishmen then living in India he experienced not only an emotional and psychological crisis, he shared with them a sense of shattered identity. Masters's ancestors had been in India since 1805. His father was a Lt. Colonel in the Indian army. His brother, several uncles and numerous other relatives had been living all over India for generations. John Masters had therefore no reason to think that he should be living anywhere else except in India.

In order to objectify his emotional crisis in his novels, John Masters went back in history in search of his roots. He thus created the fictional Savage family whose men (spread over in seven of his novels) have lived in India from the 17th century onwards in various capacities. The fact that each of Masters's novels has a protagonist from the Savage family, provides a sense of historical continuity as well as a deeply imaginative quality to his stories.

The protagonist of *Coromandel !* Jason Savage is a restless, ambitious youth who runs away from home in the Renaissance England and lands at the Coromandel coast in search of a treasure. He is an adventurer and a mercenary who is ready for break with a dead past. In his irreverence for traditional values and his totally pragmatic attitude, he is a modern man. The first three things he asks of the natives on landing in India are food, pearls and women. We are told that he is a dreamer as well as a doer, which is the rarest gift of conquerors like Babar and Jehangir. His wit and ingenuity help him survive in an alien land and although he doesn't find his treasure, he marries a Portuguese nobleman's daughter, thus laying the foundation of a dynasty of Savages who would be the future rulers of this country.

Next, we meet William Savage in *The Deceivers* who in 1825 as a district officer in Central India roots out the widespread evil of *thuggee*. (William's character is based on the real William Sleeman who had actually tracked down and eliminated the thugs in the early part of the 19th century.) William is unconventional as he feels cramped among his own English people but is at home with the Indian villagers of his district. He claims to have a 'feeling' for the country. He is imbued with a sense of the white-man's burden from which flow his devotion to duty, sense of service and sacrifice. He is the only one amongst Masters's protagonists who imperils his life by impersonating as a thug in order to unearth their secret ways of ritualistic killing of innocent people.

William's son, Rodney Savage is the young and ambitious army Captain in *Nightrunners of Bengal* who escapes the massacre by the Indian sepoys in 1857 at Bhowani and ultimately helps defeat the rebels through ruthless power. There is also mention of a Jonathan Savage who had fought alongside Clive at Plassey. Rodney's son Robin in 1880 spies for the Empire in the rugged north-western region against Russian infiltration in *The Wind and the Lotus*. In Robin we see a new trend in the delineation of the Masters hero. In a break with the usual Savage image of the heroic man, Robin is cast as a confused and tortured creature. He is a misfit as a soldier and has no faith in the traditional values of honour and bravery. He is a dreamer and a wanderer who is looking for something--truth, God, peace of mind--but never finds it. There is also a suggestion that his fractured spirit is the result of the horrors and bloodshed he witnessed as a child in the Mutiny. He is one of Masters's most psychologically complex characters.

Robin's son Peter Savage is a deputy commissioner in Panjab in 1905 in *Far, Far the Mountain* Peak. Like his father, Peter also carries a psychological scar that is manifest in his driving, alienating ambition to 'get to the top.' He is called 'koi-hai Napoleon' by the other English and a 'daemon husband' by his wife. In his burning idealism to change the face of India and to be good to the natives, he wants to be thought of as a 'shining antithesis to General Dyer.' His son, another Rodney Savage is a Lt. Colonel in *Bhowani Junction* who helps maintain peace against the Congress agitations in 1946. The same Rodney finds himself as an unemployed adventurer in *To the Coral Strand* as his personality is shattered by his refusal to accept the reality that after independence, power has gone from the English hands to those of the Indians. Rodney is the most tortured and mixed up of Masters's heroes. His feeling of emptiness and loss is heightened by his sharp awareness of the historical and traditional position his people have held in this country. He now feels like an anachronism, a leftover, having been " thrown on a rubbish heap."[1] In his violent and naive efforts to stem the march of history, Rodney symbolizes the agony of the Raj in its death-throes.

Whereas John Masters's autobiographical background has an obvious correspondence with the Savage family, he meant the Savage dynasty to be fully representative of the entire English community in India with its strength, weaknesses and contradictions. His typical protagonists are therefore bold, ambitious, ruthless, self-reliant and almost totally amoral, although the last three evince confusion and bewilderment in not being able to cope with the reality of their circumstances. Being creatures of intense historical compulsions, they fail to grasp the onward march of history ! Most of them are products of the English public schools which made them competitive, loyal and capable of mastering any situation. Except Jason, all other Savage men follow the typical pattern of being sent to public schools in England from where they return fully equipped to handle the exigencies of the Empire. They are dreamers and idealists of sorts--the kind whom Philip Woodruff[2] describes as cast in the mould of Plato's 'guardians' and who ruled with a kind of benign despotism. Masters leaves us in no doubt that Englishmen like them provided the solid bedrock on which the Empire firmly stood.

Following largely in the 'Kipling' tradition, Masters's novels are primarily concerned with the plight of the English in India. The focus is on their struggle and hardships in adjusting themselves to a harsh climate and alien society. Most of them feel that they are in 'exile' and are always 'homesick.' They are martyrs to the cause of the Empire. Their typical women folk are constantly grudging against heat, flies and the ignorance of Indian servants. They are on the move all their lives and fail to identify themselves with any one place. Gradually, they begin to feel like strangers in their home country after prolonged stay in India. Thus, their problem is 'alienation' whether they are in India or England. Rodney in the last novel cannot face the prospect of going back empty-handed to England to lead a purposeless life, "having nothing, being nothing." (p. 270) The other alternative for such Englishmen is to 'stay on' in India, a theme that begins to emerge in the last three novels and was later so effectively dealt with by Paul Scott. But the fate that awaits those 'staying on' is still worse; their pathetic struggle to survive is made difficult by their inability to accept the changed reality and is fed largely by memories in a world that grows hostile every day. *To the Coral Strand* is, in fact, a dirge on the demise of the Raj, but a dirge that expresses anguish and frustration, arising from its protagonist's realization at the loss of a glorious past; Rodney shouts to a crowd of Indians celebrating their independence: "It is not your country. It is mine. I made it, from a hundred countries, I and my great-great-grandfather, and my great-grandfather, and so on." (p. 16)

But the most important aspect of John Masters's fiction, one that is of the greatest interest to the Indian reader, is his attitude towards India and its people. Masters claims to love India, like the protagonists of his novels, but his love is only skin-deep. In his autobiography *Bugles and a Tiger* Masters declares that he had no intention of spending all his life in this 'godforsaken' country.[3] Towards the people of India Masters's attitude is ambiguous, although it is obvious that in his world too, the twain shall never meet. Jason falls in love with the temple girl Parvati but realizes that they can never unite. Rodney and Sumitra in *Nightrunners* or Rodney and Janaki in *Coral Strand* will never come together. Victoria's break with Rodney in *Bhowani Junction* has the author's complete approval: "She couldn't desert her people . . . when we English left India they could look beyond the telegraph lines and the railway lines." [4] Victoria is only half English; so, for Masters, she is not good enough for Rodney. The English boys end up getting

English girls of good stock who are their saviours and guardian-angels.

There is some historical basis for the view that throughout the imperialist era, the influence of English women on their menfolk has largely been negative. The English women in India were more supercilious and contemptuous of everything Indian. They hated living in this country and made their husbands's lives miserable. They were overtly racist and were responsible for creating a wide gulf between their men and the Indian people with whom they had to deal. All this gave birth to the idea of the stereotype female known as the 'memsahib.' Masters shows awareness of this common variety in depicting 'memsahib' type characters whose lives are full of mediocrity and empty gossip. Rodney's wife Joanna *(Nightrunners)* is interested in money, parties, and her own appearance. 'The Battle of the Bedpan' in the same novel, depicts the utter triviality of existence of such females.

Against this standard image, Masters has created the myth of what can be described as the ideal woman. It is demonstrated again and again in his novels that the ultimate salvation of man is in finding a 'perfect' woman. Further, that such perfect women do exist, at least in Masters's fiction, and one has only to recognise them. In fact, so significant is the role of the perfect woman that none of his heroes achieves completeness and maturity without the active aid of such a woman. Catherine becomes Jason's self-appointed guiding spirit who never lets him forget his dream. She is a personification of devotion, selflessness, love and wisdom. Mary is a friend, companion and a guide, who chooses to face the embarrassment of her husband's disappearance so that he may succeed against the thugs. Caroline Langford *(Nightrunners)* is perhaps the most forceful of these women characters. In direct opposition to the notions commonly held, she believes that the main flaw in the English presence is that they haven't identified themselves with the Indians. Her stamina, grit and uncompromisingly human approach make her a missionary and a moral crusader. Her insistence on love, charity and service finally prevails upon Rodney so that he regains his humanity after having been reduced to a beast by the violence and bloodshed of the mutiny. In a way, Caroline's lonely voice is the voice of the English conscience. She represents the best and the purest of whatever goes into the fabric of the English civilisation. However, even in her case, John Masters stops short of facing the real issue concerning the moral right of the English to be in India. Caroline's anger is not directed at the colonial idea, as it is against English prejudices and their aloofness and snobbery. When Rodney wants to leave the village of Chalisgon where cholera has broken out, Caroline's appeal to him reads like a direct lesson on the theme of the 'White man's burden'

> We'll be risking our lives here, as many unknown servants in unknown places have done before us. It is not showy. No one will ever hear of it. We may all die. But if we're to be accepted in India it will be because of things like this--not victories or dams or telegraphs or doctors. Don't you see that *this* is the great thing to do, come to our hands ? We can leave something here which will live when all the fighting's done, and our places are ruins, and we've gone home, as some day we will.[5]

Anne *(The Lotus and the Wind)* and Emily *(Far, Far the Mountain Peak)* although lesser characters, are cast in the same mould. Margaret Wood *(Coral Strand)* in her self-sacrificing devotion almost achieves the grandeur and spiritual beauty represented by Caroline. Quite often these women take the action into their own hands when the men crack up in the face of crisis or failure. In normal conditions they fade into the background though never taking away their watchful eyes from their men.

The English characters of John Masters by and large share the prejudices of their race towards the Indians. Although the Savages are several shades better than the average Englishman, even they cannot hide their true feelings at times. Jason thought Indians to be stupid and ignorant. [6] Angleworth, a Collector in *The Deceivers* thinks they are 'swine.' The more sympathetic Rodney *(Nightrunners)* claims to love his soldier but as 'half-witted sons.' (p. 31) In the same novel, Masters depicts the majority of English women as Club gossips, petty-minded and a 'pack of vixens.' But then he justifies their condition by suggesting that it was a way of "armouring their minds against this filthy country." (p. 122) Most significant is the symbolic character of the Silver Guru who is a whiteman afflicted with leprosy. "India had touched him" and gave him "fecund squalor, diseased and germinating dust, circling vultures, grey glowing sky, hot rain, and rioting lust and a silver skin." (p. 168) Even the Anglo-Indians of *Bhowani Junction* who are treated shabbily by the English, crudely ape some of their prejudices: for them those 'black bastards' and 'niggers' are lazy and filthy creatures who wipe their bottoms with hands ! Victoria's struggle to Indianise herself invites Rodney's sarcastic remarks on her sari. He also calls her Miss Starkie-- a name that he borrowed from a racist song about a white woman who after an affair with a 'darkie' gave birth to black, white and khaki babies. Masters throws away all pretense of sympathy and historical truth by suggesting (in the same novel) that perhaps General Dyer had not meant to kill any Indians and that the deaths were the result of panic in the public ! (p. 230)

It must, however, be mentioned that *Bhowani Junction* is, by far, Masters's best novel on India, largely because it truthfully reflects the dilemmas and predilections of the Eurasians in India who are, to a large extent, presented sympathetically. So forcefully is their situation presented that the 'Savage' theme is relegated to the background. The Eurasians, now commonly called Anglo-Indians, were the by-products of the historical process of imperialism. Half-English, half-Indian; they were the lost children of the Raj, the left-overs; they were despised by the English as "cheechees, half-castes, eightannas, blacky-white" etc. (p. 8) In turn, these Eurasians thought of the Indians as inferior and despised them thoroughly. And in 1946 the Eurasians stand on the brink of a first-rate identity crisis. Even the cocky and boastful Patrick Taylor who talks of going 'Home' to England (which he has never seen) and wore his solar hat all day and most of the night (so that he would be recognized as an Englishman), has a remote sense of the coming events. "What are we going to do ?" he asks Victoria in sheer frustration. (p. 42) Knowing that they could neither become English nor Indian, Taylor's conclusion ("we could only stay where we were and be what we were." (p. 21) shows his sense of having become total prisoners of circumstances.

The crisis in Victoria Jones is deeper. She represents more fully the conflict of identity, loyalty and self-respect--within the Anglo-Indian community as a whole. To begin with, she shares the sub-conscious inferiority complex of her people that they are descended from the "Indian loose women of a hundred years ago." (p. 79) Her character depicts a dramatic movement towards the attainment of freedom (from prejudice and self-delusion) and self-respect, although in the process she pays a heavy emotional price: Macaulay's murder releases her from the chains of her so-called English connection and her attempt to attain an identity leads her to almost marry Ranjit in a sikh gurdwara. In the next phase of her quest, she forms a sexual liaison with Savage with whom she recognizes common cultural factors. Her cyclical return to a consciousness of selfhood has a striking similarity with her initial state of mind when she had declared: 'Why must we torture ourselves with ideas that we are better than some people and worse than others? I don't despise anyone now and I don't fear anyone." (p. 22) Victoria (notice the irony of her name !) thus emerges as a dignified character who subsumes the built-in tragedy and the rootlessness of her people. It is a pity that John Masters would not allow them a place of unblemished future, and tarnish an otherwise sensitive treatment of the Anglo-Indian community as he makes his favourite gurkha Manbir remark to Victoria (apparently with Savage's full approval): "Most of your people are like jackals who follow the tiger (the English) but are always yelping, always frightened."

There is, however, some evidence that Masters struggled against his racial consciousness. In a revealing passage in his autobiography, Masters thinks that Kipling, in many ways his mentor and model, was at times a "colour-crazy ass." "Why had Kipling gone out of his way to underline with sadistic approval attitudes of mind and habits of race-consciousness that must have caused pain to anyone who loved India ?" (p. 88) One is disappointed that in spite of such feeble protestations, Masters remained the most faithful disciple of Kipling in every respect, including his racial attitudes. The disappointment is more painful, because Masters was writing in a post-independence period, almost at the same time that Paul Scott was beginning to write his novels on India, but unlike Scott, he fails to reflect a frank and liberal appraisal of the Indian-English relations. Masters's approach is mostly steeped in nostalgia and breast-beating over the loss of the Empire.

The India of 1628 is lurid, improbable and chaotic. Old men stand on their heads at street corners and naked temple girls roam around. In the later periods, erotic images and free sex abound. Above all, India is a place of poverty, hunger, crime, intrigue, sexual perversion, cruelty and total chaos. The thugs kill more than forty thousand persons per year on the roads and have done so for more than three hundred years. The Rajas's camp in *Nightrunners* is pure fantasy. It is only in the later novels that Masters's claim to authenticity and historical verisimilitude can be sustained. The best example of realism is *Bhowani Junction* that depicts the life of the Anglo-Indian community who are caught in a dilemma: they cannot identify themselves with the rebellious freedom fighters and the departing English have disowned them.

The Indians in Masters's novels fall into three broad categories. The Rajas, Nawabs and the feudal lords, form one extreme of the Indian social fabric. At the other extreme are the very poor--servants, primitive tribals, beggars, etc. In the middle are the educated, middle class Indians who are given more coverage in the last three novels of the series. Masters can barely conceal his contempt and derision for the last named category that includes politically conscious Indians who have been educated in England, regular dhoti-clad politicians, professionals, etc. Most of them receive comic treatment. Patrick Taylor the Anglo-Indian is a bumbling fool; Surabhai the congressman is a pompous clown with his pidgin English. Adam Khan *(Far, Far the Mountain Peak)*, Govindaswami the Collector *(Bhowani Junction)* and Gen. Ran Singh 'Max' *(Coral Strand)* receive better treatment, largely because of the extent to which they have imbibed western influence.

The English, however, find the company of Rajas and Nawabs as quite congenial. Their lavish hospitality, fabulous feasts and shikars and their permissive ways appealed to the English who could, with a little effort, consider these royal-blooded Indians as their own equal. The English smiled at their odd rituals, petty intrigues and immense decadence. The oversexed scheming Rani of Kishenpur *(Nightrunners)* who has her husband murdered, "Mole" the Raja in

Bhowani Junction, Mohan, the Raja of Deori with his dark, mysterious past in*The Venus of Konpara*, the old fashioned Nawab of Chambal who spends the day hunting while his State is under attack--these are some of the Indians of high society who look out from the pages of Masters's novels. Masters's treatment of them is of benign ridicule though often sympathetic.

But the only Indians whom the English knew intimately were the servants. Masters's English characters form their opinions of the Indians on the basis of what they know of their ayahs, cooks, sais and chowkidars. In spite of their petty pilferage and unbearable airs towards other Indians, these servants as a class are treated with affection, their status being no better than that of pet animals. The common stereotype is therefore the figure of the 'faithful servant'--one who stands by the side of his master in all perils, is his constant companion, and at times, guide and protector. This includes soldiers of the Indian army who formed life-long attachments to their masters. Thus we have Hussain the ex-thug who lets his body be torn into pieces for his master's success in *The Deceivers*. There are Sher Dil and Piroo, (another ex-strangler), who whisk away Rodney to safety when the mutiny begins. Jagbir the gurkha orderly *(The Lotus and The Wind)* bends to dust off his master's shoes even when he himself is going out to be decorated for bravery. Birkhe and Manbir, the two gurkhas of *Bhowani Junction* have all the qualities of ferocious pet dogs. The disloyalty of the gurkha servant Ratanbir *(Coral Strand)* is seen by Rodney as the snapping of the delicate-most ties between two human beings; it is also a signal for Rodney of a total break with India.

In fact, Masters's self-claimed love for India has a strange and twisted idealism. He believes that the best of India is in those places and people where old cultures and ways of life have remained in pristine primitiveness, totally untouched by change or modernity. Thus his characters have fond kinship with such tribal people as pathans, gurkas, gonds, bhils, nagas, etc. Even the utmost primitiveness, and animality of these tribes have some virtue. It is this aspect alone of India that is worth loving. All agencies of change are evil and to be hated. Educated Indians, the Brahmins, the Congress Party--all of them represent meanness and mediocrity of the spirit. Kendrick the resident of Konpara believes that the lessons of the Mutiny taught the British not to meddle with the primitive cultures of India. Since then the English have gone out of the way to preserve caste, so that they are not suspected of destroying Hindus. In a way, the whole of *The Venus of Konpara* is about the superiority of the pre-Brahmanic culture of India. Rodney *(Bhowani Junction)* believes that change in India is unnatural--it was better "to make Indian wood into better wood, not change it into bakelite." (p. 353) For the same Rodney *(Coral Strand)*, the accession of princely states to free India is wrong as it would destroy old cultures by modernizing them. William Savage *(The Deceivers)* has a 'glow of respect and admiration' for sati. His homage to Gopal's widow on the burning pyre is nothing but glorified, romanticized nonsense, although Masters expects us to take it seriously.

John Masters is rather evasive on the most moral and politically important aspect of the Raj--why should the British rule in India ? This moral issue that forms the very core of the novels of writers like E.M. Forster and Paul Scott, is dealt with by John Masters in passing only. The English in his novels never for a moment question their right to be in India and believe that it is their 'manifest destiny' to rule over such backward nations. Only Rodney *(Nightrunners)* who, when he is sheltered in an Indian village, makes a direct probe in this area. "Do you think," he asks the villagers, "it is not right for the English to rule India ?" (p. 287) The village bania's answer is what Masters himself would like to say in reply, that "we do not care who rules us as long as he rules well." (p. 288) We also know that when Rodney asks this question he is full of hatred and his purpose is to bring out the treachery of the Indians. He himself knows the answer; that the Indians are not fit to rule themselves and if the British leave there would be total anarchy and civil war. Even his 'awareness,' brought on by the affection of the villagers, is deceptive in its apparent innocence. For him a foreigner was a man who did not love. And that "to the men of English blood had been given an opportunity such as God grants but once in a thousand years" to prove themselves as "giants of understanding, forerunners of a new world of service." (p. 305) One can see where the catch is. The definition of a 'foreigner' eliminates all objections to the British presence in India and makes them a nation of guardians, reformers and well-wishers who acted out of love and at great cost and sacrifice on their part. Rodney of *Bhowani Junction* believes that the British who are leaving India in 1946 are deserting their responsibility. In *Coral Strand* he tries to regain the lost glory of the past by becoming 'gora raja' for the gonds.

In his autobiographical *Bugles and a Tiger*, Masters attempts a more elaborate reflection on the subject. He claims that in a country of India's size and diversity, its people have no sense of unity; it was only the British who felt the *oneness* of the land. (p. 326) He also claims--as if he expected any one to believe it--that the British interest in India was more in rendering service than in domination. He goes on to assert that the British had a strong claim here because "the land was irrigated with British blood." (p. 327) However, he concedes that the British could never *feel* at home in this country, although they no longer remained strangers. They were serving a kind of historical necessity and their 'guest- ship' in India was justified by the service they rendered. (p. 329) In a final and not inappropriate summation Masters declares that for the British, India is not a *mother*, (in the sense of a motherland) but "a lusty, disinterested mistress." (pp. 329-30)

In the ultimate assessment, John Masters's response to the Raj is disappointing: it is lacking in moral sensibility which is a pre-requisite of all great literature. There is sometimes a serious desire on his part to understand and sympathise with the Indian cause. Quite often the Indian characters who defy the power of the English attain dignity and respect. But on the whole, John Masters remains an imperialist at heart, glorying in the heroic achievements and noble sacrifices of the English in India. This is all the more disappointing when we remember that Masters wrote his novels when the independence of India had become a reality. It was a good opportunity for him to break free of the Kipling tradition of writing about India.

It must be mentioned, however, that Masters's novels were widely read in the 50s and 60s. His racy and absorbing narrative, vivid descriptions having strong visual quality and ample use of history contributed to his popularity in no small measure. Each event described has the flavour of drama and excitement. History comes alive, though in exotic colours of romance and mystery. The choice of major events and their treatment is very effective. The mutiny of

1875 is re-created in all its horror and bestiality. Earthquake, the first world war, political violence, sabotage, etc. give a larger than life dimension to the fictional scene. Journeys, chases and flights add to the flux and excitement of the situations. Read together, the novels have the sweep and force of an epic.

The narrative method is mostly straightforward and linear. There are only a few false notes and structural oddities. In *Coromandel* ! the episode of the monks is ridiculous, bizarre and irrelevant. Masters hardly seems to know how to end the narrative. The *Lotus and the Wind* is unsuccessful as a novel mainly because it deals too narrowly with a personal problem that does not arise from the given situation. Moreover, the symbolism of the lotus and the wind is over-stretched. The meanings of the *wind* (a power that moves in men and makes them restless) and of the *Lotus* (whatever gives emotional calm and sense of security and stability to women) make up a theme that is too abstract. It does not explain Robin's compulsion to leave home and family. Thus the resolution depicting Robin's separation, is poor and unconvincing. On the whole, however, Masters's handling of his material is mature and effective. In artistic maturity, the best work is *Bhowani Junction* in which each of the three principal characters are presented through first person narrative. The section dealing with Victoria Jones is the longest, thus making her the central character. The first and the last sections belong to another anglo-Indian, Patrick Taylor. *Bhowani Junction* is therefore the only novel in the series in which an Englishman is not the protagonist. Rodney's role, though important, is secondary. This enables the author to achieve complexity and seriousness, since we approach the volatile situation of 1946 through the consciousness of three diverse characters. Also noteworthy is the technique of epistolary narration. It enables the reader to get into the character's consciousness and the author achieves quick jumps of time without leaving any gaps in the narrative.

One of the strongest appeals of Masters's fiction, against his own claim to realism and historical truth, is the effective use of symbols and metaphorical images. Through such artistic achievement, Masters manages to convey what remains unstated in conventional narrative. One such important element is the mythical mountain Meru that Jason seeks. The climbing of this mountain relates to ascendancy and power, two important constituents of the Empire. As Ishmael aptly puts it (in *Coromandel!*) if not Jason then his son or grandson may climb it one day. The metaphor of climbing is continued in *Far, Far the Mountain Peak* that, when translated into reality, means that mountain climbing can take the shape of Empire building. The symbolic character of the Silver Guru, mentioned earlier, conveys Masters's sense of what India could do to the whiteman. Then there is the subtle symbolism of the Railway in *Bhowani Junction* through which is conveyed the sense of the unsettled times. The movement of trains, their coming and going, reflects the going away of the English and the coming of the Indian rule. The coral strand becomes a point in a circle: it was on the coral strand that Jason had landed and it is here that the last of the Savage men stands, looking out to the sea, ready to depart. The coral strand is thus the starting as well as the finishing point in Masters's story of the Raj.

NOTES

1. *To the Coral Strand* (London: Michael Joseph, 1962), p. 148
2. Phillip Woodruff, *The Men Who Ruled India: The Guardians* (Vol. II) (New York: Schocken Books, 1954)
3. *Bugles and a Tiger* (London: Michael Joseph, 1956), p. 39
4. *Bhawani Junction* (New York: The Viking Press, 1954), p. 372
5. *Nightrunners of Bengal* (London: Michael Joseph, 1951), p. 296
6. *Coromandel!* (London: Michael Joseph, 1955), p. 165.

Salmam Rushdie's Novels: From Fantasy to Reality

SUSHILA SINGH

Combining the elements of magic and fantasy, the grimmest realism, extravagant farce, multi-mirrored analogy and a potent symbolic structure, Salman Rushdie has captured the astonishing energy of novel unprecedented in scope, manner and achievement in the hundred and fifty year old tradition of the Indian novel in English.[1] Rushdie must portray reality, and in this endeavour fiction and non-fiction overlap boundaries. Salman Rushdie, the writer of the three novels, *Grimus*, *Midnight's Children* and *Shame*, and a book on Nicaraguan journey, *The Jaguar Smile*, emerged with the publication of *Midnight's Children* in 1981 as a new phenomenon in the genre of fiction. The book was awarded 1981 Booker McConnell Prize and literary critics compared Rushdie to novelists like Milan Kundera, Gabriel Garcia Marquez, Gunter Grass, John Irving, V.S. Naipaul. He has been hailed as a creator of epics. Starting with *Grimus*, a work in fantasy, Rushdie went on to create the real sub-continent condition in his phenomenal works *Midnight's Children* and *Shame*. His investigation of life led him to the uncovering of the true circumstances in India and Pakistan. Individual human personality, the novelist realized, proved meaningless in the present global situation. Thus, he personified India and Pakistan for the true realization of life in the two countries. "True great realism depicts man and society as complete entities, instead of showing merely one or the other of their aspects."[2] In his endeavour toward the adequate presentation of the complete human condition, Rushdie adopts non-linear, non-naturalistic forms to meet the challenge of portraying reality.

Like Gottfried Keller, the great Swiss writer, Rushdie believes that "Everything is politics." As in Balzac's and Tolstoy's, so in Rushdie's "every action, thought and emotion of human beings is inseparably bound up with the life and struggles of the community, i.e., with politics; whether the humans themselves are conscious of this, unconscious of it or even trying to escape from it, objectively their actions, thoughts and emotions nevertheless spring from and run into politics."[3] To Rushdie literature is referential and therefore he resists the label of western post-modernism where the world outside the text does not exist. In an interview he said "I do think books are about the world."[4]

The cultural displacement and its results have dominated Rushdie's creative self. He says: "I can't avoid the fact that my life has been constructed in a series of such displacements--of which only the last, the decision to stay in England, was my own choice. You have a Kashmiri family that comes to Delhi, then goes to Bombay, then to Pakistan, and meanwhile I end up in London--there's a lot of dislocations there !"[5] He further adds "I do feel that physical and geographical displacement makes you self-conscious about your position, obliges you to establish the ground you stand on, in a way which is very different for, say, a Tagore or whoever, who simply stand on that ground and write about it and grow out of it, like plants."[6] The three novels that Rushdie has produced so far present somewhat his over-reaching interest in his cultural displacement.

Grimus is a bit unusual for a writer's first novel. Rushdie has his own reservations about this novel. The work is remotely autobiographical in the sense that the protagonist, Flapping Eagle, is an expatriate like its author. Rushdie complains that he does not hear his own voice in the novel. But *Grimus* has its role in the making of the novelist. It is a part of his experiment with the structure of the novel. Starting it as a fantasy/science fiction Rushdie took ten-eleven years to write it and completed it in 1974. *The Sunday Times* and Victor Gollancz publishers organized a competition for fantasy/science fiction. Rushdie entered the book for the competition. Though it did not win the prize, it got published by Gollancz.

Grimus is a tale full of blown up images. There is a kind of hallucinogenic intensity--conjuring rock like creatures called 'Gorfs' who riddle human minds with anagrams, phantasmogoric time travel with a stone rose that makes things materialised out of thin air--the world of magic. The hero of the tale is Flapping Eagle who swallows the elixir of immortality and wanders the face of the earth for over seven centuries. He survives because of his adaptability which also compromises his past. He reflects, "I was an adaptable sort of man, more a chameleon than an eagle, better at reaction than action."[7] (p. 25) He sees things "most men miss in a mere life time" but one day explains, "I want to grow old. Not to die; to grow old."(p. 33) He falls from his yacht, falls through a hole in the sea and is washed ashore on Calf Island. "When Flapping Eagle arrived at Calf Island his body was thirty four years, three months and four days old. He had lived for a total of seven hundred and seventy seven years, seven months and seven days. By a swift calculation, we see that he had stopped ageing seven hundred and forty-three years, four months and three days ago. He was a tired man."(p. 37)

The mythical world of Calf Island, populated by people who have drunk the elixir of immortality, has a town called K. Before Flapping Eagle reaches K, he undergoes a state of paranoia that envelopes his expanded state of mind. He survives the onslaughts of the "inner dimensions." There seems no obvious reason for his hallucination. The hangover of the dimension fever is a whine which is no more than a tingle in the ear but which increases in intensity the closer one gets to Grimus who is somewhere on the island. But who is Grimus ?

Grimus remains a mystery to Flapping Eagle and to the reader. Before meeting Grimus, Flapping Eagle encounters the inhabitants of K, immortal like him, but immune to the Grimus "effect." The town K is a place of obsession. Obsession is the path of self-realization. It composes symphonies and creates paintings. It writes novels and moves mountains. It is the supreme gift of the human race. In the town K the Grimus effect was survived by obsessed minds. Flapping Eagle meets Ignatius Gribb compiling a compendium of aphorism and his pretty child-wife Elfrida. There is Irina Cherkassova, a Russian countess, who hates her husband.

The Count is the titular head of K, who is invariably found at his favourite whorehouse. The name given to it by the novelist is the House of the Rising Sun. Then we have Hunter, alias "two time kid" whose obsession is doing every thing twice; P.S. Moonshy, who distributes the rations in K, is obsessed with the revolutionary rhetoric of a communistic society and burly Sam Peckenpaw is obsessed with capturing the North American counterpart of the Yeti: Bigfoot. These obsessions shut out the bizarre effects of Grimus's existence from the minds of the K town inhabitants.

K is conceived as a utopia that works harmoniously despite the pecking order. Flapping Eagle wonders at the way the town has dispensed with a system of rewards and incentives. The fertile lands of the town produce food which is distributed according to needs rather than status and many such things. Flapping Eagle is tempted to give up the search for Grimus and to settle down to a life of hedonism. By then he becomes aware that utopias are sterile societies because permanence means unchanging sameness. The edifice of stability breaks when one of the inhabitants of K deviates from her obsession. Elfrida tells her husband that it is not him she loves but Flapping Eagle. This is more than Ignatius Gribb can bear and he dies. Three more deaths occur and Flapping Eagle is held responsible for having wrought the catastrophe. The Amerindian has to escape from a murderous crowd bent on revenge and retribution.

Flapping Eagle journeys up a mountain where he eventually encounters Grimus. Appropriately enough, he is surrounded by mummified birds (Grimus is an anagram of Simurg, in Persian mythology the bird with reasoning power). But Grimus also resembled Flapping Eagle in certain aspects. And then Flapping Eagle realises that his entire life was a journey toward this meeting with Grimus. His life has been predetermined and free-will was just an illusion. He is told by Grimus that he has ordered the world perfectly and even planned his own death in which Flapping Eagle is destined to play a part. Grimus comes close to playing god. With the stone rose, he can travel in time and space and make things materialise in the twinkle of an eye by just thinking of them. He has created Calf Island in some such way and attends to its minutest details, like providing for Ignatius Gribb's supply of stationery. Grimus, wanting to be relieved of his god role, chooses Flapping Eagle to relieve him. In the final ritual transfer of power, Flapping Eagle and Grimus, by holding the opposite ends of a device called the subsumer, find that their personalities commingle in such a manner that Flapping Eagle has a part of Grimus in him and vice-versa--"Self. My self. My self and he alone. My self and his self in the glowing bowl. Yes, it was like that. Myself and himself pouring out of ourselves into the glowing bowl. Easy does it. You swallow me, I swallow you. Mingle, commingle. Come mingle. Grow together come. You into me into you. . . . Now we are the same." (pp. 242-43)

What does Grimus symbolize ? Megalomaniac or magus ? Rushdie shows a certain ambivalence toward him. Like the Merlin figure, conchis, in John Fowle's novel *Magus*, Grimus comes to the brink of death before a Nazi firing squad which allows him a kind of "resurrection." Cynical of human instinctual fears and drives, Grimus tries to transcend them by creating Calf Island and allowing people to opt for immortality. But the world he envisages does not come true. Because the inhabitants of K chose immortality and not exploration. Thus the rose became an instrument to perpetuate tyranny because these immortals were anchored in their obsessions not willing to journey to new worlds. The rose in the story is a symbol of some supreme gift of power discovered by mankind.

"The Rose enables you to travel, said the forms, and showed I-Eagle a thousand beautiful worlds, a thousand universes to explore. The Rose enables you to learn, said the thought-forms, and revealed a hundred new sciences and a hundred new art-forms, the cream of the infinite galaxies. You have one life, said the thought-forms. With the Rose you can enter into, and become, a thousand thousand other people, live an infinity of lives, and acquire the wisdom and power to shape your own. And they showed I-Eagle some of the people Grimus had watched and understood, showed the vicarious joys and agonies of countless lives. And one day, said the thought-forms, when you have done all you wished to do, been all you wished to be, you can pass this supreme gift on to another, choose the moment and manner of your going and give the Phoenix a new life, a new beginning." (p. 251)

But I-Eagle had seen too much on Calf Island and outside it, the centuries of wretched wandering that preceded his arrival.

For Rushdie the 60s in Cambridge were euphoric years. Recalling them he said, "there was the Vietnam war to protest about, student power to insist upon, drugs to smoke, flowers to put in your hair, good music to listen to."[8] Something of the capriciousness of those years spills over in his first novel. This novel is totally unlike his later two novels and remained unnoticed till Rushdie won the

Booker Prize for *Midnight's Children*. When people read it after reading *Midnight's Children*, they found *Grimus* totally ahistorical whereas *Midnight's Children* is steeped in history.

Midnight's Children is more on the line of *bildungsroman* dramatizing the history of independent India in the person of the beak-nosed wildly extravagant Muslim, Saleem Sinai, who was born on the stroke of midnight bringing in India's independence. *Midnight's Children* is also a story about the past of a country, of its writer's nostalgic glance back from another country from which he has migrated. Rushdie muses: "Writers in my position, exiles or emigrants or expatriates, are haunted by an urge to look back even at the risk of being mutated into pillars of salt. But if we do look back, we do so in the knowledge--which gives rise to profound uncertainties--that our physical alienation from India almost inevitably means that we will, in short, create fictions, not actual cities or villages, but invisible ones, imaginary homelands, Indias of the mind."[9] Rushdie evokes the old city of Bombay, where he was born and spent his childhood with uncanny insight. The city belonged initially to the fishermen called Kolis, before "Mountbatten's tick tock" beyond Dalhousie and Elphistone, before the East India Company built its fort. The city of coconuts and rice, of the goddess Mumbadevi was changed to Bom Bahia by its first invaders, the Portuguese, and then to British Bombay under the influence of East India Company. Bombay grew at breakneck speed acquiring first a cathedral, and an equestrian statue of the Maharatta warrior king Shivaji which "come to life at night and galloped awesomely through the city streets--right along Marine Drive. On Chowpatti sand: Past the great Houses on Malabar Hill, round Kemps Corner . . . Down Rushdie's very own Warden Road, right along side the segregated swimming pools of Breach Candy, right upto huge Mahalaxmi Temple and the old Willingdon Club."[10] (p. 93) Then came the night clubs, pickle factories and Oberoi-Sheraton Hotel and the languid resort of the film stars Sun 'N' Sand. The city of Bombay of the 50s and 60s can-not be missed: the Binaca and Kolynos ads, the Gujarati rhyme: soo che , saru che /Danda le khe maru che ! (How are you ? I am well--I'll take a stick and thrash you to hell !) This nonsense rhyme powerfully portrays how India around this time was divided anew into fourteen states and six centrally administered territories. The boundaries of these states were not formed by rivers or mountains but by the walls of words leading to frequent language disputes. Associated with the moral and cultural temper of Bombay, Nanavati case is presented in the guise of Commander Sabarmati case. Informed by Salim about his wife's adulterous affair with Mr. Homi Catrack, the Commander shot his wife and Mr. Catrack and surrendered himself to the police. His wife managed to live but Mr. Catrack died. Commander Sabarmati became the most popular murderer in the history of Indian jurisprudence. *The Illustrated Weekly of India* did a pen portrait of the Commander declaring him the man of the week. When even the Supreme Court gave a verdict of guilty, his case was taken to the President of India for pardon. The public sentiments Rushdie describes: "If Rama himself were alive would we send him to prison for slaying the abductor of Sita ?" The President did not pardon and it appeared the end of the world for the public.

Midnight's Children is a memory novel and therefore a semi-fantasy, nonetheless dealing with stark realities: "Memory's truth, because memory has its own special kind. It selects, eliminates, alters, exaggerates, minimises, glorifies, and vilifies also: but in the end it creates its own reality." (p. 211) The historical perspective enables Rushdie to reminisce backward and forward reimagining himself in the persona of the protagonist through the life cycle and a series of historical moments.

The multitudinal epical intention in the form of *Midnight's Children* and the obsessive, repetitive voice of a fragmented individual consciousness are brought together. Commenting on this aspect, Rushdie admits: "What does it mean to one person in India among so many millions ? *Midnight's Children* is a comic inversion of that notion. Instead of being an insignificant dot in this multitude, Saleem Sinai actually contains the multitude. It is an aspect of him, rather than he an aspect of it. The sadness of the book is in the discovery that this is not so. When your picture of yourself, your self-image, breaks, you die. And that is what happens to Saleem."[11] Because of this realisation perhaps the novel has been interpreted as an expression of despair.

Saleem had the gift of entering the illusion of the artist, and thought of the multitudinous realities of the land. He could leap into the heads of film stars and cricketers. He learned the truth behind the *Filmfare* gossip about the dancer Vyjayantimala, he could be at the crease with Polly Umrigar at the Bradbourne Stadium and so on and so forth. He also discovered politics. At one time he was a landlord in Uttar Pradesh, his belly rolling over his pajama-cord as he ordered serfs to set his surplus grain on fire, at another moment he was starving to death in Orissa, where there was food shortage as usual--he was two months old and his mother had run out of breast-milk. He occupied the mind of a Congress party worker, bribing a village school teacher to throw his weight behind the party of Gandhi and Nehru in the coming election campaign, also the thoughts of Keralan peasant who had decided to vote communist. Saleem became Jawaharlal Nehru, Prime Minister and author of framed letters. He sat with the great man amongst a bunch of gaptoothed, straggle beard astrologers and adjusted the five year plan to bring it into harmonic alignment with the music of the spheres.(p.174)

Thus Saleem becomes the consciousness of the whole country experiencing the life and times of the multitudes. He is born on the stroke of midnight and therefore becomes the symbol of independent India. The novel is Saleem's story, representing India's millions of people. His family emigrates to Pakistan. The 1965 war brings the roof crashing down on Saleem's family, eliminating it in an air raid and Saleem is knocked out cold. When he recovers he is found to have lost his memory. Orphaned and deprived of hundred daily pinpricks of family life, Saleem has been pulled up by roots to be flung unceremoniously across the years memoryless into an adulthood. In Rushdie's transliteration, he achieved the state of Buddha--if we pronounce the word buddha with ds hard, Saleem grew old before his time. But there was also Buddha with soft tongued ds, meaning he who achieved enlightenment under the Bodhi tree. Once upon a time a prince, unable to bear the suffering of the world became capable of not living in the world as well as living in it. In ancient India, Gautama the Buddha sat enlightened under a tree at Gaya; in the deer park at Sarnath he taught others to abstract themselves from worldly sorrows and achieved inner peace; and centuries later, Saleem the buddha sat under a different tree unable to remember grief, numb as ice, wiped clean as slate. (pp. 349-50)

In the state of amnesia Saleem accepted military life. Later he was fated to suffer corruption, terrorism and conflicting political interests and the onslaughts of Emergency, a state of suspended civil rights and press freedom. This too at the hands of the saviour of human rights in Bangladesh. Janata Party coming in power did not seem to represent a new dawn because its visionary was trapped in a kidney-machine. Naturally, totally drained of his powers, the hero of *Midnight's Children* felt that an age, which had started on that long ago midnight, had come to an end. He had shared the privilege and curse of midnight's children, to be both master and victim of his times, to forsake privacy and be sucked into the annihilating whirlpool of the multitudes. He became incapacitated to live or die in peace.

After his nostalgic glance at India in *Midnight's Children*, Rushdie shifts his attention to Pakistan in his next novel, *Shame*. In a way *Shame* has its genesis in *Midnight's Children* when Rushdie could not forgive Karachi for not being Bombay, and had the realisation: midnight has many children; the offspring of Independence were not all human. Violence, corruption, poverty, generals, chaos, greed and pepperpots. I had to go into exile to learn that the children of midnight were more varied than I--even I--dreamed. (p. 291) The hero of *Midnight's Children* had already passed his judgement on Pakistan: "Pakistan . . . what a complete dump" and was fated to help change the fate of the Land of the Pure. (p. 287) Therefore in a way *Shame* is a continuation of certain parts in *Midnight's Children* and Rushdie's verdict on the subcontinent.

Unfolding the truth about Pakistan, the novel is a queer combination of free-flight-fairy tale and a savage political indictment. Though dealing with historical facts, the novel is not written in chronological order. Jumping forward and backward in time is as deliberate as its apparently disorganised form. Rushdie takes care to explain that he is not writing a realistic novel about Pakistan. "But suppose this were a realistic novel," Rushdie exclaims between the passage of his fanciful narrative, "just think what else I might have to put in."[12] (p. 6)

Rushdie expatiates upon the sins of Pakistan on the basis of his dubious spiritual bond with that country. He creates a convenient facet to analyse the gloating absurdities taking place in the so called modern era of the 20th century. The happenings take place in the fourteenth century. He says, "I'm using the Hegiran calendar, naturally; don't imagine that stories of this type always take place long long ago. Time cannot be homogenized as easily as milk, and in those parts, until quite recently, the thirteenth hundreds were still in full swing." (p. 13) Pakistan becomes the fictional country of Q. Rushdie says that the country of "my story, My fictional country exists like myself, at a slight angle to reality. . . . My view is that I am not writing about Pakistan. I have not given the country a name. And Q. is not really Quetta at all !" (p. 29) Meaning thereby that *Shame* is an exposé of the bleak nightmare in Pakistan. The corruption of both army and civilian rule, neo-colonialism and the dependence on foreign aid, religious fundamentalism as chauvinist political strategy, US support of Islamic fundamentalism, the projection of Pakistan in western media, the festering violence leading to a kind of horror at Pakistan's impending destruction.

The story of *Shame* is the story of Sufiya Zinobia, the elder daughter of General Raza Hyder (Rushdie's fictional General Zia) and his wife Bilquis about what happened between her father and chairman Iskander Harappa, (or shall we say Zulfikar Ali Bhutto) formerly Prime Minister, and about her surprising marriage to a certain Omar Khayyam Shakil, physician, and for a time, the intimate crony of Isky Harappa, whose neck had the miraculous power of remaining unbruised, even by a hangman's rope.

The novel begins with the death of old Mr. Shakil and the birth of the hero Omar Khayyam. He is peripheral to the story. Rushdie does not allow him to dominate the story in the manner Saleem becomes the focus in *Midnight's Children*. Omar Khayyam, conceived in sin, was fated to be born to three mothers because no one could ever discover, not even the child who was born, who was his real mother. The Shakil sisters displayed passionate solidarity and transformed the public shame of unwedlocked conception into the private triumph of the longed-for-group baby. He was fated to be tormented with an unabated fear of nothingness.

Rushdie found Iskander-Raza plot totally macho "all about careerism, cops, politics, revenge, assassinations, executions, blood and guts." As the story progresses Rushdie discovers female characters who dominate the novel. It is an inverted criticism of the woman condition in Pakistan where males refuse to be born. Hyder's first son is still born, strangled by his own umbilical cord. Their second child is Sufiya Zinobia, who is retarded by brain fever and the third is also a daughter who, on the day of her wedding, decided to drop her groom and marry someone else.

Sufiya Zinobia is the most disturbing character in the novel. Sinister and frightening because of flashes of violence and blinding anger, she grows into something demonic. She is presented as a metaphor for mob violence in the country. She combines in herself the shame and violence that resulted in the doom of Pakistani dictatorship. Rushdie says, "humiliate people for long enough and wildness bursts out of them." (p. 117) But Rushdie views an ennobling side also in her. Consuming herself in the shame of those around her, she becomes a saint: "For what is saint ? A saint is a person who suffers in our stead." (p. 141)

The climax is reached with the hanging of the Chairman Iskander Harappa. His destiny, Rushdie sums up, "six years in power, two in jail, and eternity underground." He came to power through elections which were not totally straightforward. "How could they be in that country divided into two wings a thousand miles apart, sundered by the land-mass its greatest foe, joined by nothing but God." (p. 178) The country was ripped into half after the civil war and people suspected Isky's complicity in the whole affair. Isky in due course became the undoing of himself. He put Raza Hyder in control of the defeated army and thus Iskander Harappa was overpowered by time. He ushered in A New Man for a New Century, though he himself was ahead of his time and therefore out of tune with it. Time took its revenge: "It hung him out to dry." *They* hanged him in the middle of night, wrapped up and gave him to Rani Harappa and his daughter Arjumand. They saw the evidence of shame--"on a hanged man's neck the rope leaves its mark. Iskander's neck was clean." (p. 187) Why the rope did not mark Iskander Harappa, because *they* had hung a corpse.

Raza Hyder rose, consequently, as a dictator who banned political parties, muzzled the media, subverted the judiciary and then postponed, re-postponed, then shelved and finally cancelled the election: "It was in this period that the initials CMLA, standing for Chief Martial Law Administrator acquired a new meaning. People began to say that what they really stood for was Cancel My Last Announcement." (p. 227) Elections were not held and Raza Hyder became President. He tried to bring stability to the country; and during the next four years of his Presidency imposed the laws of flogging and cutting of hands in the name of Islam. The whole world termed these laws as barbaric but the President said: "These are the holy words of God, as revealed in sacred texts. Now if they are holy words of God, they cannot also be barbaric." (p. 245) Rushdie believes that the Islamic revival has failed to unite Sindhis, Baluchis, Punjabis, and Pathans because the Islamic fundamentals have not sprung from the people in that country; it is imposed by autocratic regimes for their convenience. This leads to the fall of the dictator in the novel bringing God down with him. Ultimately the truth of liberty, equality and fraternity prevails. Raza Hyder, running away from his avenging daughter, Sufiya Zinobia, seeks shelter at Nishapur in Q. along with Omar Khayyam and there he is slaughtered by the agile knives of a hoary contraption. The story of *Shame* has taken a full swing at a note of prophecy and apocalypse.

Thus the stance of a fantasist, a fabulist, the guise of the fairy-tale writing, all contribute toward the novelist's way of seeing. What is the ultimate goal ? To unfold the truth. Rushdie himself writes in *Shame:* "The book would have been banned, dumped in the rubbish bin, burned. All that effort for nothing ! Realism can break a writer's heart. Fortunately however, I am only telling a sort of modern fairy-tale, so that's all right; nobody need get upset, or take anything I say seriously. No drastic action need be taken either. What a relief !" (p. 70)

NOTES

1. William Walsh, "India and the Novel," *The New Pelican Guide to English Literature: The Present*, ed. Boris Ford (Middlesex, England: Penguin Books, 1983), p. 258.

2. George Lukacs, *Studies in European Realism* (London: The Merlin Press, 1972), p. 6.

3. *Ibid.*, p. 9.

4. Kumkum Sangari, "Interview with Salman Rushdie," *The Book Review*, Mar/Apr 1984, Vol. 3, No. 5, p. 251

5. *Ibid.*, p. 252.

6. *Loc. cit.*

7. Salman Rushdie, *Grimus* (London: Granada Publishing, 1975)

8. Dilip Fernandez, "Such Angst, Loneliness, Rootlessness," *Gentleman*, Feb 1984, p. 100.

9. Ibid., p. 102.

10. Salman Rushdie, *Midnight's Children* (London: Pan Books, 1981)

11. *The Book Review*, p. 247.

12. Salman Rushdie, *Shame* (London: Pan Books, 1983)

Yatra: Nina Sibal: A Rites of Passage *Bildungsroman*

SHALINI GUPTA

Nina Sibal's interesting first novel *Yatra* (The Women's Press Limited, London: 1987; Roli Books, New Delhi, 1988) is complex, many-stranded, dense-textured. It weaves together narrative, history, image, ideas and symbol in an intriguing mixture of invention and reality. Ms. Sibal's writing gives off whiffs, at times, of Marquez and Rushdie in its touches of magical realism, at others of Nayantara Sahgàl in its concrete localization of time and place, and finally, of Jhabvala in its overt and often arbitrary sensuality. Though the novel is *manque* as regards style--this is in fact Ms. Sibal's Achilles's heel--it proves ultimately a fascinating *pot pourri*--a multi-layered onion of a novel: peeling off its successive layers is a taxing exercise in mental agility and readerly ingenuity. The novel, from start to finish, compels attention, its images often graphic, vivid, sometimes startling. It hurtles back and forth in time and place with all the chaos of an irregular heartbeat. Yet within this subtle chaos, it crystallizes its own order, a hard clear reality as cold and palpable as frozened glass.

The heroine of the novel, Krishna Chahal, is half-Greek, half-Indian, like Ms. Sibal herself. Yet there the resemblance ends. This is clearly a provocative work of imagination, not a fictionalized autobiography. Between the beautiful Sonia--"the most beautiful girl in Paris"-- and her dark-skinned progeny, Krishna, named after the blue god of Hindu mythology, there is little resemblance, save that of sexual promiscuity. Krishna's unprogressively darkening skin is symbol for the political *sturm und drang* of Indian historical events since Partition. Imaginative Rushdiesque touches of magical realism are, Kailash Kaur's dancing eyes behind the lattice of Pakistani star singer Karishma's black satin *burqa*, or the magical bridal *phulkari*, with its "strangely perfect beauty," steeped in human blood; the blood of beloved brother Manmohan Singh flowing across the courtyard to the room where his sister Swarnjit Kaur sits weaving her *khes* is a distinctly Marquezian touch. In such places the language becomes rich and resonant, or puckish and magical. The beautiful green-eyed boy Prakash, incestuous lover to his aunt Kailash Kaur, is again one of *midnight's children*; or perhaps a figure out of Mario Vargas Llosa. The snake that is Rai Bahadur Bhim Lal Whig, "crawling up mountain paths, dodging invaders, hiding out in deserted villages" before reaching Srinagar, and the slaughtered lovers locked lovingly together in *rigor mortis*, are, again, whimsical and effective images, like the needle and thread imagery used throughout the book to sew together people, situations, events. This, then, is a novel of magical realism.

However, Ms. Sibal fails to sustain this vision continuously, and brilliant chapters such as Chapter 4, "The story of Kailash Kaur" are succeeded by chapters of patchy, inconsequential and banal writing, for example, the long and boring train journey of Chapter 5, which achieves little but Theroux-like glimpses of Indian railway station tea and fails significantly to further the narrative. In fact, style and symbol often fail to coalesce, which makes the writing "come apart at the seams."

In Chapter 12, for example, we have the introduction of Father Sherifis, a priest from the Mediterranean, described as a powerful figure with a "tremendous vitality," a monocle of "utter elegance" (incidentally a very weak phrase), "beautiful white robes" and a "vibrant healthy skin." An impressive figure with his tribe of six nuns who "unfolded like a flower, a bunch of white petals opened around him, smooth and impassive." This image, beautiful as it is, is, however, neither elaborated nor left to stand as it is: instead it is undermined by the makeshift weakness of the next line which leaves the reader hanging in mid-air, as it were: "He was the central force, the dancing, powerful spirit that twirled round and round, holding them together." A more experienced writer would have rounded out the image like a bell--Ms. Sibal ironically undercuts its power by a follow-up line that is ineffective, if not inane. Patchy writing such as this destroys the beauty of the whole. Take again, for example, the final sentence, at the end of the novel: "Her head was light, she was twirling in one place, like the laburnum three from her father's jungles, complete and whole, dense and yellow with silence"--

whatever force the image of the laburnum tree--incidentally another flower image--"dense and yellow with silence," may have had, and whatever symbolic impact it may have possessed, are destroyed by the inanity of the first part of the line. Ms. Sibal seems obsessed with the word "twirls," which she uses thoughtlessly, indeed risibly. It is the thoughtless use of word or phrase in the wrong place, then, that detracts from the impact and consistency of the writing as a whole. Thus, often the writing fails to convince. This then is the central weakness of the novel: a failure of style.

The novel embraces in its wide emotional, political, cultural, historical and geographical sweep many levels of metaphor: metaphors of travel, change, progression, transition. It is a voyage of adventure and discovery by one woman across the dark heart of the Indian sub-continent: the journey of the Indian woman in search of herself. In Rushdiesque fashion, it also delineates a parallel between Krishna's history and the history of a nation--with her darkening skin a metaphor for the politics of the Indian subcontinent. It also traces Krishna's ancestral history down five generations of the Sikh Chahals of Kohat, with their business and political affairs, their social, amorous and domestic intrigues. It is a novel of transition and change: a "rites of passage" *Bildungsroman*.

There are, however, passages of infinite tedium. The introduction of Ranjit Dhawan, Krishna's sorely-needed lover, is prefaced by a long and infinitely boring account of the activities of Krishna's doctor father during the 1971 Bangladesh war--an account that could well have been omitted altogether, and which is reminiscent of Paul Scott's equally tedious 100-page narrative in the first book of the Raj Quartet, *The Jewel in the Crown*, a dreadful chapter entitled Civil and Military. Mercifully, Ms. Sibal's narrative extends to only 30 pages, though as extraneous. One suspects it is brought in as a touch of local colour, added to give authenticity. It fails to achieve either objective.

On the other hand, I rather liked the chapter entitled "Dear Images." Perhaps its artful inconsequence appealed to my feminine sensibility, with its fast-paced imaginative cinematic technique. The woman in the blue Fiat is the *doppleganger* tactics of the lost woman in Krishna--of all she once was, and all she aspires again to be. The image of Krishna's car hurtling over the phoenix-like green city of post-Asian Games New Delhi, risen from the ashes of its arid past--of Krishna in search of her alter ego in the blue Fiat--of Krishna ending in a crash--not here fatal--is expressive of emotional release for long pent-up energies. In this symbolic accident, Krishna is resurrected. But, again, much more could have been done with this brief chapter, far more symbolically expressive than many others, concretely realized as it is in its successful capturing of a fleeting, vivid, graphic image--an image of self-destructing in the moment of release--an image of life itself ?

Time and again, Rushdie comes to mind. Saleem Sinai, changeling, and Krishna Chahal, collector of fathers: "Who was her father, white man or Indian ? Her darkening skin, moving from pink to brown and black, had fooled them all, confusing them; there was no way of telling which one had shot his genes into her, had bestowed the original patrimony." It is a marvellous confidence trick, pulled off with panache. Sibal is at her most successful when she is most Rushdiesque.

The Chipko movement, and Krishna's *padyatra*, associated with it, are again successful symbols. Walking is a metaphor of life, again--this time an Indian, a Gandhian metaphor. Krishna's *padyatra* is like Gandhi's Dandi march--a journey with a purpose, this time into the heart of a feminist movement. Krishna, in her association with Chipko, becomes symbolic of the liberation of the Indian woman. Gandhi liberated the nation; Krishna tries to do the same for Indian womanhood. She is even called Krishnaji. She becomes symbolic, also, of the body of "Mother Earth," wounded through deforestation landslides, floods, drought and soil erosion. Her darkened skin becomes a metaphoric analogue of this terrestrial devastation. The Chipko women, with Krishna as their fountainhead, are symbolic of a predominant desire for self-preservation, for self-liberation. Through ecology to selfhood: Krishna becomes here a symbolic expression of the spirit of the Indian earth, of Indian womanhood, to liberate itself. But she becomes more--mysterious, magical, mystical: "the woman of the trees," they call her. Chapter 19 is, in fact, one of the most lyrical, effective and symbolic. Indeed, in it, Krishna almost attains god- head. She becomes almost a Buddha, a Mahomet, a Gandhi, or a Christ. And she attains her terrestrial aim: becoming at the end of the book, because of this, a potential candidate for the Tehri seat for Parliament, a potential politician, a potential M.P.

With Chapter 20, the novel moves from the geographical and ecological Indian realities back to magical realism. After a lyrical passage of great beauty, comparing Krishna to her Hindu namesake, "the passionate, colouring god," comes this paragraph: "With Houdini-powers she could escape from anywhere, even chained in an iron box let down into the sea. She could travel out to others, bound and gagged and fired with life. Connected thus, touching the world, wrapped with love, she would pirouette in the streets. Out in the open air, willing to be assaulted by light. They say Houdini died by drowning, but she was not about to die. Not yet."

A fleeting note of existential angst ? It passes. Krishna loses her family and gains a nation: "Denied patrimony, deprived of inheritance, land grabbed from under her feet, she was earning the right to a whole country. Slowly, inch by inch, she was drawing India into her with love. Mother India for the orphaned girl." Again, the Rushdiean image comes to mind, and Sibal is the female Rushdie.

Then comes the supreme "hubris." One day she might be Woman of the World, distinctions blurring between country and country, her skin encasing the whole twirling earth in a faint dark film, visible from space-ships and the dulcet eyes of extra-terrestrial beings. Who is this Krishna Chahal, self-created being, separated from chaos by her own skin ? Or, in Whitman's phrase, "I am large, I contain multitudes." In other words, will the real Krishna Chahal please stand up ?

The chapter ends with Sibal's Bombay, which, unlike Rushdie's is an unreal city of squalor and tawdriness, in which the evil presence of Chaman Bajaj, "silent wind of destruction," "had blown straight through walls which had seemed impregnable." Here are whiffs of Marquez's culminating cataclysm at the end of *One Hundred Years of Solitude*.

Chapters 21-27 take the narrative back to a recounting of the tale of Krishna's ancestors, not especially memorable or visible. Sibal's depiction of the Punjab in these chapters is fairly evocative of history and the spirit of place, but these are not personally my favourite chapters. I found them dull. Her successful portrayal of the

New Delhi of the 80's is far more lyrical and poetic than the sketchy glimpse she gives us of a sordid, seamy Bombay.

Lastly, Bibi Chinti. Along with Chaman Bajaj, she is an evil wind blowing nobody any good, present as a portent of death and disaster; at Poonam's death, she weeps paradoxically for her dead buffalo, blown to smithereens by the same blast that killed Poonam. In the final chapter, she is present when the dogs tear apart Chaman Bajaj. She also occurs as a false alarm earlier in the novel when Krishna and her lover Ranjit visit Humayun's Tomb. An ominous figure of doom, she is a character straight out of the dreamland of magical realism.

What then are the novel's weaknesses and strengths ? First, the weaknesses, as they can then be somewhat if not entirely dismissed: lapses of style that are legion, and certain chapters of marked dullness and boredom. Its strengths, however, are what remain in mind as one turns the last page: several passages of great lyricism and beauty, a successful recreation of India's demography, geography and history, a skilful construction of character, situation and incident, a contemporary eye for local colour and detail, a complex weaving back and forth in time, ancestral history, and political events, an effective use of idea, image and symbol, an often poetic evocation of the spirit of place, and, finally, a graphic depiction of the deracination of the Indian woman. At times, the novel overstates the case. At times, the writing doesn't quite jell. At times, "between the conception and the creation . . . falls the Shadow." And yet, I must confess, somehow I couldn't put the book down.

Rich LIke Us: A Note

NINA ARORA

Within the span of just one year Nayantara Sahgal has bagged two prestigious awards for her new and sixth novel, *Rich Like Us* published in 1985. In that very year, she was awarded Sinclair Prize for Fiction and in 1986 the prestigious Sahitya Akademi Award was bestowed upon her for this novel.

During Emergency, Sahgal resigned from Akademi's Advisory Board in protest, because her suggestion that the Board should pass a resolution to condemn censorhip of Press and imprisonment without trial was not acceded to. Ironically, the same Akademi has now honoured her for her novel which subjects the Emergency to a rigorous critical scrutiny and launches a seething attack on the excesses committed by the political dragons during the period.

Sahgal has the honour of being the first Indian Woman novelist writing in English dealing with political themes. She started her literary career in 1954 with her autobiographical work, *Prison and Chocolate Cake*. Since then, she has consistently been engaged in writing novels and journalistic columns for newspapers dealing with the contemporary political themes. *In Rich Like Us*, she vividly and pungently delineates the socio-political scenario of India particularly during Emergency the backdrop of which is Delhi.

Emergency meant opportunity, plenty and power for a handful of loyalists. While the hero-worshippers prospered, the majority of common, simple-minded, straight-forward people were being exploited and deprived of civil liberties. The sincere officers and civil servants had become virtually "like cherry stones on a plate, not like people," (p. 86) or to say in the language of Sonali (the protagonist of the novel), "the automatons," who were forced to indulge in corrupt practices just to please a handful of hangers-on. The state-of-affairs, the suppressed cries under the rule of rod, have been aptly symbolized by the recurring image of a handless, helpless struggling beggar in a street being dragged by society ladies into a mobile vasectomy clinic.

Besides depicting the anguish during Emergency the novelist takes the reader to the scenario of the second World War and nostalgic pre-partition days and describes the magnetic, transforming influence of Gandhi on the masses. The portrayal of the upper strata of society who are as usual indifferent, insensitive to the chilling upheavals around, lost in their own small, rich, glamorous world of clubs, parties and get-togethers is unsurpassable.

Sonali--a sincere, senior civil servant, is pained to see the murder of democratic ideals. The sudden apocalypse of her well-to-do grandparents's especially her grandmother's submission to 'Sati'--an evil social system leaves her dumb-founded for sometime. The entire political drama during emergency is seen through Sonali's eyes.

The love-triangle of Ram, Rose and Mona, the tears and bleeding heart of Mona--Ram's first wife and her religious fervour, her regular fasting peculiar of a traditional Hindu wife--and later the development of friendship between co-wives are some of the incidents carefully blended into the mainstream of the novel.

Sahgal has special regards for patriots like Mahatma Gandhi and Pandit Jawahar Lal Nehru (her maternal uncle). Some passages in the novel reveal her true respect for Pt. Nehru. She pays a tremendous tribute to his overall personality:

> What a man, what character, what integrity, what ability, what democracy ! What refinement such as never-before-seen ! . . . Relationships, anecdotes, encounters with Panditji popped up like jack-in-the boxes. (p. 146)

She vividly recalls the matchless patriotism, selflessness and sacrifices of freedom fighters before partition and contrasts them with greed, selfishness and shamelessness of contemporary politicians.

After a gap of eight years, since the publication of her earlier novel *A Situation in New Delhi* (1977), there is a marked development in her prose here, which is complex, deep, rich with apt images, symbols, gentle humour and irony. Her description of events is marked with accuracy and foresightedness. *Rich Like Us* is, in fact, one of the best novels Sahgal has so far written.

Plans for Departure: A Study

M. G. HEGDE

Mrs. Nayantara Sahgal's seventh novel *Plans for Departure*[1] which has won the Eurasian regional award in the Commonwealth Fiction Prize registers an important stage in her growth as a novelist. While each of her earlier novels, as has been stated by herself, "more or less reflects the political era we are passing through,"[2] *Plans for Departure* takes the reader back to the colonial past and presents a picture of the subcontinent poised for revolution in the backdrop of the world on the edge of a cataclysmic war. In choosing a context of vital significance and possibility, Mrs. Sahgal assumes an ambitious position which has the danger of dissipation as well as the possibility of synthesis and the novel itself has little resemblance to anything she has written before.[3]

One of the assets of Mrs. Sahgal's fictional art is a definite perspective with which she views men and matters. Often the perspective is offered by the principal woman character in the novel. In *Plans for Departure* a significant chunk of history i.e. 1914—is presented as the experience of an emancipated Danish spinster Miss Anna Hansen. Mrs. Sahgal's scrupulous selection of the period as well as the protagonist is perfectly matched by her enviable understanding of the history. Selection of a British character or an Indian character as the central consciousness would have marred the facility which she enjoys now. While Anna's sojourn at Himapur, an imaginary hill station in the Himalayas and the decisive impact of this stay on her life is the major note in the novel, themes like human relationship, status of the woman, East-West encounter, British imperialism, the Indian National Movement, and the steady growth of a sombre mood in which the whole world is moved towards the catastrophic war of 1914 make for the symphony. Most of the action in the novel takes place in a period which Forster has called 'the sinister corridor of our age.' It is a period when the whole world is on the brink of change. Commenting on the significance of the period, in 1961, Jason, Anna's grandson-in-law, who is working on a conference paper on

Tilak's leadership of the Congress, says: "nothing would have turned out as it did afterwards if these particular things hadn't happened before." (144)

Anna, in whose witness we get a memorable picture of the troubled times is, in terms of the novel's theme, of special significance. It is very important that she is a Dane. Coming as she does from a little unimportant country, she can view from a common man's standpoint 'the Great Powers who had their greatness and power to preserve.' "It is not at all clear to me," says Anna to Henry, "who wants war and who wants peace . . . why do countries have to be Powers, and why do Powers have to be Great ?" (129) And Henry, in his turn, says that none of these things are clear to him either. "But we aren't alone, Anna. There's such a tremendous future awaiting for people like us." (129) The other way out is, according to Anna every country should shrink into 'total insignificance,' 'Danish unimportance' as fast as possible.

Secondly, because of her Danish unimportance and as she is 'born nine centuries after Denmark gave up raiding, colonizing, and lusting after worlds to conquer,' she displays a potential for tolerance, wisdom and objective view of pride and prejudice of both Oriental and Occidental. Her indomitable independence and her sense of freedom provides a striking contrast to the British imperialism and the suffocating political situation of the 1914.

Anna is a happy choice in other ways too. She is conscious of the span of India's history, its cultural tradition as well as its present. She reflects:

> The struggle for self-mastery was all that was really real. If that was Hinduism in a nutshell, it was a pity it had not stayed grand and simple, in the nut. (47)

She knows her India very well: 'Whatever else it (India) needed, it did not need one more religion.' (51) Evidently, Anna is more Indian than any other Indian character in the novel. Moreover, she has come to India for self-realization—the age old Indian concept of the ideal of life. Thus she celebrates the necessity of facing up to the complexities of life and stands for the new image of woman which was then in the making.

II

Plans for Departure is a many-faceted novel. At one level it is about human relationships. Miss Anna Hansen sets out on a travel for one year—Copenhagen, London, Madras, Calcutta and finally Himapur, where she gives secretarial assistance and company to Sir Nitin Basu, (whose resemblance to Sir Jagdish Chandra Bose is quite plain) the eminent Botanist working on the psychology of plants. In England she has a suitor Nicholas Wyatt, an English diplomat who firmly believes in 'the white man's burden.' His "order of priorities was fatally clear. Food, drink, and the wedding date, followed by life in a jeweled status quo . . . whereas her priority was life and freedom first." (62) When Nicholas calls her idea "infantile," she protests:

> "It is not silly wonders I am after. But what other way can I break out and be me ?" (62)

After her arrival in India she spends several months at the Theosophical Society in Adyar in the South and finally comes to Himapur.

The novel begins at this point. It starts as a social comedy. For Sir Nitin Basu, "who had never had any woman, her presence was alarming as invasion." (14) Despite his Western education, study of science, and knighthood, he has 'long Hindu habits.' (12) He is needlessly worried about Anna's age and is disturbed by the attitude of this unconventional feminist towards religion and church, by her six miles walk up and downhill everyday and by the 'indicators of unsupervised upbringing' in her. She almost gets on his nerves and it takes a long time before they are able to adjust to each other.

Making up the small European community in Himapur with whom Anna comes into contact are the District Magistrate, Henry Brewster, 'the sum total of officialdom in Himapur,' and the missionary Marlowe Croft and his wife Lucilie Croft. Madhav Rao, a photographer-cum-chemist, is probably the only Indian who is in Anna's small circle of acquaintances in Himapur.

Henry Brewster, 'a mold-craker' as Anna would call, is ill-at-ease with the imperial authority he represents. He has been posted to Himapur where there are 'more pine and deodar woods than human habitation' because Henry has 'an annoying tendency to keep making a case for the fox.' (22) But Stella, his wife, has opposite political commitments which got muddled with other reasons. Their relation is, as Henry appropriately puts it, "like being on opposite sides in the American Civil War." (128) In spite of Henry's devoted love for her which makes him give up his dreams of a new political life in England, she develops an affair with Robert Pryor, the Home Secretary. Even when they tell Henry that they are "fond" of each other, Henry is not ready to leave her:

> I said to Pryor, since Stella wouldn't talk, "Is she pregnant ? Is that the trouble ? Because if she is, I'll adopt the child." They looked at each other as if I were dangerously unbalanced, and this the final travesty in my dementedness. (195)

The inevitable does happen. Pushing Henry to the depths of desperation Stella makes her journey downhill only to marry Robert. Thus by the time Anna comes in contact with Henry, all is said and done, and Henry is left all alone chaotic, desperate and dwindled.

Anna comes to Henry's office every day to collect mail and borrow books from his personal library. She is moved by Henry's predicament as she always sympathised with grieving souls. She writes to Nicholas, "He is quite nakedly suffering and it is hard to watch him and remain unmoved." Moreover, she appreciates and shares the anti-imperialistic stand of Henry. Their relationship develops and comes dangerously close to loving. She even begins to reconsider her future. But at this point she stumbles on vague evidences of two unnatural deaths on a faraway hillside and imagining them to be associated with a secret crime she makes plans for her departure. On returning to England, she marries Nicholas.

The case of Marlowe Croft and his wife Lulu is another story. Marlowe comes in the life of Lulu in rather a dramatic way. He opposes her father in favour of 'indigo.' Consequently he is arrested and he loses church affiliation. Thus he has no backing and is accountable to no one. Still Lulu marries him as if she has been under 'a hypnotic spell.' Marlowe is bent upon 'making something out of nothing in Himapur.' (85) He is busy with his school, carpentry, his soul-saving activity: the 'Christian Endeavour' and of course, with his 'obsession': building a Christian church in the hills. Lulu Croft, diametrically opposite in nature, is 'universally disliked' and she 'could undo years of good will in five minutes' (31) as she raises 'solid phalanxes of hostility every time she opened her mouth.' (119) 'Two such diametrically opposed nuisances could ever have got together at any level, much less in matrimony.' (31) For all her shrill foolishness, Lulu has been a good wife. But when Marlowe baptizes a sweeper's child and thinks of adopting it Lulu finds it unbearable. 'With her good wifeliness gone, and her loyalty to his loyalties at breaking point . . . the life she had made with him was over.' (147) She plans to depart. But before she could depart, she meets with an accident in a forest glade.

In England, in the late autumn of 1916, Anna receives Henry's letter which apart from lifting the clouds around Stella's departure, gives a picture of the 'real' Henry from his own stand-point. The covering letter informs her of Henry's death in the Allied offensive on the Somme. A visit by Stella and Robert further unravels the mystery and puts the record and Anna's fancies straight. Peter, the only son of Anna and Nicholas, marries an Indian political activist. Nicholas and Anna have their political career too and sit on the opposite sides in the Parliament. Gayatri, Anna's grand-daughter continues Anna's own self and Jason, Anna's grandson-in-law is working on a conference paper on Tilak. That is 1961. The novel ends sometime after Anna's death, Gayatri thinking much in the line of Anna.

Evidently, Mrs. Sahgal's major concern is clash of human beings—the clash of the opposites. She juxtaposes characters diametrically opposite in nature: Henry and Stella, Marlowe and Lulu, Sir Nitin and Anna, Anna and Nicholas. This device helps her to register the contrasting responses to the East and the West, the role of Church, British imperialism and the Indian National Movement and of course, status of the woman in India and abroad. Furthermore, a pattern is clearly discernible in these conflicts. Also, all the plans for departure have a bearing on varying degrees of "change" at varying levels.

III

'Freedom' and 'Change' are the key words in the novel. To begin with, the title of the novel itself is suggestive of change. Anna's character emerges a symbol for struggle for change and freedom. Her priority is "life and freedom first."(62) Gayatri tells that Anna "was so disappointed the world hadn't changed enough in her life time, she had to hurry it along."(211) Contrasted with this are the attitudes of Robert Pryor who says "No reason why there should be any changes," (204) and Sir Nitin Basu who 'believed in the slow, majestic forces of progress under the grand glorious British' (142) and Nicholas who 'belonged to the breed that had simply imagined constitution and traditions into being' (165) and in a word, "wanted permanence." (198) Writing to Nicholas Sir Nitin's one of the findings that carrot is highly excitable and the most reacting while celeries don't get so easily excited, Anna states, "I have come to the conclusion I'm a carrot and you a celery." (177) Henry Brewster, on the contrary, is 'the theatrical extreme of Anna's effervescence.' (200) Once, Anna and Henry get so carried away talking about the changes they were going to see during their lives that 'they forgot the time on a walk to a view Anna had never come across." (137) There is Tilak's new interpretation of the *Bhagwad-Geeta* that one has to 'hurry back from private bliss to public duty and spend the rest of one's life making the world a better place.' (123) Finally, there is Madhav Rao with his typically Indian attitude couched in mysticism that the world changes, "when our perception of it changes." (154)

Romantic idealist as she is, Anna confronts in Emily Davison, Tilak and Tulsidas, the sixteenth century poet-saint some hitherto unconscious yearning in herself. That is the reason why she develops a kinship with Tilak though 'she wasn't anywhere near politics' (143) and 'didn't meet anyone politically important'(142) including Tilak. When Emily Davison, the famous suffragette, threw herself under the hoofs of Kind George's colt, her suicide does not 'touch a single nerve or chord' but leaves Anna's life up by the roots. She imagines the kindred spirit of Tulsidas in Henry Brewster. Jason quite appropriately diagnoses this:

> "And were the people real, apart from Tilak ?"
> "They must have been. Gran always said she met a kindred soul in Henry Brewster."
> "Kindred spirits are hard to find. We sometimes have to invent them out of sheer need", murmured Jason worriedly into his pillow. (210-211)

One finds Anna's imagination in full bloom when she finds herself in her daughter-in-law, a political activist and when she says she "invented" Gayatri, who is Indian to the core.

Thus, Anna yearns for change on a grand scale. As she herself is incapable of such a grand endeavour in her given situation, she identifies herself in the people who have such possibilities. In seeing "a priest emerging out of that pale fire, a consuming religious dedication taking the place of his love for Stella" (117) in Henry, one finds the same instinct operative. This being true, she is made to conclude when she herself is made politically active and elected to the Parliament:

'The world would remain more or less as it was.' (211) This could be the sign of her maturity, while it is also arguable that it is the sign of her defeat. The defeat of Anna, nevertheless, is the defeat of the novel itself which becomes obvious when Gayatri, much against her character, and also probably too early for her age is made to remind herself, only to conclude the novel that

> 'we can't even hope for things we can't imagine, one world out of many, love everlasting, and all the rest.' (213)

IV

Departure, operative at different levels, becomes a unifying metaphor in the novel. As Anna herself emerges a symbol for the struggle for change the novel easily achieves structural unity. The contrasted responses to "change" have been discussed in the previous section. At the level of action too there are departures. Henry is the first to plan his departure. "There was a time a few years ago when I was all ready to quit," he tells Anna, "But Stella was against it." (126) Though Stella is the one who wanted to stay, ironically, she is the first to depart—'the only accomplished—departure' and her departure clouded with mystery heralds other departures. "Stella Brewster isn't the only one who can walk out," (139) Lulu warns her husband. But 'she had been a fool to imagine she could leave Himapur.' (148) Clouds of mystery around the departure of Stella and the death of Mrs. Croft become the immediate cause for Anna to plan her departure. She does depart only to lead a cozy life in England. As for the British stay in India, Henry reflects, 'apart from rights and wrongs of being here there's no future in it. I'm convinced we'll have to clear out in my life time.' (126) But while the British continue to stay on the subcontinent Henry himself is slaughtered in the battle.

The novel is teemed with references—to myths, legends and

incidents from the epics—which are functional. Mrs. Sahgal has an elegant and graceful style. The dialogues of Anna, Madhav Rao and Nicholas show how the author is at home with different varieties of English. Anna's English, in particular, creates a comic effect. The imagery in the novel is quite evocative. Few of these images are redolent of feminine sensibility: Anna finds the footpath encircling the hill 'like a loose, uneven girdle around bulging hips.' (19) Anna's hair had 'the innocence of fresh butter.' (154) Imagery is used to evoke situation (e.g. Henry's bedroom is 'sterile as a gauze bandage,' [76]) to realize character (e.g. Marlowe waited about 'meek as a lamb,' [23]) and to denote the attitude of characters towards other characters (e.g., For Lulu her husband 'looked like a huge, wet dog.' [145] Gentle humour and wit pervades the narrative. Madhav Rao's perpetual obsession with bringing about 'fundamental to character' in photos, the conflict between Lulu and Marlowe, Sir Nitin's attempts to correct Anna's manners show Mrs. Sahgal's sense of humour operative at its best.

Serious limitations in the novel, however, cannot be glossed over. As the novelist has 'too many irons in the fictional fire' most of the issues raised are not convincingly resolved. An ambiguous shift in Anna's response to change has been already discussed. Also there are sudden shifts of emphasis in Anna's career—from interest in India's past to the present to the active politics of England—which are neither prepared for earlier nor are they convincing in her context. Lack of action and telling episodes has resulted in the introduction of flat characters like Henry and comic caricatures like Madhav Rao. While Nicholas, Sir, Nitin, Robert Pryor are types, Henry, Stella, and the whole lot of younger generation, as has been shown earlier, have existence mostly in Anna's imagination. Though the back-drop of world politics has astounding historical fidelity, at times the back-drop itself is focused while no drama takes place on the stage. Hence moments of appeal and illumination come only when the human relationships are treated. Issues, public or private, should be particularized. Fictionalised. Else they become a parade of scholarship and remain at the level of statements.

Secondly, the element of mystery in the novel appears contrived because when they are resolved, those which should have evoked serious response, disappoint the reader and sound comic by their sheer triviality. For example, much ado around the death of Stella's spaniel remains an incident contrived to create cinematic effect. What after all is the significance of much sound and fury around Lulu's death ? Anna's response to these mysteries and her consequent departure also remain ambiguous. It is surprising as well as unconvincing that without a second thought she lets fly her imagination and arrives at easy conclusions.

Thirdly, distant echoes of Forster (a curse on the novelists writing on the theme ever since the publication of *A Passage to India*) are clearly heard. While the muddle in the character of Madhav Rao and the romantic idealism of Anna remind us of Prof. Godbole, and Aziz respectively, minor details like 'Aunt Anna' becoming 'Tantanna' for the villagers (reminding "Esmiss Esmoor"), the District Magistrate's liberal ideas and his dinner party. and the ending of the novel correspond to the details in *A Passage to India*. As for the mystery in the novel, Forster's ghost must have played the trick. However, the novel has neither the symbolic richness nor the structural sophistication of Forster's classic.

To conclude. In spite of contrived mysteries, unsatisfactory ending and lack of action, in its vision, sure insight into the politics of the times, elegant style and gentle humour, *Plans for Departure* registers a definite stage in Mrs. Sahgal's fictional career. *Plans for Departure*, in a way, shows Mrs. Sahgal's plans for departure: "It has left me with the feeling that there are all kinds of fresh pastures ahead, and that in a sense, I have only just begun to write,"[4] says Mrs. Sahgal in an interview. One only hopes she will take the reader to the 'fresh pastures' soon in the novels to come.

NOTES

1. (London: Heinemann, 1985).

2. Quoted by M.K.Naik, a review of *Rich Like Us*, *Indian Literature*, Vol.XXX, No.5, Sept.-Oct. 1987, p. 29.

3. Quoted by Jehanara Wasi, "A Writer's World," *Indian Horizons*, Vol. XXXV, Nos. 3-4, 1986, p. 44.

4. *Loc. cit.*

Sahgal: The Novel as Political Biography

JASBIR JAIN

Nayantara Sahgal's *Rich Like Us* (1985) and *Plans for Departure* (1986) are different from her earlier work in several ways. Though on the face of it they continue the thematic explorations of her earlier work, they are different in both character portrayal and narrative structure. Sahgal appears to have successfully thrust aside the autobiographical element, what she is now writing is political biography. *Rich Like Us*, like the later novel *Plans for Departure*, is the story of a country told with interest, humour and sardonic wit. None of the traditional approaches will work There are no protagonists in the conventional sense. The protagonist is India—and it provides a centre for different points of view to converge on.

Biography attempts to reconstruct the life of a person and to trace the major influences which may have shaped his character and life. The narrative approach is analytical, trying to put the various pieces of the puzzle together to form a pattern. It differs from autobiography for it need not have the element of self-reflexivity autobiographical narration may have. It also does not necessarily follow a linear development, and may at times be meticulously concerned with the details which appear significant with the advantage of hindsight. Biography necessarily looks at events from a distance. In these novels, Sahgal is concerned with India and its past, and attempts to account for the course of events in interpretative terms.

Rich Like Us is a double-edged title, ambiguous and divided even in its double meaning. Who is "rich," and who is us ? From the point of view of foreigners, Indians are aspiring to be rich like them. But the title from the Indian point of view is ironic in another sense. It is a pity to be rich in the way we are. From amongst the Indians, the rich, corrupt business people, bureaucrats, politicians are rich in a material sense, but bankrupt in terms of human values. The poor cripple, in contrast, is rich with his own wealth of defiance, courage and loyalty. The novel, even through its title, moves further back into India's 'rich' heritage and examines its present 'richness' of economic and political manipulations. It raises several questions: who is rich like us ? are we really rich—and if so, in what way ? and finally, is it worth being like Rose's stepson Dev ? The reference is right in the beginning of the novel. Neuman had been briefed before the trip:

> The first thing those local elites do . . . is to get themselves the biggest, latest model foreign cars, and why not ? We like the way we live. We can't blame them for wanting to live like us.[1]

Beginning with an ironic title with multiple meanings, the novel moves constantly between the past and the present through two consciousnesses, one of Rose and the other of Sonali. Rose is an Englishwoman from a working class background, speaking Cockney English, but bold enough to cross all racial and class barriers. Rose had broken an almost settled engagement with Freddie in order to marry Ram, a Lahore businessman, when the British were still ruling India. She had married for love, and had incongruously enough, done so with full knowledge of Ram's first marriage and the existence of a son. Thus the adjustment required of her was at many levels, requiring not only the acceptance of a joint family system, but also the feeling of guilt aroused by the presence of Ram's first wife and her child. She had abandoned all—her home, her country, her parents, even the familiar structure of love and marriage. The only thing she had not abandoned was a feeling of herself as a person, as a human being. Sonali is contrasted with Rose. She is an IAS officer in a free country and has all the advantages—parental support, an education abroad, and above all a mind of her own. But having all this, she is willing to detach herself from her background and look at it critically—her mother's caste feelings, her sister's social graces, her colleagues's manipulations—all leave her cold. But Sonali and Rose come together in the battles they fight in post-independent India, with the area of their freedom becoming smaller and smaller as the battle gets fiercer.

There are other characters and other points of view which reveal the helplessness of the bewilderment of the past in the face of the new uncertain future. These include figures like Dev's father-in-law, and Sonali's father. But for the main part there is Rose's part of the story, narrated in the third person, with Sonali's first person narration moving to and fro between the past and the present. There is also the middle ground inhabited by Dev, Rose's stepson, and Ravi Kachru, Sonali's childhood friend, colleague and one-time suitor. The meeting point is provided by the foreign collaborator Neuman.

Neuman is responsible for the generation of action. Sonali is in political disgrace because she has failed to understand the importance of this collaboration; Kachru is on the rise because of his ability to have understood it. Dev's financial position begins to improve from this point onwards, and politics for once rules all other spheres of life, ranging from the economic to the personal. It is not merely the perpetuation of power, but it is the calling into the being of new alignments and those who fail to accommodate these are left out in the cold. What is it that goes into the making of a people—their past heritage or the present pressures of existence ? And, more important than this is the question, what goes into the making of history: the quality of men, or the events ?

Rose's life provides some of the answers. She never had the advantages which accompany family background or education, or even marriage, but she proves herself quite capable of bridging the inequalities at two levels—the economic inequality where Ram has all the advantages, and the political inequality where she belongs to the race of the rulers. She is able to do this because she is conscious of herself as an individual and compels others to recognise this. Her husband had "learned to respect her for the individual she was." (40) Life is harsh: her parents die, there are moments of doubt, of being and remaining alien, the country's division, shift to Delhi, Ram's illness; all these happenings take their toll but she is still capable of reaching out to people and extending sympathy and warmth.

Alternating with the accounts of Rose's life and thoughts are Sonali's accounts of her life (Chapters 2, 4, 7, 9, 11, 13, 19 and 21 are all first person narrations by Sonali). Sonali realises that her administrative training has not prepared her for handling the new situation which has arisen out of political concerns dominating the administrative:

> Once upon a time who had thought of the civil services as "we" and politicians as "they," two different sides of the coin. "We" were bound by more than discipline. We partook of a mystique. Our job was to stay free of the political circus. We were successors to the I.C.S., the "steel frame" the British had ruled India with, but with more on our hands since independence than the steel frame

> had had in two hundred years. . . . The distinction between politics and the service had become so blurred over the last few years it had all but disappeared. The two sides were hopelessly mixed, with politicians meddling in administration, and favourites like Kachru, the prime example, playing politics as if his life depended on it. (24)

Sonali is unwilling to bend the rules to suit people, or to liberally interpret them. Therefore she has to be transferred and demoted all in one stroke. All along she is against the current. Idealism, heritage, character, integrity, value structure, even personal relationships—all are outdated ! Sonali's problem is that she has to unlearn all that she has learnt so far. The quality she is being asked to give up is courage—a quality which she has inherited and has nurtured. Though individually idealistic and brave, she has also been naive and politically ignorant. Now when she is pushed out of the corridors of power, she begins to realise how the rot had set in, how silence had led to further demands on one's loyalty—and how loyalty and courage had begun to seem incompatible:

> Nothing anywhere made sense, since in a moral universe either everything must have meaning or nothing. Memory dragged me backwards to reports I had read with momentary shock and then deliberately pushed away because they were too terrible to remember. . . . (29-30)

Reports of bride burning, of prisoners being murdered, of justice being denied, of resistance being suppressed, reports she had ignored perhaps in the interests of survival, which survival is also being threatened now:

> And how naive the cast-iron idealism I had been brought up with, believing we were moderate, tolerant people, steeped in civilized ways, I should have been differently taught, told how casual we are about cruelty, depravity. I had grown to adulthood nourished on monumental lies. By the end of my illness I had sloughed off my upbringing, the orgy of idealism I had been fed, the second skin of it I wore. It was a relief to tell myself in the dark on one of those interminable nights, "In many ways we are barbarians. All the evidence says so." (30)

There was no logic in the happenings in the political world. The only logic that worked was one of power. Against it, heritage, human values, idealism, justice were all nothing. Even marriage was a way of reaching the right people. If the civil services found the bottom knocked out of its structure, the intellectuals and the upper classes also crumbled like nine pins. Political rights, it was felt, were the privilege of the upper classes and if the lower classes were being sacrificed, there was no cause to be unhappy. After all social justice had to begin from somewhere. Conversation at dinner party at Kiran's house "was milky and mild, the leisurely exchange of people on the winning side, who don't have to lose their tempers in the argument." (82) The lawyer and the editor talk about the hereditary principle in politics, not worried about the value of character at all. Dev was successful, and as a winner he was exempt from all criticism. There was no need to consider his *bonafides* as a man. In Sonali's opinion he's a dunce, but his unreliability and mediocrity no longer have any importance. They cease to be negative qualities because he is now chairman of the New Entrepreneurs. It is the strategic "location" of a man which is valuable: nothing less and nothing more. People had ceased to be individual or to have opinions; there were simply two categories, those in power and those out of it.

The question which is asked over and over again is "what has gone wrong ?" Several answers are posited: men are cowards, economic divisions have won, the upper classes have betrayed the country, the civil services have succumbed to political pressure, Western concepts have overlaid the national heritage, our understanding of our own culture is vauge. The problems of the present are blamed on colonialism. We have not really stopped to make the right distinctions. There is plenty that is wrong with the past. But instead of analysing its shortcomings, first we idealised it then chose to bypass it. Sonali's narrative as it progresses, throws up several possible answers, but each one in itself is complete and unsatisfactory. Each successive attempt at trying to identify the problem, takes her further back into history. First it is her job and the civil service, then the intellectual elite, then the Western value structure, the vague and hazy understanding of the past. She travels into the past through her own memories, her father's memories, and the records in his files of the 'sati' episodes in 1822-23. The rot has not set in now, it has been there all along with nobody paying attention to it. Looking through her father's files, Sonali comes across his explanation. At the beginning of the first world war he had written:

> The world is at war as I wrote at the start and some changes are expected in India. We have been promised political reforms. I believe in gradual progress towards self-government, but underneath there will be the subterranean layers of ourselves we cannot escape. (135)

The indifference to human beings has not descended on us all of a sudden, the contradictions lie in India's past which holds ample evidence of greed, cruelty, apathy and wrong. There is need to be more analytical and self-critical. Sonali is fighting not only against the stranglehold of the political system but also against the myths which persist about a glorious past. In the end she realises that it has to be a constant fight. Others who have nurtured their idealism have been fighters like her father, the boy in the Connaught Place, the cripple Rose has adopted, and Rose herself.

From a narrative point of view though the two strands adopt contrastive techniques, both move backwards in time. Sonali's memories of the past and her father's records allow us to say the idealism nourished by idealism. Rose has her own memories, of England, of her English friends, and her husband's business. The cleanness which invested these relationships contrasts sharply with Dev's collaboration with Neuman. Rose and Sonali are two of a kind and their affinity goes to prove the value of individual strength.

In terms of time the period covered is less than a year, but in terms of history it stretches back into the past. Ravi's shamefaced confession of failure gives Sonali her freedom, the possibility of a continuity of the hope and idealism of the past makes her look forward to the future. India has been through a lot and has recovered from many setbacks. There is every reason to hope that it'll come out of its present political crisis where values and value structure have been jostled and shelved. There is hope that people may be able to conquer narrow claims, or narrow preoccupation with the present—as people like Dev are. Rose saw the symptoms of this malady in Dev:

> He had nothing in his head except the present. There's no more to him than that, she thought, no dreams at all. Even—especially—the mad have dreams. He hasn't even the saving grace of natural,

> harmless madness. Locked up in the present like in a cell, he's a lunatic of another kind, cut off from continuity before or behind. (141)

"Especially the mad have dreams." And *Rich Like Us* examines the possibility of going on dreaming against the current. A kind of activity which now needs to be supported by action. It is not enough to dream by itself.

Plans for Departure adopts a different narrative mode, but here also there are at least two points of view projected through the narration. One in Anna Hansen, who like Rose, is an outsider to begin with. She is, again like Rose, outside the imperial ruling class. Thus her version is one of a sympathetic and yet an objective narrator. Anna Hansen is Danish, and not directly involved in colonial issues. She stands outside both—the native and the imperial circles. India, Sir Nitin, Tilak, Brewster and his estranged wife Stella, Marlowe and Lulu—she sees them from outside until she goes on being drawn towards involvement. The second consciousness is that of Sir Nitin in the background—gentle, perturbed, feeling things are getting out of control—but there it is. The novel opens with Anna Hansen landing up as a secretary in Sir Nitin's household. The tall foreign girl puzzles him, appears to be of indeterminate age and an indeterminate religion. He wonders why she has come to India. Anna, on the verge of getting married to Nicholas, suddenly decides to travel and to discover her own identity, "to break out and be *me*."[2] As a result Anna comes to India, and is now involved in the Brahmo-Samaj movement, the efforts of the local missionary, the woman question, Tulsidas's biography and the concept of love, Henry's wife Stella and the mystery which surrounds her disappearance, and Tilak's six year term of imprisonment.

Anna is the narrative centre where thoughts and actions converge: her letters to Nicholas are censored by Henry (in his official role), and while talking to her Brewster reveals his view of the British rule. He is aware of another England, one that doesn't preside "over executions on soil where it has no right to be in the first place. There's new world in the making at home." (128) On the other side is Sir Nitin, formal and upright, and astonished by the speeches of Tilak, not only by their style but also by their content. To him they appear to be seditious. He is surprised that "such a tone and sentiments should come out of the Congress, one of the noblest monuments to British rule !" (135)

Like Forster's *A Passage to India* and Orwell's *Burmese Days*, Sahgal's *Plans for Departure* is about the divided conscience both of the Indians and the British. Henry and Stella disagree on the road to power, and the values of power itself, Sir Nitin and his countryman Tilak have very little in common. The basic conflict is between love and power: it is also between freedom and power. Anna loves Nicholas but is unwilling to submit to a power relationship. What is applicable to her as a woman, is also applicable to the country to which she has come. Henry loves Stella but the barrier between them is the size of an empire. There is need to know oneself, a need which cannot be sacrificed. Tilak with his demand for a half-loaf is just doing that, as Anna through her visit to India. Even Tulsidas's wife, when she turns away from his obsessive love, is doing just that. It is character which is important. It is important to have the awareness of oneself, and to make a protest against the power structures no matter how private or how feeble the protest. Anna points this out in her comment on Tilak: "There must be something extraordinary about a man who can set even these words ablaze, so far from Delhi, and after so many years of absence." (143)

The division of conscience and of opinion is there on every plane, at every level—amongst the British (to every Henry Brewster there are many Pryors), amongst the Indians (the Tilaks are outnumbered by the Sir Nitins), and every Marlowe seems to be hounded by a Lulu.

Idealism and oratory have a dangerous habit of getting mixed and confusing issues. Even the very intelligent are taken in. Sir Nitin was one of them. He had spent

> the years of national protest against the partition of Bengal in his laboratory, while the fanatics seized arms and ammunitions from wherever they could and took to revolutionary violence, and Bengal's greatest poet marched across Calcutta at the head of a procession singing a song he had composed for the occasion. (162)

What was wrong with India was not merely the wrong kind of people in power, but also the stooge Indians, the ones who had been taken in by oratory, and promises of equality, the ones who had been charmed by the show of liberalism.

Anna Hansen is like a mirror reflecting the lives around her, and like a mirror is often ruthless and distorts the reflections to reveal the reality behind the pleasant cover. Anna Hansen is, in herself, an idea—an extraordinary woman, more humane than political.

Though the main events in the novel concern the passage of a year, it moves both into the past and the future. Anna's grandchild Gayatri and her husband Jason (note the name and its association with the classical myth of Jason and the golden fleece), continue the efforts of distinguishing right from wrong. It is the continuity of this approach which is Sonali's mainstay amidst the disruptive political actions in *Rich Like Us*; in *Plans for Departure*, the continuity and the hope are evidenced in Gayatri's lineage. Anna's spirit seems to be pushing the world forward. It is as Gayatri says.

> She says she invented me. She was so disappointed the world hadn't changed enough in her lifetime, she had to hurry along. . . . My father was not the sort to branch out and marry a dynamo on the other side of the world all on his own. (211)

A lifetime is not enough. There have to be others to push the world forward, to continue the battle.

Even though Anna Hansen becomes the main consciousness through which the narrative is unfolded, she remains intangible and abstract. It is India, with its confusing ideals, and England with its divided conscience which are real. The war in Europe reflects some of the issues of the sub-continent. The Bosnian youths "stuffed with socialism, nationalism, and anarchism," trained to blow up bridges and to blow up the empire. The Austrians's philosophy of life is echoed by other imperial races, "Timely small wars prevented big wars." (63-64) The Balkan issues, somewhere, in some mysterious way linked up with the struggle of the suffragetes, with the need for freedom and love. It is when men want power not love that the result is violence.

At the narrative level the recurring references to Tilak, his speeches, his followers, his imprisonment, his ideals provide one line of continuity, while the wars, the Pryors, the tyrants form another line of narration. Sahgal is not merely giving an account of happenings, or elaborating upon historical events. She is also not describing a political situation, as she has done in some of her earlier work both autobiographical *(From Fear Set Free)* and fictional *(A Situation in New Delhi)*. Irving Howe, in *Politics and the Novel* defines the political novel as one in which political ideas are dominant, the kind in

> which the *idea* of society, as distinct from the mere unquestioned workings of society, has penetrated the consciousness of the characters in all its profoundly problematic aspects, so that there is to be observed in their behaviour . . . some coherent political loyalty or ideological identification.[3]

Sahgal's main concern is not with politics, or with ideology. Her concern is with values, and with analysing what has gone into the making of a country. To this task she applies herself, bringing in little known facts, ferreting the past, filling up the gaps, interpreting happenings and what has led to them, reconstructing in fact, a whole country with its complexities of men and views.

The Plans for Departure referred to in the title are many, the title works at various levels. The beginning of the realisation that the British would have to leave India is forced on them by such men as Tilak, and women like Anna. Earlier Anna leaves Nicholas in 1913 and comes to India. Stella also leaves India and Henry Brewster. Finally Anna summons her grand daughter to her deathbed and is thus planning for her departure. Journeys are begun, never ended, and every arrival at a destination is a new beginning. But primarily long before the British became consciously aware of the need to free India, at a subconscious level, and also at a personal level it became increasingly clear that they would have to leave.

In both these novels the multiple vision and point of view of a political biography is at work. It is a narration of history-in-the-making with the advantage of hindsight. *Rich Like Us* has a multiplicity of narrative techniques in addition to the variety of point of view, while *Plans for Departure* has Anna as the centre of consciousness. The techniques of fiction are used to arrive at an understanding of a country and its life, to understand the happenings and events which appear to be separate and limited in scope but actually relate to each other in order to weave a pattern. The novel adapts itself to the techniques of biography, or one can say the other way round that a biographical approach governs the narrative. There is thus a similarity between the approach of the creative writer and the historian, the creative writer using events in order to comprehend the reality of the world. Sahgal's work is different from an ordinary biography on two counts: first the protagonist is not a person but a country, second the focus is not on major historical happenings, but on the psychological processes and the emotional conflicts which have gone into them. Judith H. Anderson in *Biographical Truth* asserts that the essential truth of biography "is a matter of perception, insight and judgement, never reducible to fact and at times, like life itself, irreconcilable with certain kinds of fact. . . . To a greater or lesser extent, biography is inseparable from fiction."[4] Sahgal depends not only on fact, on psychological understanding, on cultural analysis, but also makes no attempt to present a unified picture. She presents India with all its contradictions, depicts the political situation with all the ulterior undercurrents, and succeeds in presenting the ideal and the real working against each other, the real undermining the ideal and the ideal resisting erosion. There may not be fidelity to fact, imagination and ideology have a dominant role to play, but there is in the end a comprehensible totality.

NOTES

1. Nayantara Sahgal, *Rich Like Us* (London: Heinemann, 1985), p. 7.
2. Nayantara Sahgal, *Plans for Departure* (London: Heinemann, 1986), p. 62.
3. Irving Howe, *Politics and the Novel* (New York: Horizon Press, 1957), p. 19.
4. Judith H. Anderson, *Biographical Truth* (Yale University Press, 1984), p. 13.

The Nature of Brother-Sister Relationship: *Untouchable, A Bend in the Ganges*, and *A Situation in New Delhi*

SANGEETA GUPTA

1

This paper attempts to show that brother-sister relationship in the Hindu household borders on incest. To illustrate the point, three novels have been chosen: Mulk Raj Anand's *Untouchable*, Manohar Malgonkar's *A Bend in the Ganges* and Nayantara Sahgal's *A Situation in New Delhi*. Deliberately two men and a woman writer have been chosen to show both masculine and feminine sensibilities towards the subject. The three novels cover between them, the lowest of social classes, the outcastes of *Untouchable* to the urban upper class of the other two novels.

The theme of brother-sister incest can be traced back to the *Rig Veda*, the oldest of the *Vedas* and also the oldest surviving record of Hindu Literature. In it, there is to be found an old myth about the origin of human race from a first pair of twins. Yami (who later became the river Yamuna) tries to tempt her brother Yama (who later came to be known as the god of the underworld) to incest, in order to prevent the dying out of the human race. In passionate words, glowing with desire, the sister draws the brother on to love:

> My friend I would draw near to me in friendship,
> Should he have gone e'en to the farthest ocean,
> That he beget a grandson to his sire
> On earth, remembering wisely future days.[1]
>
> (*RV*, X, 10, i)

Thereupon Yama replies:

Thy friend loves not the friendship which considers her who is near

> in kindred as a stranger. . .[2]
>
> (*RV*, X ,10, ii)

Yami further tries to persuade her brother saying that the gods themselves desire their union.

The conversation between Yama and Yami is an incomplete fragment, but even as it exists it endorses the fact that the subject of incest between brother and sister is as old as the tradition of Hindu Literature.

The myth of Yama and Yami still lives amidst Hindus in the form of the Bhaiya Duj (Bhratri Dvitiya or Yama Dvitiya) festival, celebrated on the second day after Diwali. This festival is celebrated in remembrance of Yama and Yami, the first pair of brother and sister. On the Vishrama Ghat, in Mathura, on this day, thousands of brothers and sisters take a dip in the holy Yamuna praying for the longevity of their ties. One wonders how many of them know about the actual story behind this festival and this dip !

P. Spratt, in his psycho-analytic study on *Hindu Culture and Personality* notices "the exceptionally strong attachment between brothers and sisters, of which there can be no doubt. "To corroborate his observation he refers to sociologists like Nivedita, Stevenson, G.M. Carstairs and M. Cormack. Spratt talks about the Bhratri Dvitiya festival and states that

> In Gujerat similar customs are observed on different days. In Maharashtra on Manasa Panchami worship is offered to snakes; a boy was killed by a snake when gathering flowers for his sister, but he prayed to the snake-goddess Manasa; who restored him to life. Haldar notes sculptured representations of Shiva's daughter, Bhattasali together with the linga and yoni, and infers an unconscious wish for incest with the sister.[3]

From the *Rig Veda* if we come to the epics, we find that though Valmiki's *Ramayana* and Tulsidasa's *Ramacharitamanasa* do not have it so, there exist several versions of the epic which show Rama and Sita as brother and sister:

> Narayan Aiyangar mentions variants of the story in the *Uttara Vasista*, *Skandottara*, and *Bhargava Puranas*, and in the Dasaratha

> Jataka, in which Ram and Sita were brother and sister. . . . In the *Trishashtishalakapurushacharitra* of the Jain teacher Hemachandra a Sanskrit poem of the twelfth century A.D., Sita had a twin brother who had been her husband in their previous lives; another king carried him off and adopted him and later tried to bring about his marriage to his twin sister, but Rama foiled the attempt. Exactly the same story is narrated in the *Ramayana* of the Jain author Pampa, a Kannada work also of the twelfth century. This occurrence of twins . . . is suggestive.[4]

Spratt links up these stories of brother and sister becoming king and queen, to the creation ritual reconstructed by Lord Raglan in his book, *Jocasta's Crime*.[5] According to this ritual, "from which most of the later rituals and legends connected with the divine kingship must have evolved," a youth and maiden play the parts of king-brother and queen-sister" and are made to have "ritual intercourse."[6]

It is amazing that stories in Hindu mythology, related to incestuous brother-sister relationship could find parallels in pagan rituals. J. G. Frazer, in *The Golden Bough* also refers to a Greek custom according to which it "often happened that a prince married his own sister, the princess royal, in order to obtain with her hand the crown which otherwise would have gone to another man, perhaps to a stranger."[7]

When talking of incest Freud comes immediately to mind. He has made a strong case for incest proving through several case studies that incestuous desires are a natural part of the process of growing up: "Psycho-analysis has taught us that a boy's earliest choice of objects for his love is incestuous and that those objects are forbidden ones—his mother and his sister."[8] It follows, as Simone De Beauvoir confirms in *The Second Sex* that for a girl, the earliest objects of admiration and adoration are her father and brother.

Yet there is a taboo on incest. In *Totem and Taboo*, Freud studies "the most backward and miserable of savages, the aborigines of Australia" to note that even among them exists "an unusually great horror of incest."[9] This Freud naturally finds quite strange because "we should certainly not expect" that the sexual life of these poor, naked cannibals would be moral in our sense or that their sexual instincts would be subjected to any degree of restriction."[10] But he goes on to explain the sensitivity of these savages towards the subject of incest by the fact that they "are probably liable to a great temptation to it and for that reason stand in need of fuller protection."[11]

Some customary taboos extend far beyond the totemic races of Australia. In Leper's Island, one of the New Hebrides, there are unusual restrictions on brothers and sisters. These begin with puberty ceremonies and are maintained throughout life. They are not allowed to meet each other openly or talk to each other or take one another's names. Similar customs prevail in New Caledonia and among the natives of the Gazelle Peninsula in New Britain. Among the Battas of Sumatra it would be considered "shocking," "were a brother to escort a sister to an evening party."[12]

In *The Old Testament*, in Book of Leviticus, chapter 18, verses 9, 11 and chaper 20, verse 17 as well as in the Book of Deuteronomy, chapter 27, verse 22, incest between brother and sister is clearly, strictly prohibited.

From the law of savages—to the law of Moses—down to Hindu Marriage Laws, one finds that incest between brother and sister is considered illegal, irreligious, tabooed. According to Hindu Marriage Law, marriage between brother and sister, and "Sapindas" comes "within the degree of prohibited relationship."[13] But is not prohibition needed only where a desire exists ?

> The law only forbids men to do what their instincts incline them to do; what nature itself prohibits and punishes, it would be superfluous for the law to prohibit and punish. Accordingly we may always safely assume that crimes forbidden by law are crimes which many men have a natural propensity to commit. If there was no such propensity there would be no such crimes, and if no such crimes were committed what need to forbid them ? Instead of assuming, therefore, from the legal prohibition of incest that there is a natural aversion to incest, we ought rather to assume that there is a natural instinct in favour of it, and that if the law represses it, as it represses other natural instincts, it does so because civilized men have come to the conclusion that the satisfaction of these natural instincts is detrimental to the general interests of society.[14]

Having proved that incest between brother and sister is a very old phenomenon; that it is considered a taboo and is generally accompanied by a sense of horror that there is yet a natural inclination in man towards it—we will now go on to examine some twentieth century works by Indo-English writers to see how they treat the theme of brother-sister relationship.

II

To start with, let us consider Mulk Raj Anand's *Untouchable* which is the story of one day in the life of Bakha, the eighteen years old sweeper boy who lives in the outcastes' colony with his father, brother and younger sister Sohini. Bakha's mother has died and the household responsibilities have been taken up by Sohini. She is "meek," "docile," "patient"[15] and treats her elder brother with reserve, love and respect. Outwardly, in terms of action the novel does not show any signs of incestuous relation between the elder brother and younger sister, but in terms of Bakha's thoughts, suggestions are put forward. Bakha is acutely away of his sister's femininity:

> She had a Sylph-like form, not thin but full bodied within the limits of her graceful frame, well rounded on the hips, with an arched narrow waist from which descended the folds of her salwars and above which were her full, round , globular breasts, jerking slightly, for lack of a bodice, under her transparent muslin shirt. Bakha observed her as she walked along swaying. She was beautiful. *He was proud of her with a pride not altogether that of a brother for a sister* [italics mine]. (p.32)

When Sohini is molested by the priest in the temple, Bakha is "livid with anger and rage." (p.86) "I hope he didn't violate my sister" he suspects fearfully and this thought is immediately followed by a pang of guilt. "He was stung to the quick when he suddenly felt that he too had looked at her with desire." (pp.86-87) Feeling helpless, weak and angry, Bakha starts walking towards home with Sohini. Now follows a passage which explicitly illustrates Bakha's incestuous desire for his sister:

> The sight of her walking along with him, however, sent a wave of

anguish into his soul. So frail she looked and so beautiful. Bakha was conscious of the charm of his sister. Her pale brown figure, soft and warm and glowing, shot through with a lustre that set off her ornaments, the rings in her ears the bangles on her arms, to a ravishing effect, was so silent and subtly modest and full of a strange tenderness and light. He could not think of her being brutalized by anyone, even by a husband married to her according to the rites of religion. . . . He loathed the ghost of her would-be husband that he conjured up. He could see the stranger holding her full breasts and she responding with a modest acquiescence. He hated the thought of that man touching her. He felt he would be losing something. He dared not think what he would be losing. 'I am her brother,' he said to himself, to rectify his thoughts which seemed to be going wrong. *But there seemed no difference to his naked mind between his own feeling for her and what might be a husband's love.* He dismissed the whole picture. [Italics mine] (pp.88-89)

Such thoughts arise but are suppressed by Bakha. He is in agony thinking of his sister's shame and his inability to take revenge or protect her "I could have sacrificed myself for Sohini," (p.90) he cries silently to himself, anticipating the sense of commitment Sundari has for Debidayal in *A Bend in the Ganges*, Devi has for Shivraj in *A Situation in New Delhi*, and Bim has for Raja and Baba in *Clear Light of Day*.

Bakha is tormented with the beauty of his sister. At one moment he wishes she was born ugly so that no one could be attracted to her, but the next moment "he couldn't bear the thought of her being ugly. His pride in her beauty seemed to be hurt." (p.90) When he sees her "[w]ith a sudden burst of tenderness and humility, he grip[s] her arm close and drag[s] her along writhing with the conflicts within his soul." (p.90)

In his sensitive portrayal of Bakha, Mulk Raj Anand displays a keen understanding of the social and psychological constrictions working upon an individual. It is significant that in a novel whose main issue is untouchability, the novelist should have devoted considerable attention to relationships within the family and one cannot ignore the above-quoted instances which portray the brother-sister relationship as bordering on incest, at least in terms of thoughts and desires.

Becoming conscious of the woman in one's sister as Bakha does, is noticeable also in Raja Rao's *The Serpent and the Rope*—the novel about a South Indian Brahmin. Following is a description of Saroja as viewed by her brother Ramaswamy who has returned to India after four years and finds that his sister has grown up into a beautiful woman:

> Saroja had grown so lovely. At seventeen, Lord, how beautiful the world could be ! . . . Saroja was a strange sensation for me. Here was a mystery which I had never observed before: the girl becoming woman, and the thousand ways it shows itself, in shyness, in language, in prime presence. . . . Saroja's presence now obsesses me sometimes, like one of those nights with the perfume of magnolia. Rich and green seemed the sap as it rose, and it had a night of its own and a day. That Saroja was my sister made the knowledge of her womanhood natural to me—natural to see, to observe and even to breathe. I would myself pluck flowers for her hair and take her out on long walks and speak to her of Europe and of Medeleine. . . . I was intoxicated with Saroja's presence like a deer could be before a waterfall, or an elephant before a mountain peak; something primordial was awakening in a creature, and I felt that maturity in a girl was like the new moon or the change of equinox, it had polar affinities. There was something of the smell of musk, of the oyster when the pearl is still within, of the deep silent seas before the monsoon breaks. There was too the feeling of the temple sanctuary, and I could now understand why primitive peoples took the first blood of mensturation for the better harvesting of their fields. And why Indians gave such beautiful names to their women. . . . I could bow before Saroja and call her Queen.[16]

Bakha's description of Sohini is direct, almost crude in its sensuality; Ramaswamy, the well-read Brahmin, says almost the same thing but in a more evocative and poetic language.

Manohar Malgonkar's *A Bend in the Ganges* is largely about the violence and turbulence that shook India during independence and partition but it makes a significant contribution to the theme of brother-sister relationship. Reflecting about her childhood, Sundari remembers that

> It had always been so . . . ever since they were small; she was always

> doing things for him, taking the blame for him. But then in all honesty, that was something she herself had loved to do, and *at times she wondered if there was not something a little unnatural in her fondness for her brother*. [Italics mine][17]

These thoughts are coming to Sundari on the way to her honeymoon and so are additionally significant. Sundari goes on to remember her jealousy towards the Stanley sisters, his brother's friends, and is "still thinking about Debi" (p. 144) when she reaches the small forest bungalow beyond Mahabaleshwar where she is to spend her honeymoon.

> She tried to shake off her despondency, to step into the part of a newly married wife. But she did not feel excited or happy or eager, as a bride was supposed to, nor did she even look attractive . . . how could she prepare her mind for the delights of their honeymoon . . . beautify herself to receive this strange man, who had now become her husband, when Debi's ship was heading for the Andamans. (p. 144)

Gopal, her husband, behaves in a very understanding manner and tries to comfort her, to kiss away her tears "but she felt clumsy and unwanted. Her thoughts were obviously far away and her body remained cold and unimpressive."

Sundari's married life begins as game of "let's pretend" but gradually even the pretences are dropped. She just cannot get herself to care for her husband. Her deepest love is her love for her brother. The others come after him—Gopal too. Before Gopal comes to "see" her, she is happily humming to herself embroidering Debi's initials on his handkerchief in black silk. She thinks about Gopal's photograph which she had seen and in which he had "looked handsome, in a somewhat big-boned, heavy jowled, wavy-haired way, but that, she told herself, was because she was used to associating good looks in men only with the sensitive, eager, sharply chiselled face of her brother." (p. 96) In her thoughts Sundari keeps comparing her image of Gopal with her knowledge of Debi. Her brother "the baby with spaniel eyes and soft, chubby hands" had now grown into a man:

> He had grown much taller than herself, now, and his hands were

hard as teak planks. The thin-limbed body now rippled with muscles, and the round, wide eyed face had become sharp, insolent and yet somehow eager—like that of a Spanish film star, she had always thought, or a bullfighter's; his movements no longer gawky but graceful, even the way he walked was oddly like a panther's prowling.

Thinking of Debi like that, Sundari felt a little disloyal to the man whose photograph her mother had shown her. (p. 97)

She feels the same pride in her brother's manhood as Bakha and Ramaswamy feel for their sisters's womanhood.

In such a frame of mind she goes into Debi's room and almost the first thing that strikes her mind is that her brother has perhaps secretly concealed some contraceptives in a package placed behind some books. However, she discovers the hidden explosives and is shocked into the knowledge of her brother being involved with the terrorist movement. Gopal seemed "of so little importance now." She can only think about her brother, wanting to know how she could help him. "She was not singing as she came out, nor did she care what sari she would wear for the afternoon."

One of the chief factors responsible for making the bond between brother and sister so obsessively strong is the fact that they do not share a very good relationship with their parents. There is a gap between the two generations resulting in the brother-and-sister depending on each other for understanding love, approval, love and protection. Sundari remembers Debi's childhood habit of waking up during night, of pretending that he saw ghosts in their nursery, and not sleeping till Sundari got into his bed. She wonders if there was "anything sexual" (p. 142) in their relationship and dismisses the fact by saying that had there been, she would have found herself resenting his growing independence rather than feeling proud of it. But one cannot deny that there existed a sexual attraction at least, if not a sexual relationship between the brother and sister. When Dewan Bahadur comes to know that his son had become a revolutionary, he wonders where he had gone wrong and painfully realizes that neither party had understood the other:

He had never understood him.

But he was conscious that his son had not understood him either;

> the only person who had been close to him was Sundari, even as children, they had always stuck together, he remembered. He and his wife were both ousiders, however hard they tried. (p. 246)

In *Clear Light of Day* by Anita Desai, we see this repeated in an intenser form, in the case of Bim and Raja. Neglected by their parents, they come close to each other, the elder brother becoming a hero, an obsession for the sister. James Bossard and Eleanor Boll have studied the behaviour of siblings in *The Large Family System*[18] (large family meaning houses in which there are six or more children) and they observed that in the absence of parents's existence or care, children naturally fall back upon each other for love and leadership. However, *A Bend in the Ganges* and *Clear Light of Day* show that even in small families children can behave similarly.

Sundari remains obsessed by her brother throughout the novel. The introduction to the Orient paperback edition of the novel states that Sundari "is half in love with her own brother." The only boys she is shown as meeting before her marriage are her brother's friends. She first feels attracted towards Gian because he had befriended her brother in jail, and starts hating him after she comes to know that he had once betrayed her brother so cruelly.

Though Debi-Sundari's relationship is not incestuous in the way brother-sister relationship is portrayed by John Ford in *'Tis Pity She's A Whore* yet it is almost obsessive in its intensity and borders on incest. Belonging to a traditional orthodox Hindu family, one cannot even think of marrying one's brother or sister, and so the attraction they feel for each other is subject to repression. Debi dislikes Gopal for no reason at all except the most obvious one that he is going to marry his sister and take her away. A small but nevertheless noticeable example of repression is Debi's reaction to certain swear words he hears when in jail:

> 'Sons of whores/ Pigs from Hell ! Sister rapers !' the swear words came from below, hitting his eardrums with almost physical force. Almost perversely he thought of his sister, shocked at the connotation, inwardly guilty at associating someone like Sundari with the foulness of the warder's language. (p. 157)

Spratt points out that the "commonest term of abuse in North India is one which accuses a man of incestuous relations with his sister, somewhat less common but frequently used words accuse a man of such relations with his mother and with his daughter. These usages probably point to repressed feelings of uncommon intensity." [19]

In *Clear Light of Day* Bim expresses once a desire to lie down beside her retarded brother Baba. Though one agrees that this is the only tangible way in which she can reach out to an almost unresponsive being, yet the language in which the desire is expressed is very sexual.

> She felt an immense, almost irresistible yearning to lie down beside him on the bed, stretch out limb to limb, silent and immobile together. She felt they must be the same length, that his slightness would fit in beside her size, that his concavities would mould together with her convexities. Together they would form a whole that would be perfect and pure. She needed only to lie down and stretch out beside him to become whole and perfect. Instead she went out. [20]

In *A Situation in New Delhi*, the brother Shivraj is already dead when the novel opens and his relationship with his sister is reported rather than dramatised, by a series of reflections—chiefly his sister's and Michael Calvert's.

Incest is not the main theme of the book (as it is not in any of the books under consideration). It is mainly a political novel—a novel about different ideologies and the last part centres mainly around Rishad and Priya's relationship. Yet whatever we get to know about Devi, and Shivraj makes it obvious that their relationship was bordering on incest, they behave like lovers in the flashback scenes where we see them together.

Devi wakes up one morning, thinking of Shivraj and the unexpected day:

> long ago when Shivraj . . . had spoken, drenched, to the huge wet unmoving gathering of women, and Devi had ecstatically pledged, mixing up her life with his, 'I'll follow you to the ends of the earth,' while rain plastered her hair and clothes against her. [21]

Her marriage to Ishwar had been a passing interlude of happiness. Her parents had chosen her husband for her but fortunately she had fallen "tenderly, distractedly in love with him." (p. 41) However, this was a short-lived episode in her life and Ishwar dies, leaving behind his wife and a son. After Ishwar's death, Devi's only thoughts are of Shivraj. She feels no need or desire to remarry:

> While Shivraj had lived she had thought of the years ahead as being many and varied, a glowing mature time to come, when things not necessarily visible or tangile would bear fruit. She and Shivraj would grow old together—as she and Ishwar had never been allowed to. They would read books there had been no time for, listen for hours to music, make a garden, enjoy Rishad in his manhood and then Rishad's children. (p. 15)

Michael had observed Devi closely in relation to her brother. One evening in Kashmir he met Shivraj face to face. With Shivraj was his sister. Michael

> had observed her with interest as she watched her brother not five yards away, her face showing pride and concern. . . . They did not look particularly alike. . . . The two of them were yet somehow similar and when they had looked at each other, Michael had known that other deeper resemblances bound them. He wanted to say impetuously, 'You love him dearly.' It would have been a natural affirmation. (p. 48)

This was the observation of an objective Michael. He soon became friendly with Devi and Shivraj and learnt more and more about them. Once he asked Devi if a certain view she had just expressed was hers or Shivraj's and she had replied:

> 'What does it matter, Michael ? It's the same thing. We were twins [cf. Yama and Yami] born six years apart. . . . Maybe he was the inside and I was the outside of the same person. (p. 51)

Michael remembered Devi as a youthful, radiant girl, who had many admirers but chose only her brother as a companion. He could remember her enjoying boat rides and horse rides with her brother and he could also remember

> a picture as distinct, of a family enlarged by friends and relations at a long polished table reflecting light from the candelabra above it, the boy and girl, cherished as roses, facing each other across it. Leaving it later to walk arm in arm in the light of the stars. The Pharaohs had married their sisters. (pp. 51-52)

Michael's meetings with Devi were always tense because Devi seemed "all given to her brother, his life, his needs. She had no other life." (p. 52) On being asked by Michael to marry him, she "had looked shocked and strained" and had replied

> 'I can't do things other people do.' In an ugly scene, one of the last, he had shouted at her, `what are you, the ghost of your brother ?' `If that's what I am it's enough for me.' She had said it in a stricken way but he knew there was no changing of her mind. (p. 52)

Her commitment to her brother was too powerful. Michael had noticed that "physical contact" between the brother and sister "was so constant, hand touching; his head bent to hers." (p. 54) Duty to a husband, or wife or child, Michael could understand. But what duty was this ?

> With herself, with Shivraj, it was all the same thing, they were so much flesh of each other's flesh, their very souls mixed. He [Michael] had been jealous of Shivraj. (p. 55)

Michael felt that there was a "primitive," almost "unreasoning attachment," (p. 163) between brother and sister. They behaved like lovers, or rather as husband and wife would behave towards each other. Whether their relationship was sexual or not is never clearly shown but references to Pharaohs marrying their sisters, Devi-Shivraj being "flesh of each other's flesh" recalling Adam's description of Eve in Book of Genesis—are clearly suggestive of a relationship, quite close to incest.

What Michael felt is corroborated by Devi s own thoughts about her brother. She remembers the beautiful moments she shared with Shivraj. If we read the following passage carefully, the picture of Devi-Shivraj which emerges is less of brother and sister and more of lovers:

> Even their times together were few and far between by then, a great personal loss to her. Michael had not understood when he quarrelled so fiercely with her that Shivraj was both rest and excitement, new and familiar, longing and fulfilment. . . . Once he became the country's she had had to wait for him. Unlike earlier, when she'd be able to argue with him into an outing, when they had got into the car because the day sparkled and she at the wheel had swung it out toward the river, toward freedom and salvation. They had carried lunch and spent the afternoon in their boat and had known as if a clock had struck, the exact second when the apricot light would drain upward . . . she and Shivraj, motor switched off, would lie in the boat under her white woollen shawl. Borne along by the deep flowing current, they talked in murmurs or not at all, the sky of contentment above them. . . . Devi's tears had made wet diagonal paths down her cheeks, and she had been glad, glad that today she had given him the sky and the world beneath it. (pp. 75-76)

Surely anyone reading this passage cannot ignore its implications.

Usman Ali's affectionate name for Devi is Shahbano. "Persian for the King's Consort," (p. 22) to which she objected strenuously because "Shivraj was not a king and this was no kingdom but a republic." It is interesting to note that her objection was not to the word "Consort" which would have been any sister's natural objection but to the word "King's" because officially Shivraj was a Prime Minister. Now what does one say to this !

Devi's friendship with Usman Ali is prompted primarily by the fact that he was a close friend of her brother and was so much like him. Her physical relation with Michael, while Shivraj was alive was very dissatisfying for Michael because he felt he was "never alone with this woman. She had always put a man, her race, her family between them." However when he returns to India after Shivraj's death, he realizes that "nothing stood between them any more." (p. 95)

Shivraj had been an obsessive influence on her. She had once called herself his twin, and if we accept Spratt's view, she was in some ways Shivraj's alter-ego "with whom identification, and therfore love, are particularly easy."[22] Like Devi confesses at one point: "In some ways he lived through me." (p. 87)

III

European history carries records of several renowned personages who are known to have incestuous attachments. Shelley fell in love with his cousin and later formed a strong attachment to his sister. He was fascinated by the idea of incest, and made it the subject of *The Cenci*. He idealized the brother-sister relationship in *The Revolt of Islam*. Nietzsche was strongly attached to his sister and is known to have had physical relations with her. (He never married). Byron is believed to have had such relations with his half-sister, and Wordsworth made his sister his life-long companion.[23]

The novels which have been discussed have examined the brother-sister relationship in the context of the Hindu household as depicted in twentieth-century Indian English fiction. In *Untouchable*, we have seen that Bakha's thoughts about his sister are clearly incestuous. In *A Bend in the Ganges* we have seen Sundari herself wondering if her fondness for her brother "was not . . . a little unnatural" (p. 142)—a fondness which disrupts her marital happiness also. *A Situation in New Delhi* has clear evidences of a brother-sister relationship bordering on incest.

The scope of the paper does not allow a discussion of the brother-sister relationship in the context of Muslim household but if we turn briefly to *Midnight's Children* by Salman Rushdie, clear parallels can be drawn. Saleem Sinai feels incestuous desires for his sister Jamila Singer. Though she is not his real sister—"the blood in his veins was not the blood in hers,"[24] yet having lived for so many years as brother and sister, he is conscious of the fact that his feelings for her were unnatural

> Is it possible to trace the origins of unnatural love ? Did Saleem, who had yearned after a place in the centre of history become besotted with what he saw in his sister of his own hopes for life ? Did much-mutilated no-long-Snotnose . . . fall in love with the new wholeness of his Sibling ? Once the Mubarak, the Blessed One, did I adore in my sister the fulfilment of my most private dreams ?[25]

The paper has already traced the origins of unnatural love to the myth of creation and the oldest records of Indian Literature—*The Rig Veda*. Hence it is not so shocking to see suggestions of it in the worlds of Indians writing in English. But these writers are not very bold regarding it and the relationships they write about still border on incest and one feels that the writers are still hesitant about the subject. They want to and yet do not want to write about it. Salman Rushdie takes a bold step forward because at least he calls incest, incest yet Saleem's desire for Jamila occupies a very small portion of the vast epic-like narrative and it is treated largely in a comic manner. Perhaps the most clear statement made about this topic is by A.K. Ramanujan in his poem "Love Poem for a Wife I" and a selection from this poem will be an apt conclusion for the paper.

> Probably
> Only the Egyptians had it right.
> Their Kings had sisters for queens
> to continue the incests
> of childhood into marriage.
> Or we should do as well-meaning
> Hindus did,
>
> betroth us before birth,
> forestalling separate horoscopes
> and mothers' first periods,
> and wed us in the oral cradle
> and carry marriage back into
> the namelessness of childhoods. [26]

NOTES

1. Maurice Winternitz, *History of Indian Literature, I* (New Delhi: Oriental Books Reprint Corporation, 1972), p. 105.
2. *Ibid.*, p. 106.
3. P. Spratt, *Hindu Culture and Personality: A Psycho-Analytic Study* (Bombay: P.C. Manaktala and Sons, 1966), p. 138.
4. *Ibid.*, p.118.
5. Lord Raglan, *Jocasta's Crime* (London: Watts, 1940).

6. Spratt, pp. 107-08.

7. J.G. Frazer, *The Golden Bough: A Study in Magic and Religion* (London: Macmillan, 1957), p. 437.

8. Sigmund Freud, *Totem and Toboo: Some Points of Agreement between the Mental Lives of Savages and Neurotics*, trans. James Strachey (London: Routledge and Kegan Paul, 1960), p. 17.

9. *Ibid.*, pp. 5-6.

10. *Ibid.*, p. 2.

11. *Ibid.*, p. 9.

12. *Ibid.*, p. 11.

13. Jaspal Singh, *Law of Marriage and Divorce in India* (New Delhi: Pioneer Publications, 1983), p. 27.

14. Freud quoting Frazer in *Totem and Taboo*, p. 123.

15. M.R. Anand, *Untouchable (*New Delhi: Arnold-Heinemann, 1981), pp. 31-34.

16. Raja Rao, *The Serpent and the Rope* (New Delhi: Orient Paperbacks, 1968), pp. 48-50.

17. Manohar Malgonkar, *A Bend in the Ganges* (New Delhi: Orient Paperbacks, 1964), p.142.

18. James H.S. Bossard and Eleanor Stoke Boll, *The Large Family System: An Original Study in the Sociology of Family Behaviour* (Philadelphia: At the University Press, 1956).

19. Spratt, p. 138.

20. Anita Desai, *Clear Light of Day* (New Delhi: Allied Publishers, 1980), p. 166.

21. Nayantara Sahgal, *A Situation in New Delhi* (New Delhi: Himalaya Books, 1977), p. 14.

22. Spratt, p. 119.

23. *Ibid.*, p. 137

24. Salman Rushdie, *Midnight's Children* (New York: Avon Books, 1980), p. 387.

25. *Ibid.*, pp.377-78.

26. R.Parthasarthy, ed., *Ten Twentieth-Century Indian Poets* (New Delhi: Oxford University Press, 1976), p. 102.

Irresolvable Bi-Cultural Conflicts and Other Ironies in Narayan's *The Guide*

JOHN OLIVER PERRY

When a Third World writer—or his reader—chooses English for dealing with a non-English-speaking indigenous culture, then special intercultural and bi-cultural political issues are bound to arise. There are intercultural political considerations for criticism arising just from the inevitable competition of Third World English writing with the two main established national literatures in English, and bi-cultural issues arise from its inevitable comparison with less widely known literatures in one or another of the indigenous languages that the post-colonial writer (along with his indigenous readers) uses in much of his everyday life. In India, although (and also because) much of the bureaucracy, intellectual life, technology, trade, education and news media are carried on in English by a tiny (under 3%) educated elite, the act of choosing to read or write an Indo-English novel is laden with inherent bi-cultural significances. An Indo-English novel, by my definition here, first of all, is set and draws its chacracters mostly from inside the sub-continent, and, secondly, is written by someone who lives in India and thus necessarily uses another language besides Indo-English for everyday life; even in New Delhi only 25% of the population knows English. Bi-cultural ironies thus arise simply from a reader accepting or a writer importing Western literary forms—e.g., the novel—as well as the mixed bi-cultural medium—the Indo-English language—in order to deal with an Indian sub-culture, including the overwhelmingly predominant Hinduism. Key parts of the literary process—writing a text or deriving an experience from it—will be profoundly affected according to whether the perspective adopted is that of the unavoidably elitist, partially alienated culture embodied in the distinctive *Indo-English language* or that of some predominantly indigenous culture, in which presumably the *fictional events* occur.

Though modern writers are renowned for their cultural alienation and divided loyalties, every Indo-English novelist necessarily operates with a special kind of cultural split; his is necessarily an ironic bi-cultural expression—both someway Indian in subject and attitude and yet inevitably English to some degree by the language medium with its inherent social attitudes, its distinctive cultural, idiomatic, rhythmic and lexical comprehensiveness, and so on. A novel embodying such a bi-cultural authorial expression also necessarily is read by a doubly bifurcated bi-cultural audience, by both English-educated Indian readers and by so-called "foreign," mainly Anglo-American and Commonwealth readers where English predominates culturally. Even if written for an Indian audience, and even if the action and experience fictionally represented occur totally within an untrammeled indigenous Indian culture, to some extent the Indo-English writer, because of the medium and its elitist audience, is implicitly dealing with his own cultural dualities; he cannot just reject non-traditional splits and attempt to revive traditional unities and simplicities, as Mishima may try to do in his native Japanese. Some Indo-English novelists may try to ignore these issues, but others may revel in bi-cultural complexities and ironies; they may decide not to attempt to resolve them within their novel, perhaps only within themselves. Knowing clearly where he stands culturally, such a supremely ironic author, and any reader who wishes to stand aside from the controversies these ironies generate, can enjoy the controversies about ambivalences and ambiguities of interpretation that will necessarily occur for either type of reader—those taking the Hindu (Indian) traditionalist perspective or those attempting an English (Western) modernist one. It is this situation of clarity about the author's own cultural stand along with awareness of his ironic amusement about the confusions and complexities his novel generates that occurs in a careful reading of Narayan's *The Guide*.

The special complexity of bi-cultural perspective within Indo-English writing makes it as perplexing as it is enriching for any audience that reads English. The foreigner may experience interpretative confusion as somehow related to "the mystery of the East," but it is both less and more than that. For in part the bi-cultural perspective means that, in ways more emphatic than in literatures wedded to one culture, both the tiny English-educated audience in India and the foreign audiences for Indo-English fiction are themselves split, into two ultimately political camps: there are those who will lean with the author in his chosen cultural direction (whether toward the more modern, progressive Indo-English kind of urban sophistication or toward some other highly civilized outlook among the more traditionbound indigenous Indian cultures) and there are those readers who will favor (for, at bottom, political reasons) the other cultural option. (I am presuming that any so-called 'balanced view' or any response of interactive tension will inevitably lead to the incorporation of one culture into the other.) This unavoidable intercultural dimension in Indo-English fiction brings with it a consequent need, rather than a mere potential, for readers as well as authors to choose a political perspective for their interpretations of central cultural ironies. Because all readers necessarily side, perhaps unconsciously, with one culture or another, certain key points of interpretation and of value judgments in Narayan's *The Guide* turn out to be quite irresolvable. Though Narayan, for his own reasons, may appreciate this additional irony, it remains for critical readers to work it through as far as possible.

Nowhere is irresolvable confrontation among bi-cultural ironies more unlikely than in the case of Narayan's novels, for the texts themselves are superbly revealing and clarifying about the strains in present-day South Indian Hindu life carefully placed through a wide range of subordinating ironies of tone and action, as M.K. Naik, among many others, has shown. Narayan's conservative bias toward traditional South Indian Hindu values is clear-cut, offering little hope for the progressivist culture of his chosen English-language medium. A word of caution: though clear in its support of the ancient indigenous culture, *The Guide*, written in 1958, may not fully and accurately represent Narayan's comic-ironic writing, which extends from 1935 to the present. For one thing, it is the most widely and deeply read of Narayan's novels in India and elsewhere in part because it seems a very serious, though not tragic, work, while by no means less comic or ironic than others in method. For another, the work is extraordinarily controversial: because of its textual ironies, some being irresolvable, basic disputes have arisen about the psychology of the main character, and even whether this traditional trickster character becomes good in the end (see Chandra and Gupta). Other controversies among Indian readers if not critics have arisen because rumor has it that Narayan drew on the scandal experienced by his well-known brother, the newspaper cartoonist R.K. Laxman, specifically his marriage to and divorce from a South Indian dancer: not that the novel is a *roman clef*, but that such apparent revelations in fiction are not considered proper by some Indians.

Perhaps most crucially, as Narayan reveals in *My Dateless Diary* (1960), the conditions of production for *The Guide* were peculiarly intercultural: first of all, it was written in Berkeley, California, and, secondly, the supremely controversial Catholic novelist Graham Greene firmly insisted that Narayan's hero—a sometime English-using tourist guide-entrepreneur-convict who becomes a Hindu *guru-sannyasi-swami* should certainly die at the end. Among the Western cultural patterns Narayan plays with here—perhaps, like Graham Greene, enjoying and prizing the controversy the novel provokes around profound cultural and religious issues—is the trick of turning the trickster con-man, the anti-hero, into some kind of transcendental paragon of faith. Indeed, it is precisely in Greene's recommended dying of the hero, Raju, that certain irresolvable bi-cultural ironies are implied: is his last act a possibly miracle-working death, or a transcendentally religious self-sacrifice, or, at the very least, a final triumph of moral self-transformation ? In fact, the ironies there generate two or three coherent, complex, comprehensive understandings of the final crux that are necessarily and irresolvably controversial, and thus dependent for their meaning on the reader's cultural bias toward modernism or traditionalism.

As a further qualification about its general significance for Narayan's work *The Guide* is not typical in its carefully fulfilling a great many conventions of the realistic novel, understood as a Western-born, bourgeois-progressive, highly individualistic genre. Narayan's novelistic technique is also particularly modern here in its Conradian interweaving of time schemes and hence of multiple perspectives by shifting the narration back and forth from omniscient to first-person (sometimes, as in Conrad, not entirely consistently, but without damage to achieved meaning). And though the trickster-god is found throughout many traditional literatures, including some in South India, Narayan's con-man hero whose personality dissolves in many different roles does have characteristics that echo modernist and post-modernist anti-heroes in novels by Greene, Joyce Carey, Saul Bellow, Samuel Beckett and many others.

Three major characters are concerned with reviving indigenous Indian art forms, and this connection helps give a formal structure to the several non-traditional, even anti-traditional or rebellious personal relationships in the novel. But these very rebellious activities ironically become individual or private means toward achieving different kinds of selflessness, and even contribute to the common good: Marco, Rosie's soon deceived husband, obsessively studies ancient cave art and thus loses his wife, but ultimately his work illuminates older culture for present audiences; Rosie betrays her husband in order to foster what she vaguely calls "cultural traditions" through her inbred, caste-decreed dancing profession, and she is quite successful aesthetically, personally and socially. Raju's more irregular successes as a guide to local cultural sights and to Rosie-Nalini's traditional dancing lead directly to his virtual apotheosis as god-man fasting to death to bring villagers desperately needed rains. Playing on the ambiguities of the word 'guide' in English—with multiple significances of '*guru*' in the background—Narayan further structures the action by tracking Raju through various activities as some kind of "guide" (If you are lucky enough to be guided by Raju, you will know everything. . . ." [6]) These *guru*-guide roles include helping tourists like Marco find the enigmatic caves (a pervasive Hindu symbol long before Forster's use); helping Rosie as her lover, manager and entrepreneur (most paradoxically when he tries to control her by forging her name); and finally, after imprisonment for fraud, helping Velan and the villagers at Mangal by reluctantly acting as their nameless 'Swami.'

Although clearly set after Independence, in a post-television South Indian time, it is not clear in what state Narayan's fictive town of Malgudi lies. It is on the rail-line to Trichy (Trichirapalli, T.N.) over the Mempi Hills, but after several states were linguistically re-defined in 1956 that could be either Tamilnadu or possibly Narayan's own Kannada-speaking Karnataka state (formerly Mysore). Because it is a generalized small town of today rather than a village, Malgudi is bi-cultural—age-old South Indian ways mixed with newer English artifacts. It is touched, if not overpowered, by English-medium government (for example, in the court house and *Talak* [district] office, now neo-colonial centres of control), by English-medium newspapers (we hear of The *Illustrated Weekly of Bombay* and *The Hindu),* by English-using railways and telegraph as well as out-of-state and foreign tourists, and by an English-medium Christian school. Raju would have preferred attending this Albert Mission College rather than the traditional Brahminical one his father chose for him—held under a tree, no doubt using an indigenous language, at times, Sanskrit. Still he has acquired some English: he brags, "I . . . earned while I learned" (54) by acting in his chosen profession as "Railway Raju." Not inconsequentially, he thereby superseded his father's established work as purveyor of snacks at the station, in order to become more and more exclusively a roaming, English-using guide for mostly Indian tourists.

When Raju's mother, whose family is from a village near Madras, asks Rosie, whom Raju has brought home to Malgudi, "Don't you understand Tamil ?," the highly educated city girl—M.A. in economics—answers, apparently demonstrating her Tamil, "Yes, it's what we speak at home." (124) So multilingualism is expected in this traditional South Indian society, but not necessarily English. Narayan, in these ways, subtly confronts and connects specific bi-lingual and bi-cultural issues that pervade urban and small town life in India.

Because Narayan aims for "purity of English diction" and uses very few non-English words like *sadhu*, Mahatma (not italicized) or *pyol* (entry verandah or stoop), the distinctive feel of Malgudi small-town life is conveyed mostly through the consciousness of the central character. Raju's mentality is conspicuously non-analytical, and though culturally divided, not highly ironical or even very self-aware. Despite his devious, and finally criminal, manipulativeness as lover and entrepreneur and his confused lack of single-mindedness, Raju is marked by a basic innocence. A certain simplicity of moral feeling, apparently deriving from his traditional heritage, protects him from utter corruption by modern ways and values, as well as from any debilitating sense of guilt for his youthful rebelliousness. From discovering such ironic contradictions within the psyche of Raju and, less so, of Rosie, Narayan can develop a positive, not a cynical comedy about what matters and what does not in life, that is, life as understood in a profoundly religious unified culture, understood from the traditional Hindu perspective. As in most well-made modern novels, the action leads this central consciousness through a series of thematically related adventures, until by the final situation—an absurd media event wherein the nameless, long-fasting Swami dies standing in the river praying for rain—the characteristic values of the hero and those of his society are revealed for us.

Raju's last guiding role of "reluctant holy man" that Velan and the villagers initially impose on him soon begins to fit. It cannot be shaken off despite his telling Velan (for half the novel !) the shameful story of his deserting traditional duties to parents and customs (especially to marriage rites) and adopting modern entrepreneurial, finally criminal forms of "guiding." The needy and extremely simple-minded villager Velan understands Raju from the start to be quite altruistic and helpful as a traditional spiritual and social guide—and, in fact, as the novel's first four words say, "Raju welcomed the intrusion." Lonely and cut off by a two-year prison term from family and friends, Raju desperately needs the mere food his culturally pregnant words and silences earn him. For almost despite himself—despite, anyway, his well-developed individual personality or ego-identity (unusual in Hindu India according to Sudhir Kakar's view of its *Inner World*, [104ff]—Raju somehow has retained traditional wisdom, often in cryptic forms which the villagers are ready to interpret and resolve their disputes.

Though we are not shown the transformation, like Raskolnikov, Raju possibly attained the capacity to transmit this accumulated cultural wisdom in prison, where, as he reports to Velan, he was also fed without working and "they came to refer to me as Vadhyar—that is, Teacher." (202) Pressed by the villagers's needs, Raju's rejection of them is abrogated by an idiot boy's self-defensive lie (ironically a better communication of his underlying sense of connection). More crucially, Raju is also deeply touched by Velan's intense effort in support of the Swami's fasting, so that, finally without reluctance, he resolves to pursue the ritual whole-heartedly. Exhilarated by his own resolve and lack of food, "For the first time in his life . . . he was doing a thing in which he was not personally interested." (212) He is, in fact, performing for the villagers's sake and at their insistence the role of Mahatma or great soul—more specifically, chanting prayers, songs and mantras until, as it happened, the whole "world around became blank." Achieving unexpectedly that ideal state of enlightened non-attachment, becoming a *sannyasi*, to use Hindu religious terms not in the novel, he should also be able to perform the ultimate death-rite *(samskara)* of self-sacrifice. Such a *sannyasi*' s death could gain him *moksha*, liberation from the cycle of *karma*--that earthly fate of repeated rebirths into the delusion of our living as separate beings apart from the unchanging, all-inclusive One.

Thus this plot seems designed, as already suggested, quite in the Western tradition of the novel as a means to test inner "character" in relation to outer "world"—both terms being Western cultural and literary conventions. The deepest resources of Narayan's brilliantly individualized guide "character" are drawn upon for his finding his proper place in a dynamic moral and social system, the South Indian Hindu "world." But there are ironic implications in this conventional Victorian pattern, for Raju moves from the more complex bi-cultural small town society to a much simpler village and temple. In Malgudi, and in the larger cities in South India where Rosie dances, the social structure and manners differ markedly from those in Velan's village of Mangal, across a drying, crocodile-infested river from a ruined temple, the ironic final haven where Raju is never quite alone. The framed success-defeat story of Raju with Rosie, as narrated to Velan, reveals the railway culture with its free enterprise rewarding supposedly individual effort as a system deeply divided against itself. The highly educated Marco and Rosie have some isolated successes in that sphere, but an ordinary man like Raju, to tradition born and bred and otherwise self-educated, is defeated there by his own ambitious efforts. (This piously anti-individualistic moral pattern marks much Western fiction from Macbeth through the Dickensian villain.) The traditional Hindu social structure with its karmically assigned family and work roles persists untrammeled in the villages. Even in Malgudi it appears to have some solidity, is not total illusion. Though clearly unimaginative and even hidebound, Raju's unusually small family (father, mother, mother's brother), as well as the tourist-retreat caretaker Joseph and the taxi-driver Gaffur, all merit some respect for their relative social and moral caution; even the low-caste barber crouched outside the prison walls knows much just from staying and watching in his given social place. Laws and customs that distinguish this traditional culture, the *dharma*, comprise a network of limitations and duties holding everything and everyone together.

In the mixed bi-cultural life of Malgudi this Hindi "world" is fairly successful in absorbing or coping with the modern world of technology and other associated values; thus, it is not undergoing the radical social change most commentators would worry about. However, "character" there, even though a bi-culturally well-established (and novelistically conventional) social construct, is not only unstable and divided, but also not quite real. In fact, individualistic "character" is ultimately rejected as a value, quite contrary to the eighteenth century and Victorian premises of the novel genre. Narayan achieves this result partly by drawing on newer Western conventions of both the ironic anti-hero and the fragmented or dissolving personality. These modern or post-modern ironic forms offer Narayan and his audiences sufficient novelistic means for projecting onto and revealing through Raju quite ancient non-Western understandings of character, identity and Self.

The more readily recognizable dimensions of Raju's personal being—his knowingness, his ambitions and frustrations, his loneliness and so on—are treated so comically and ironically by Narayan that they seem morally trivial. Despite suggestions of characterological indeterminacy and comic anti-heroism, Narayan is far from promoting the anti-establishment, cynical or possibly transcendental tenets of a modern existentialist. In fact, precisely because of the comic a-moral diminishing of his *personal identity,* Raju works properly as a traditional Western novelistic character, but one who achieves his distinctive moral meaning only in his unchangeable Hindu Self. Since he is so persuasively trivialized as an individual, he can achieve a believable moral status outside the traditional heroic or anti-heroic molds of "character" measured in relation to "world." Having worked out the absurdity of Raju's self-serving worldly attitudes, Narayan can convincingly show Raju abandoning at the end all those traits that have distinguished this brilliant con-man. Raju achieves his almost miraculous selflessness by drawing at the end on a residuum in him of village-based non-ironic simplicity. This simplicity, as we see it first in Velan, centers on a capacity for unquestioning belief in someone else's power, ultimately in a power outside the normal human self. It is readily apparent that some such simple other mindedness always underlay Raju's more sociable character. His ironically self-defeating activities are best accounted for by splits and ambivalences in his naive ambitions and his personal character. By uniting his life with the simple but paradoxically helpless power in the Hindu tradition, he attains a triumphant moral status in a persuasive fiction that defies modern sceptical disbelief.

Hindu traditional psychology understands that neither an essential or morally defining trait of personality, what Christians call the soul, nor an individually or existentially created self makes up human beings. Though *karma* and *dharma* deal with an inborn social self, one's true being is not separate from all that is being. This silly man is defeated by his conflicting ambitions and desires, but his habit of offering guidance can work for the benefit of others, so that in isolated and deadly circumstances, he is enabled to find his True Self (Atman) within, as part of, identical with the Whole Self (Brahman). Dying in the process of fasting and praying for rain, he thus may lose the burden of personality and its consequences and achieve *Nirvana.*

The Swami's last act is clearly virtuous for any attentive reader. Though it is not the cautious way of his mother and other traditionalists in Malgudi, it contrasts sharply with all the socially mobile, overly resolute, confused ways of life offered in the novel and compares very well with the similarly self-transcending, culture-transmitting roles of Marco and Rosie. The act of self-sacrifice draws on cultural resources and reasons that Raju does not examine but we can, and so it is not simply simple. It would defeat intercultural analysis only if it required unquestioning belief in the long and complex Hindu mystical tradition. Interpretations short of our willfully suspending modern disbelief in the merely miraculous are generally available with a modicum of cross-cultural communication and inter-cultural awareness. When an aggressive newsman asks, for example, "Have you always been a Yogi ?," Raju's weak and weary answer—"Yes; more or less."—is neither error nor evasion. The capacity or tendency has always been there for the stupidly self-defeating, manipulative simpleton Raju to take life seriously—or, rather, not seriously at all, but in the proper unattached Hindu way. His ridiculous and definitive infatuation for Rosie, we realize, manages to capture her attention when he explains his feeling with a cliché of romantic hyperbole: "Because life is so blank without your presence." (63) Raju develops his obsession with an idea even more ironically related to the Hindu ideal: "She could make me forget my surroundings." (101) Coming back to this pathetic love story after his final act, we can recognize the potential ironic truth behind his absurd romantic exaggerations and behind too the moral comedy in this self-serving exploitation of conventional Hindu ideals: "while I watched her perform, my mind was free, for once, from all carnal thoughts; I viewed her as a pure abstraction." (101) Thus, the final sagging of Raju into death or unconsciousness, convinced of the miracle of rain (whereas earlier he had only wondered why a miracle of food should not appear in his panier), is not patently ridiculous, despite its ultimately religious claim on our sceptical intelligence. Nor is his action so transcendentally plausible as to compel our faith in the fictional fact of a practical miracle engineered by the Swami tradition. His action of fasting to bring rain springs from attitudes he has shown before, but now under a new guise and without selfish aims, so that everyone can recognize his clear moral triumph.

It may not be possible for any fiction to persuade a sceptical reader that such a life-ending act is transcendentally valuable (perhaps after all Graham Greene was wrong and Raju should live). As C. D. Narasimhaiah has said of a similar hero in Raja Rao's fiction, "Now how can one seek to convince positivist critics about the validity of a life which must look like anti-life to them !" Even a religious sceptic or an uninitiated foreigner, with ever necessary imaginative humility, must admit, however, that some profound moral meaning just short of the religious point is fully achieved by Narayan's art. It also seems clear that—just as the *Bhagavad Gita* advises doing one's duty without concern for the consequences, good or bad—the whole action of *The Guide* implies that Raju's final self-sacrifice is morally inconsequential; it does not necessarily cause miracle and bring the reward of needed rain. The merely temporary salvation of rain for the villagers, as Raju knows, will come sooner or later, only as fate or the gods decree. Still a believable moral change clearly occurs in the deep, if short-lived, transformation of character within Raju, ironically death-inducing and in a new sense self-defeating, along with a lesser change in those who rever him without questioning.

We watch the last stage of that transformation from within Raju's consciousness, and because the dramatic interaction, the interpersonal psychological processes, are similar to those in his first meeting with Velan, we can believe that he accepts the Swami role thrust upon him down to the last deadly detail. What he can and does do, climactically, is enjoy his work as Swami without thought of manipulating others or of the food his performance used to earn. The "floating feeling" from lack of food gives Raju an enjoyment that, he says to himself, "Velan cannot take away from me." (212) At the same time he brings to the villagers in their troubles another opportunity for exercising their collective faith, hope and peace of mind (though the intrusions of the modern world—newsmen, telecommunications, larger societal demands—make that difficult). The last almost comic words in the novel are:

> It was difficult to hold Raju on his feet, he had a tendency to flop down. They held him as if he were a baby. Raju opened his eyes, looked about, and said, "Velan, it's raining in the hills. I can feel it coming up under my feet, up my legs—" He sagged down.

Passage to More Than India: Shifting Perspectives in *Kim*, *A Passage to India* and *Midnight's Children*

RATNA RAMAN

As a third world student/teacher/critic of English literature, one has been increasingly aware of the power that the language and literature wield in countries like India, where it remains the predominant medium of instruction and education undertaking the dissemination of ideas in most fields. While one cannot wish away the political/cultural history that has been responsible for one's appropriation of English, one has nevertheless registered discrepancies between lived experience as an Indian in India and recorded by imaginative writers (writing in English) on India and Indians.

Somewhere along the way, while eagerly acquiring, the knowledge that the English language and literature offered access to, one had lost grasp over one's own immediate context—something not very difficult to do in a subcontinent that has had a complicated history, mixed cultures, different languages and disparate lifestyles. The result was a dormant critical understanding of oneself as an Indian, and an inability to articulate one's self-image in the language that shaped our lives. This dilemma has been compounded by the fact that English literature has been taught to us in the best humanist tradition, obscuring its potential as a political weapon. Viewpoints offered by non-Indian authors on India and Indians have been enshrined as canonical truths. Such texts and such readings, ironically, have survived, dominating university syllabi and reading lists in spite of the laudable achievements of Indo-Anglian writing.

It was at the outset difficult to accept that the language and literature that so comprehensively documented information ranging from the scientific to the factual and the imaginative could be mistaken in its observations on one's own country and countrymen. The problems lay not so much in the language *per se* but in our mistaken conferring of authority upon it, to the extent of explaining us to ourselves.

The critique I have offered and the cry for a *Bharat* brand of

English are by now sign-posts in the past. Despite a long established critical awareness of the misconceptions and misrepresentations present in the so-called canonized texts, we have suffered greatly from the absence of a creative vocabulary in English that could imaginatively reconstruct the experience of being an Indian in India.

In spite of the controlled success of an R.K. Narayan or the appeal of a Raja Rao, most Indian writers in English who appropriated the novel form, were hampered and inhibited by the great literature in whose tradition they sought to accommodate themselves. This resulted not only in insular visions where the novelist turned away from mainstream writing but also in the creation of derivative mediocre fiction with very little to offer. A case in point is Manohar Malgonkar's novel *A Bend in the Ganges* which deals with pre-partition days and the horrors of partition. The protagonist of the novel, Gian, in a moment of self-inquiry sees himself as shallow and inadequate. He wonders: "Did he in some way represent the average Indian, mixed-up, shallow and weak ? Like someone out of *A Passage to India*, Aziz or someone even more confused . . . now even his nationalism was wavering, just because the British officials he had come into contact with so far had been of sterling character."[1] Again, travelling on a prison ship to the Andamans he finds repulsive "the typical Indian sentry drunk with authority." (p. 118) Recalling the "corrupt, sub-human, minor officials" of India he wonders what "would happen if the steel frame of British officialdom was ever removed." (p. 119) Predictably, Gian, at the end of the novel would not have survived the holocaust of partition, were it not for the efficient handling of the situation by Patrick Mulligan, a stereo-type of competent, selfless British officer.

I would like to argue that these notions of how the 'average' and 'typical' Indian functions in a hierarchy where the white man invariably occupies the upper echelons, are derived from readings in which Indian characters have been similarly portrayed.

It is in the context of such writing that *Midnight's Children* distinguishes itself as an extremely important arrival on the literary scene, at the tail-end of a host of novels on India, written by both non-Indians and Indians. To understand the relevance of *Midnight's Children* it becomes necessary to look at earlier literature that has dealt with issues similar to those raised in Rushdie's novel. For the purposes of this paper, I shall examine two other novels, namely Rudyard Kipling's *Kim* and

E.M. Forster's *A Passage to India* in order to locate the distance that *Midnight's Children* has travelled in terms of its author's perspective on and attitudes to India and Indians.

All three novels under discussion evince a sustained interest in the Indian subcontinent, trace the presence and influence of Western involvement in India, and explore at length the relationships between various communities and peoples living there. Although *Kim* and *A Passage to India* were written in the first quarter of this century and *Midnight's Children* is separated chronologically from them by over fifty-five years, all three novels focus on the resultant tensions and contradictions arising due to the impact of Western civilization on India.

Edward Said in *Orientalism* points out that to "be a European in the Orient always involves being a consciousness set apart from, and unequal with its surroundings."[2] This sense of distance that separates the author from his context shows up in analyses of *Kim* and *A Passage to India*. Both novels can ostensibly be seen as attempts to explore and understand a culture alien to the Occidental world. Kipling and Forster successfully create the landscape and atmosphere of India, whether it is the dizzy peaks of the north, the hustle of a (Lahore) marketplace, the glamour of the Lahore museum or the rail journey in *Kim* or the Marabar Caves and the Gokulashtami festival in *A Passage to India*. Both novels successfully capture the multifaceted variety of India and their evocation of a disparate Indian locale is one of the reasons for their continued popularity.

Kim, in its treatment of plot and characterization, however, operates as a Westerner's approach to India. The narrative mingles and merges with the hues and colours of the land, but at critical points reveals its author's conscious isolation from the Indian ethos.

The linear narrative of Kim deals with the adventures of a young orphan boy in India. The boy Kim, in the course of a vagrant lifestyle affiliates himself to Teshoo Lama—a religious seeker, and in the course of their travels together, Kim runs into the Maverick regiment. Tracing the boy's parentage to one of the men in their regiment, Father Victor and Bennett take him into their fold, hoping to restore him to the normalcy befitting a white Christian boy. Ironically, neither of them are believers, but they nevertheless see the Christian faith as infinitely superior to the faith of Teshoo Lama. This is critiqued by Kipling who portrays the Lama as dignified and gracious in comparison to Bennett's coarseness and insensitivity. Again, Kipling's rejection of the insular world of the drummer boys and Bennett is juxtaposed with compelling sketches of the people of India, residing in far-flung areas. The problems with the narrative arise with Kipling's projection of a new hierarchy in the novel, namely, the world of St. Xavier's where young English boys are prepared for administering in India. Supervising this world are Creighton sahib and Lurgan sahib, men whose essential soundness is spelt out by the authorial voice. Kipling's view of India is increasingly propelled by the point-of-view of perceptive and adaptable 'sahibs' like Creighton and Lurgan. Through them, Kim too learns to study the Indian world and handle it. His ability to transform himself into a low-caste Hindu boy, a well-dressed Pathan, or a chela, is evidence of a similar adeptness. Whether it is his ability to coax and wheedle, or his dexterity at the 'great game,' Kim comes out with flying colours for his shrewdness, presence of mind and sharp responses that are identified and valorized as essentially English traits.

When Kim sets out on action, the narrative voice "celebrates his ability to lie like an Oriental,"[3] and yet get the better of Oriental ticket clerks. The narrative voice mocks the Oriental's sense of time, "the happy Asiatic disorder," (p. 74) and the "immemorial commission of Asia." (p. 35) It applauds Kim's rising to a challenge because while "a native would have lain down, Kim's white blood sets him upon his feet." (p. 55) Kim is trained at St. Xavier's where 'going native' is frowned upon and young boys are informed that "one must never forget that one is a Sahib and that some day, when examinations are passed, one will command natives." (p. 138)

Mahbub Ali and Huree Babu, two prominent Indians in the novel, are shown as serving the interests of the British Secret Service. The other Indian character, Teshoo Lama, is presented as a positive figure with qualifications. He is shown as naive and gullible and Kipling's treatment of Buddhism and the Lama oscillates between fascination and indulgence. The Lama's vision of life and his approach to reality remain of subsidiary interest in the narrative. The reader is allowed to emote with the Lama but it is to the world of British administrators that he must pledge his loyalties. Kipling confides: "All India is full of holy men stammering gospels in strange tongues; shaken and consumed in the fire of their own zeal; dreamers, babblers and visionaries: as it has been from the beginning and will continue to the end." (p. 40)

The above statement, like the novel itself, adopts a dismissive tone towards alternate sources of perception that are available in India. Therefore Teshoo Lama's mystical experience remains at best quaint and esoteric. It is to be viewed finally through the amused eyes of Mahbub and Huree whose tolerance for the Lama is shared by Kim. Kipling subsumes the entire experience of India under the broad and tolerant overview of a special class of sahibs to which the hero of the narrative belongs. Thus, the Lama, in spite of wanting Kim to become a spiritual seeker, is obliged to accept the boy's vocation as a scribe for the government. In *Kim*, the focus is clearly on India as picturesque, and India as quaintly mystical, but badly in need of British supervision. Any individuality that Indian characters might possess is evaluated in terms of its relevance to British administration. Both alternate modes of apprehending India and the people of India themselves are seen as existing outside the perimeters of British-India, offering very little by way of threat to its values.

A Passage to India, on the other hand, is a more sensitive delineation of the conflict between the East and the West. Forster's novel questions in significant ways the conclusions of *Kim* and engages in a far more complex analysis of Indo-British relationships on the sub-continent.

Unlike *Kim*, *A Passage to India* in its rejection of British values, records a major shift in attitude. Forster makes no attempt to disguise his contempt for "the sun-dried bureaucrat"[4] of Anglo-India. The values of the Turtons, Mcbrydes, Callendars, etc., are repeatedly questioned and Forster is disturbed by their "abysmal contempt" for "the gestures of an inferior race." (p. 216) The novel clearly exposes the unpleasant realities and assumptions underlying Imperialist attitudes.

Forster also touches upon the inefficacy of Christianity in the novel as part of his questioning of English values. In *Kim*, Father Victor and Bennett, in spite of their personal indifference to Christianity, can see no other alternative to it. There are no such double stances in *A Passage to India*. We are told that Graysford and Sorley "made converts during a famine, because they distributed food; but when times improved they were naturally left alone again, and although surprised and aggrieved each time this happened, they never learnt wisdom." (p. 98) Along with this astute understanding of how converts are made, Forster shows the limited impact of Christianity as an institution in Heaslop's and Fielding's indifference to matters of religion. Adela's "morning kneel to

Christianity" (p. 206) is in the hope of a favourable verdict at the trial. Again, Mrs. Moore's "poor little talkative Christianity," (p. 148) is swallowed up by the echo in the Marabar Caves. Forster's portrayal of Christianity as a feeble force is followed up by a rigorous questioning of Western perspectives.

Adela Quested's self-questioning at the trial: "In virtue of what had she collected this roomful of people together ? Her particular brand of opinions and the suburban Jehovah who sanctified them—by what right did they claim so much importance in the world, and assume the title of civilization," (p. 212) can be seen as an indictment not merely of Anglo-India, but of Western civilization as a whole.

A similar moment of self-doubt is faced by Fielding when he wonders whether after "he had learned to manage his life and make the best of it on advanced European lines, had developed his personality, explored his limitations.... A creditable achievement, but as the moment passed, he felt he ought to have been working at something else the whole time." (p. 187) As Fielding and Adela talk to each other after the trial, the narrative voice records: "She was at the end of her spiritual tether and so was he. Were worlds beyond which they could never touch, or did all that is possible enter their consciousness, they could not tell.... They had not the apparatus for judging." (p. 256) Their perceptions have been dwarfed in the face of the experience they undergo in India. At an extended level their limitations operate as those of Western man himself, demonstrating the inadequacy of Western yardsticks of evaluation.

The narrative form of *A Passage to India* also spells out the impossibility of understanding Indian experience through Occidental modes. Forster's use of language and symbol in the novel is a far cry from the straightforward narrative of *Kim*. Forster's evocation of landscape in the novel is not merely descriptive or decorative, but operates at philosophical and metaphysical levels. Again, in *A Passage to India*, there is a doing away with the linear narrative for a more complex projection of experience.

In the *Mosque* section, the interruption of linear narrative through introspections, evocative descriptions and speculations is important as it anticipates the complete disruption of linear narrative in the *Caves* section. The episode at the Marabar Caves remains eerie and unknown, and although various characters offer their own interpretations of what transpired, the narrative voice maintains a studied silence. Forster carefully shifts the focus from the actual incident to the state of mind of the various characters at this juncture. The experience in the Caves, Forster indicates, is as elusive and ungraspable as the experience of India itself. The novel thus becomes a metaphor for the breakdown of Anglo-Indian and Occidental yardsticks of measurement.

India has its own patterns of life and spirituality, Forster affirms, and when this is acknowledged, "the destiny of the English seems to resemble their predecessors, who also entered the country with intent to refashion it, but were in the end worked into its pattern and covered with dust." (p. 206) Against the fading ripples of Christianity and English intellectualism, Forster projects the overpowering infinity and nullity of the Marabar Caves, and the joyous frolic and ecstatic resurgence of Gokulashtami as more vital and vivid traditions of faith.

It is interesting however, that despite his indictment of British attitudes and his endorsement of Indian spiritualism, the Indian characters in the novel remain disappointing. Godbole is featured as an old Hindu professor and a singer of strange hymns. We are told that his "conversations frequently culminated in a cow" (p. 76) and that he normally "wore a turban that looked like pale purple macaroni, coat, waistcoat, dhoti, socks with clocks." (p. 74) We are also regaled with his fondness for food and his unpunctuality. Godbole's speculations on the aspects of good and evil at the end of Aziz's arrest, with a visibly upset Fielding, remain half-farcical. He is also an unsuccessful headmaster since he allows the school he is professionally in charge of, to be used as a granary. Forster, in spite of his sympathetic approach to Indian ideology, seems unable to extend his sympathies to Indian characters. His perception of them is constantly tinged with officiousness and very often the narrative voice falls back on generalizations about Indians.

This tone is also present in the delineation of Aziz. At the tea party at Fielding's house when Aziz begins to look around, Fielding takes this gesture of intimacy in his stride as "with so emotional a people it was apt to come at once or never." (p. 64) Aziz's fantasies about Moghul generosity reveal "the tenderness of one incapable of administration." (p. 70) When everything settles down on the train, the narrative voice observes that "the celebrated Oriental confusion appeared at last to be at an end." (p. 129) At the Marabar Caves we are informed that "an obscure young man had been allowed to show courtesy to visitors from another country, which is what all Indians long to do" and that "like most

Orientals, Aziz overrated hospitality, mistaking it for intimacy." (p. 141) Aziz's suspicion of Fielding is qualified as follows: "Suspicion in the Orient is a sort of malignant tumour, a mental malady that makes him self-conscious and unfriendly; he trusts and mistrusts at the same time in a way the Westerner cannot comprehend." (p. 272) When Aziz appropriates letters not belonging to him, the narrative voice explains that the "sanctity of private correspondence has never been ratified by the East." (p. 302) Aziz's mock-salute addressed to Fielding is recorded in the following words: "Aziz sketched a comic salaam; like all Indians, he was skilful in the slighter impertinences." (p. 296) Aziz is a personable man, but his looks must be identified as those of a "handsome little Oriental" (p. 150) by Adela Quested. He is a qualified surgeon, yet once he is away from British supervision his medical training and medical kit gather rust. There is very little that Aziz is allowed to do which is not explained away by the narrative voice as a peculiar Oriental eccentricity, specific to Indians and perhaps other Orientals.

Aziz and Godbole, Forster's two major Indian figures are vividly characterized, yet lack in dignity and conviction as fully developed individuals. This is largely due to the tone of condescension adopted by the narrative voice in depicting them. Elsewhere too, the narrative voice generalizes on unpunctuality, absence of co-ordination, incapacity for administration etc., as essentially Oriental traits. A telling statement in this connection is Fielding's rumination that "when he was throwing in his lot with Indians, he realized the profundity of the gulf that divided him from them. They always do something disappointing." (p. 170)

Such a statement is extremely suspect since Forster could not have been unaware of the political ferment and agitations that characterized the first quarter of the twentieth century in India. Nor could the countless prominent Indians, who took public stances on important issues have escaped his notice. Forster's deliberate portrayal of Indians as caricatures rather than individuals is because his concern remains focussed over the crisis of post-war Western humanism, typified in the failure of British Imperialism in India.

He is not particularly interested in accurate representations of Indians; India operates largely as a metaphor that allows him to interpret the reasons for the failure of the British. Forster would have us believe that one " touch of regret . . . true regret from the heart would have made . . . the British Empire a different institution." (p. 50) Even in his private correspondence Forster is more concerned over the British high-handedness which led to political unrest on the part of Indians.[5]

However, Forster's deviations from an older narrative tradition that emphasized on story and plot, to an awareness of the chaotic and complex nature of experience, lead him to evolve a new theory of the novel: "Expansion. That is the idea the novelist must cling to. Not completion. Not rounding off but opening out."[6] In doing so, he prepares the way for a novel like *Midnight's Children*. Forster's suggestion that the novelist strives to communicate through expansion rather than through any final conclusive statement is carried over by Salman Rushdie in his open-ended narrative. Dispensing with linear narrative and the myth of the omniscient narrator, Rushdie's novel moves into unchartered territory. *Midnight's Children* is an effervescent and buoyant account of over seventy-five years of the history of the Indian sub-continent.

The portrayal of Indian characters in *Midnight's Children* is very different from that of their counterparts in *Kim* and *A Passage to India.* For once, we are given the inside story of these characters as they struggle for expression in the midst of change and complexities. Through a host of figures, major and minor that dot the canvas of his narrative, Rushdie captures the atmosphere of ferment and turmoil that marked the history of India from the beginning of the century.

One of Rushdie's central figures is interestingly enough, a Dr. Aziz. Aadam Aziz of *Midnight's Children* is a far cry from his namesake in *A Passage to India.* Newly returned from Europe with a medical degree, Aziz's religious disenchantment and sense of unease are effectively portrayed by Rushdie. Aadam Aziz's dilemma is definitely more indicative of the generations of Indians who faced similar problems of realignment with their country after exposure to Western ideas and education.

What is even more remarkable is that *Midnight's Children*, while hurtling through a changing socio-political landscape, is able to present events sensitively, though the predominant tone of the novel is one of comedy. Whether it is Tai's exaggerated anger at Aziz's bringing home of strange ideas, family circumstances that compel a hitherto confined mother to go out to work, the wily Ghani's manipulation of Aziz into marrying his daughter, Naseem's refusal to come out of purdah or her fear of being photographed, all these and more are presented through light-hearted and yet compelling episodes.

Rushdie's figures are shown as being enmeshed in the predicament of their times, coming across to the reader as fallible, vulnerable, pathetic and funny. The reader is made to laugh with them and at them. Although modulated by the comic and the grotesque, the characters, however imperfect, remain credible and convincing. Although a lot of fun is poked at them, they are not seen from the omniscient perspective of the narrator of *Kim* or *A Passage to India.* Again, since there are no superior perspectives that the characters are pitted against, the Indian figures in *Midnight's Children* come into their own.

By creating characters with vitality and identities of their own, Rushdie finds for them a place in a larger, creative, literary tradition. What is more important, for the first time in our own literary history, Rushdie legitimizes and authenticates the experience of Indians. The characters in his novel are no longer segregated butts of humour or astonishment like their counterparts in either *Kim* or *A Passage to India.* They can be seen as eccentric, bathetic, credulous, sad, touching, comic, gifted, and so on, but they are very much a part of a recognisable humanity, not esoteric or quaintly 'oriental.'

The device of juxtaposing personal life-stories with the social, political and religious history of the sub-continent is exploited very successfully by Salman Rushdie. This links up persons with events in an extremely fascinating manner. In his intermingling and overlapping of personal and national histories, Rushdie effortlessly shifts gear, changing from comedy to more serious narrative in a matter of seconds. The incident of the Jallianwallah Bagh is a case in point. Aadam Aziz's accidental tumble is bathetic, yet it is juxtaposed with the horror of the massacre. Going back home, Naseem dismisses his wounds as the usual Mercurochrome stains. On being told that it is blood, she faints. Revived by her husband she asks anguishedly where he has been and his reply recreates for us at an extremely personal level, the nightmarish and frightful nature of this event from our history: " 'Nowhere on earth,' he said, and began to shake in her arms."[7] This is a brilliant reworking of history, which captures the reader's, imagination without any mawkishness, melodrama or hyperbole.

Rushdie's treatment of the white rulers of India is equally fascinating. In contrast to the usual awe and importance conceded to white men and their values that reading memory can recall, it is refreshing to see Western figures of authority in the novel, treated irreverently, whether in the case of Brigadier Dyer waxing his moustache or the bald and wig-clad Methwold, stating the terms and conditions for the sale of his estate, Rushdie is also able to turn commonplace events into metaphors for significant historical moments. Dodson's speeding car knocks down a spitoon and leaves behind a "dark fluid that congeals like a red hand in the dust of the streets and points accusingly at the retreating power of the Raj." (p. 44) Associations of declining imperialism and the violence and disturbance generated by it are successfully suggested by the mention of the pointing hand, the scattering urchins and the overturned spitoon. The handing over of Methwold's estate is also an elaborate parody of the last stages in the exchange of power between the departing colonials and the succeeding Indians.

The novel's narrative technique also enriches Rushdie's attempts to capture the multitudinousness of India and her people. Declaring that " there are as many versions of India as Indians," (p. 261) Saleem Sinai adopts various narrative modes to convey experience. Yet he is forced to confess his inadequacy as a narrator, for "there are so many stories to tell . . . such an excess of intertwined lives events miracles places rumours, so dense a commingling of the improbable and the mundane." (p. 11)

At times the narrative voice piles up an assortment of dates, facts, and figures related to private and public issues in keeping with the "narrow one-dimensionality of a straight line." (p. 149) This is also juxtaposed with several occasions of clock-hiding where the reader is shuffled between the future, present, and past in an unchronological manner.

Some events in India's chequered history like the partition riots, Hindu and Muslim hostility, the war with China and Pakistan, the trauma of the Bangladesh war, the death of L.N. Mishra, the imposition of sterilizations during the emergency, etc., are represented realistically. Yet this world of facts is often rudely disturbed by Rushdie's acknowledgement of errors and discrepancies: "In my India, Gandhi will continue to die at the wrong time." (p. 164) Acknowledging his inaccuracy as a chronicler, Saleem also indicates the contradictory nature of India itself. Checking himself from an attempt to over-simplify issues, the narrator soliloquizes: "Am I so far gone, in my desperate need for meaning, that I'm prepared to distort everything—to re-write the whole history of my times purely in order to place myself in a central role ? Today, in my confusion, I can't judge. . . . I must finish what I've started, even if, inevitably, what I finish turns out not to be what I began. . . . " (p. 166)

Consciously acknowledging his inability to render Indian experience in totality, Saleem Sinai prepares the reader towards an acceptance of the bewildering multiplicity of India. In order to communicate this multifacetedness of experience, Rushdie deliberately uses the mode of fantasy to structure and permeate into experience. This is highlighted by the use of leitmotifs like the perforated sheet, Lifafa Das's peep show, the game of snakes and ladders, the washing chest, the broken-down clock tower, pickle vats and chutneys, all of which operate as modes of perception at the literal and symbolic levels.

The emphasis on the social, political, and historical realities of the sub-continent is paralleled by an awareness of the world of magic and spirituality which defies logical narrative. Interestingly, in *Midnight's Children*, unlike *Kim* and *A Passage to India*, the fantastic operates as a qualification of the real and vice versa. The realm of fantasy in the novel is not isolated or peripheral. Often Rushdie iconoclastically uses the myths and fables of India, reworking them into the murky world of Indian politics. Yet again, the real is substituted by the metaphorical, and linear time is ruptured by the knowledge of the Mahayugas. Faced and "overwhelmed all of a sudden by an older learning" (pp. 191-2) Saleem can only ask in consternation: "And where in this scheme of things am I ?" (p. 192)

The potency of this world is also evoked through the mummified corpse of St. Xavier, the hair of the Prophet, the Tower of Silence, and the temples of Kali and Shiva, as also the horrifying and unreal experience in the Sunderban forests.

Such modes of apprehension, Saleem implies, invariably co-exist in "a country which is itself a sort of dream." (p. 117) In India, progress and prosperity are found side by side with squalor, disease, malnutrition and poverty. Here modernity is found along with inflexibility and a resistance to change. Fake gurus like Lord Khusro co-exist with soothsayer Ramram Seth and Sadhu Purushottam. Against the world of tetrapods, Alpha and Omega, and skyscrapers is juxtaposed a life of traditional participation in innumerable festivals. Little wonder that Saleem remarks: "If I seem a little bizarre, remember the wild profusion of my inheritance." (p. 108) *Midnight's Children's* success lies in its recognition that both these aspects, the logical and the irrational, the prosaic and the spiritual, the ugly and the beautiful, the sublime and the bathetic are facets of the Indian consciousness and are not mutually exclusive. Acerbic comment in the narrative, therefore, alternates with authorial incomprehension.

Rushdie's acrobatics with the narrative technique establish that the story of the Indian sub-continent cannot be easily and simplistically rendered. Saleem's own inability to chronicle his tale and the presence of several modes of interpretation in the novel, allows the reader to identify with a perspective on the sub-continent, very different from that of the author. Saleem's vision, is finally, one of the countless experiences that *Midnight's Children* offers. The novel, by positing such perspectives, remains open-ended and optimistic in its conclusion.

By recognizing the complex nature of experience that the Indian sub-continent points towards and by making Indian characters the repositories of such experience, wherein they function as centres of consciousness, Rushdie is able to authenticate their experience. In its dealing with plot and language to highlight this, *Midnight's Children*, as the blurb on the paperback suggests, is really the story of a continent finding its voice.

NOTES

1. (London: Hamish Hamilton, 1964), p. 122.

2. (London: Routledge and Kegan Paul, 1978), p. 157.

3. Rudyard Kipling, *Kim* (London: Pan Books, 1976), p. 23.

4. *A Passage to India* (Harmondsworth: Penguin Books, 1936), p. 76.

5. The letters of 1921 in *The Hill of Devi and Other Indian Writings* (London: Edward Arnold, 1983), p. 98. One letter states: "I have been with pro-Government and pro-English Indians all the time . . . and am only sure of this—that we are paying for the insolence of Englishmen and Englishwomen out here in the past. I don't mean that good manners can avert a political upheaval. But they can minimize it and come nearer to averting it in the East than elsewhere. English manners out here have improved wonderfully in the last eight years. . . . But it is too late."

6. E.M. Forster, *Aspects of the Novel* (Harmondsworth: Penguin Books, 1962), p. 170

7. *Midnight's Children* (London: Jonathan Cape, 1981), p. 36.

Nergis Dalal's *The Girls from Overseas* and Jhabvala's *A Backward Place:* A Matter of Survival

SARALA BARNABAS

Oh, East is East, and West is West,
and never the twain shall meet. . . .

Kipling, 'The Ballad of East and West'

A persistent concern for a number of writers, notably E.M. Forster, has been that of the problems faced by foreigners living in India. Two women novelists have explored afresh with insight and understanding, the issues involved. In the novels under consideration, Nergis Dalal and Ruth Prawer Jhabvala concentrate on the lives of foreign women married to Indian men. Eight women are portrayed here, one still single, one a three-time divorcee. India is seen through their eyes. After their experiences, and studying their reactions, one begins to feel that perhaps Kipling was right after all.

Of the five women in Nergis Dalal's *The Girls from Overseas* (1979), Jane and Gertrude are English, Sandy is American, Louise is Canadian, while Michelle is French. The word 'girls' is a misnomer for Gertrude, the oldest, who is in her mid-sixties, and the more youthful ones are well beyond their twenties. Widely separated by age and cultural differences, they are bound together by two factors—one, that they are all foreigners, and two, that their husbands are Indians. These facts lead them to seek solace in each other's company.

Once a week, the five women meet for coffee at one or the other of their houses. The husbands are puzzled. Louise's husband, Dinesh, wonders about it. "What did they talk about ? Why was it necessary for them to meet—five totally disparate and unlikely strangers, held together by the merest thread of their foreignness." (pp. 6-7)[1] His wife laughs and tells him that they talk about their husbands. And indeed this is so, but they also have discussions on children, in-laws, and their own myriad problems which they as foreign wives must face. "Their weekly meetings were safety valves—analyst's couch and confessional, at one and the same time." (p. 7)

Not one of the marriages is outstandingly successful. In fact, two are utter failures. The others have managed to adapt themselves with varying degrees of success. Michelle, wife of a retired general, General Rajendra Verma, has spent forty years in India, and is the mother of two grown-up daughters and a son, but "she often thought how strange it was that although she had spent many more years in India than in France, she still felt very different, very French." (p. 101) Basically not a complex personality, Michelle is pleasantly plump, no signs of grey in her dark brown coppery hair, with blue eyes which are steady and assessing. A wonderful housekeeper, "wildly successful" gardener, and fabulous cook, she still has managed to keep her identity. Clearly, her family and surroundings have adapted to Michelle, rather than they to her. She has even retained a trace of her French accent.

In his own life, the General follows an orderly routine, maintaining a rigid schedule for meals, exercise, and, most important, writing his memoirs. He has built a dream house here in Dehra Dun which his wife enjoys immensely. They have settled into a comfortable routine. With Raj locked away in his study for many hours, emerging only for lunch before going back to his writing, "Michelle found this a very satisfactory arrangement. He was at home and yet not under foot, as many friends complained their husbands were after retirement." (p. 98) She is free to shop, play Mahjong, and enjoy her own private life as she wants to. Thinking about their marriage, the General considers it a success. Yet he has realized they "had less and more need of each other in old age. They went their own ways and saw less of each other; and their different religions, cultures, had widened the gap that always exists between any two people." (p. 159)

Jane was only four when her parents were divorced. Her mother became neurotically possessive, abnormal in her demands upon Jane and her sister. From them she expected good looks, intelligence and success. The sister managed to escape by running away.

Working as a physiotherapist in London, Jane met a promising young Indian surgeon, Dr. Sunil Kumar, and fell in love with him. Marriage to Sunil offered an escape both from her parents as well as from England. There were terrible scenes at home. On her last day, her mother told her, "I would rather you were dead, than married to an Indian." (p. 16) What Jane had never anticipated was the presence in her home of Sunil's mother and sister, both widowed, and now in the traditional way, his dependents. Jane dislikes them cordially. Being of a highly nervous and emotional temperament, when things become too much for her, she resorts to tranquillizers. The Kumars have three lively little boys who keep the house in a constant state of noise and upheaval.

Marriage with Sunil has hardly been a partnership of unalloyed happiness. Sunil is devoted to Jane and, in a strictly limited way is considerate enough. Once at a party in their home, Jane is playing the piano, and Sunil begins to talk softly to a fellow surgeon. Jane stops playing with a resounding crash, and rushes out into the dark. After a fruitless search, Sunil sits with his head in his hands and says in despair, "She's so sensitive. I should have remembered it would hurt her if I talked while she was playing." (p. 41) Nothing alarming happens to Jane. She books herself into a hotel for the night and gets drunk on half a bottle of whisky. On a different level, Sunil expects his wife to provide him with every comfort. In the first year of marriage, Jane found herself constantly doing the wrong thing, "Indian men were so spoiled by their mothers." (pp. 151-152) Meals must be on time, buttons replaced, clothes brought from the laundry, otherwise "Sunil would look at her in injured silence. She would have welcomed a shout, but silence was the bluntest of instruments." (p. 151) Jane asks herself "why she ever got married and why, if she must marry, she had to pick on a foreigner, whose culture was totally different from hers and whose attitude to life was shaped by that culture." (p. 150)

If some of Jane's early experiences in India have been quite bewildering, one particular one stands out for its sheer unpleasantness. Highly westernized friends, Aroon and Savitri Sharma, announce they are coming over for Holi. They ask her to have on hand some bhang and sweets. Sunil tries to warn her and offers to take her off for the day, but all unsuspecting, and in her desire to experience all things Indian, Jane insists on staying on. When the noisy throng arrives, she can hardly identify her friends. "They looked like multicoloured fools—Holi fools—and they laughed and staggered in a way that made her think they were drunk." (p. 152) Worse is to come. "Catching hold of her Aroon poured dark red powder in a stream over her head, rubbing it in roughly with his fingers and drawing his smeared hand down her body, pressing breasts, belly, thighs with probing hard fingers." (p. 153) Others follow Aroon, drenching her with coloured water, paying no heed to her tears and rage, pressing their stained hands over her body. It is Sunil who rescues her finally, and puts an end to the rowdy display by offering the crowd sweets. When they have gone, Jane sobs with rage: "Savages, barbarians—that's what they are. I never want to see Aroon and Savitri again. Their sophistication—their civilized behaviour—are not even skin deep. I refuse to have them in the house." (pp. 153-154) Of course, the Sharmas come again, but Jane will not allow herself to be truly friendly with any Indian again. From the Holi incident, she has formed her own conclusion. "All Indians were like glaciers she felt—civilized on the surface—but deep down, beneath the surface, they were violent savages." (p. 154)

For Louise, going away with Dinesh was a temptation. A Canadian working as a highly paid stenographer in New York, Louise met her future husband, a Stanford-educated engineer employed in the same city. "That the reality was never the same as the imagined dream, was a disillusionment she had learnt to live with." (p. 19) She is totally unprepared for the onslaught of her mother-in-law and young sister-in-law. Unannounced, they invade her house, spreading their belongings everywhere, and are quite puzzled with the room she has prepared for them. "The idea of privacy was a totally foreign concept. A family lived as a family, with open doors, sharing everything. There was never any question of 'mine' or 'yours'." (p. 12) Louise is horrified when entering her immaculate bedroom, she finds her mother-in-law sprawled on the bed, dirty feet on the bed spread, talking unconcernedly to her son. The final straw is her use of Louise's towel. The two women find her subsequent fury quite strange, but then they feel they must be tolerant. "These foreigners had such strange ideas, they didn't really blame her. They expected Dinesh to bring her around slowly to their way of thinking but instead he asked them, with some embarrassment it was true, to conform to what she felt was right. They had to learn that the house was hers." (p. 122) So instead of Louise coming around slowly, it is Dinesh's mother and sister who now never come unannounced.

Louise and Dinesh have an astonishingly pretty child, Sonia, who combines the best of both parents, having inherited her mother's wide grey eyes, high cheekbones and delicately modelled chin, and her father's fine nose and curving mouth. Sonia's darkly gold skin is her own as is her lovely hair "bronze, dark brown, rust, copper, gold and even black, depending on how the light caught it." (p. 19) At first, the colour of the child's skin is a disappointment to Dinesh's mother, for she had hoped it would be fair. Indeed "(it was one of the things that made marrying a foreigner acceptable).... Indians have this curious prejudice about a fair skin which is supposed to denote descent from the civilized Aryan invaders from the north, while a darker skin meant descent from primitive tribes who had been pushed into jungles or fled south.... Two hundred years of colonial rule had done nothing to diminish this prejudice." (pp. 19-20)

Louise thinks how impossible it is to escape from one's background. It has been five years since she was married and came to India "and still she was herself, alien, separate, linked only by the slenderest of filaments to her husband." (p. 5) And yet, Louise tries to adjust to a situation so different from any she has known before. "She is young and full of ideals. She is truly in love with Dinesh, adores her small daughter Sonia, but finds India hard to take." (p. 43)

Jane and Louise have mothers-in-law living under their roofs, but in Sandy's case, it is in her husband's mother's home that she and Dilip dwell. Dilip Singh is the former Raja of Dilawar's cousin, and his mother, known as Mataji, is a gracious lady whose blue blood shows in every word and action. For years the victim of a cruel dissipated husband, Mataji in her widowhood has acquired a wisdom and serenity which touches everyone who meets her.

Coming to India, Sandy at first felt utter futility, in despair because of an identity crisis. The future stretched ahead of her bleakly, but how could she return to the States where she would be a nobody ? At this critical juncture of her life, it was Mataji who helped her.

By nature, Sandy is an extrovert. Extremely intelligent, a psychology major, she had studied at Spelman and Sarah Lawrence College. Her path crossed Dinesh's when she was working at the American Embassy in New Delhi. Sandy is no beauty with a thin angular face framed by shoulder-length hair. She has a harsh voice and tends to be outspoken. She is aware that Dilip has never been in love with her. Reputed to be a ladies's man, with her at least, he is totally impotent.

Perhaps no one among the five 'girls' is more bitter than Gertrude Das. George, her husband, is a cold cruel man, incapable of arousing any feeling of love. Marriage to him was a way to get out of a very small town. They had met in London where George was a student of history at the university. Gertrude hates him and has done so since they were married. As a young bride, Gertrude was really beautiful, the centre of attention from young subalterns and captains. George was kicked out regularly from jobs. In those early days, he was frequently unfaithful to her, jeering and laughing at her. To him she was a new possession to show off. She had run away twice, coming back because he pleaded and promised to improve. "She had married him in spite of opposition, filled with romantic longings for a new way of life and hot exotic lands. Disillusionment had come very quickly." (p. 21) There was a child. A drunken George delayed taking Gertrude to the hospital and the baby died. She could never forgive him for that. Fortunately his father left him money and property. He was able to build the house where they live now.

Then many years later, after three decades of silence, her mother dies, leaving Gertrude a small annuity which she invests with the help of a friend, Jason Skinner. Now she acquires at least a partial financial independence, no longer needing the humiliation of asking George for money. Best of all, she transforms her room into a haven of comfort where she can be alone. Hardly any communication is left between husband and wife. Gertrude spends as little time as possible in George's company, and when they are together, they seldom exchange a word. "It was an uneasy arrangement but it was the only way they could bear to live together and they needed to live together. She, for the financial security it gave her; and he, because it was not possible for him to manage on his own." (p. 22)

In her loathing for India, Gertrude has developed almost paranoic tendencies. She controls her feelings, keeping herself, at least outwardly, under a tight rein. Inwardly she is a seething mass of hatred. She has evolved her own method of making tolerable the fat sari-clad women who gape at her, the urchins who dance around her and yell, by playing an elaborate game with herself. Behind the dark glasses she always wears, she stares at these dark aliens whom thirty years have not sufficed to identify with, and carries on a "pretence that she alone existed, an explorer in a savage country." (p. 10) In her mind she conjures up a secret weapon which will make all her tormentors go up in smoke, totally annihilated—bang, bang, bang.

Nor is Gertrude on the same wave length as the other 'girls'. Something about this lean woman in her mid-sixties, her skin lined, black hair faded, always dressed in skirts or slacks, hands gloved, a scarf concealing her withered neck, and particularly those pale blue eyes which have a slightly mad look, makes them uneasy. They never establish an easy relationship with her, all of them addressing her as 'Mrs. Das' with the exception of Michelle. She does not join them in listing her grievances to the group, only listening and smiling. None of them would mind if she dropped out of the circle, but how can they stop her ?

The coffee hour is precious to all of them. Dalal lays stress on how each hostess for the week goes out of her way to make the food very special. D.R. Sharma refers to "the general impression that Dalal writes mostly on cookery." With reference to another novel she wrote, *The Inner Door* (1975), he speaks of "Dalal's relish in undulating the menu and exhibiting her culinary accomplishment."[2] In the case of the 'girls', the menus assume a special significance which perhaps the male reader overlooks. In the first account of a coffee session, held this time in the Verma home, "Michelle wheeled in a trolley laden with sandwiches, a luscious chocolate torte, cheese and bacon pastries and her own special walnut fudge. She passed around cups of steaming coffee and even those who were on diets, forgot and helped themselves greedily to all the goodies." (pp. 10-11) The selection of food is deliberate. *Pakoras* and *gulab jamuns* would hardly serve to preserve the illusion, however transient, that at least for now they are not in India. The tortes and sandwiches go a long way in providing a reprieve, no matter how fleeting it might be.

Extraordinarily important in the lives of the five are the visits to India of Jason Skinner. "He was their safety valve—confidante, accomplice." (p. 11) Jason supposedly works for the United Nations and therefore travels all over the world. A bachelor, he is immensely popular with ladies of all ages. In return, he likes them equally well. Jason brings the 'girls' all kinds of good things which are not available in India—perfume, Scotch, cosmetics, French bras and pantyhose, as well as cheese, biscuits and chocolates. But that is not all. Jason plays a unique role in all their lives. "They confided in him, complained about husbands and relations, and sometimes, slept with him. He was their very special friend, a foreigner like themselves, with whom they were safe, at ease. . . . None of them questioned his relationship with the others. They guarded their own, and were content that it did not collide with that of the others." (p. 13)

If the coffee hour offers a time of fellowship and sharing, and Jason acts as a safety valve, one more need has to be fulfilled. When life becomes too much, when problems seem insurmountable, there has to be a place to which one can retreat, to hide while one replenishes one's inner resources. In Tennessee Williams's *A Streetcar Named Desire*, Blanche DuBois finds such a retreat in the bathroom in a tub of warm water. Honey in Edward Albee's *Who's Afraid of Virginia Woolf ?* lies down on the floor and curls herself into the foetal position. For Gertrude Das, the room she has decorated so beautifully, even luxuriously, is her sanctuary. It is here that she can keep George out of sight, where she can nurse her hatreds, and where later, as her mental condition deteriorates, she secretly studies witchcraft in order to punish those on whom she wishes to take revenge. Showing Michelle the room where no one else has been before, Gertrude defines its role: "This is my refuge, and of course, my prison as well." (p. 103) She can change its appearance to match her mood. When she draws the curtain, it takes on a green under-water look. When the lamps come on, it is filled with a golden glow. Even before she hears Gertrude's revelations about her study of witchcraft, the place makes Michelle shudder, though it is in answer to her question to Gertrude "How can you bear to stay on, feeling the way you do ?" (p. 102) that she is shown the room.

When the shattering news that Jason has married Maya Kishore, not only an Indian woman but a famed Bharat Natyam dancer, reaches the five, each one takes it as a personal betrayal. For Jane, Jason has been of "her own kind, with whom she could talk and laugh and feel, as she never felt at other times, free to lower her guard. No one knew what Jason had meant to her." (p. 154) In her deep distress over Jason's perfidy, Jane takes refuge in her room. "There was comfort in lying in bed hemmed in by shadows, safe for the moment, like a child who cannot imagine that anything unfortunate could happen to her when she was safely tucked into bed." (p. 154) Subjected to some very frank remarks from Dilip when she asks him for a divorce, Sandy feels terribly lonely and restless without Jason to turn to. Going to her room, she flings herself down on the bed. "At least it was a relief to know she could lie here all evening, if she wanted to . . . she need see no one, and have her supper in her room on a tray." (p. 147) Even Michelle who has come to terms with her situation, hearing of her son Jit's sudden departure to train as an airlines steward, takes the news hard. She goes to her room. "Michelle felt that particular cherished feeling which was so important to a woman. She lay back on the pillows and in spite of what had happened, felt contentment and peace. She picked up a magazine and the stiffness of the cover was like a shield for her heart. She became a child again, loved, cared for, protected." (pp. 160-161)

If the women have such frank remarks to make about India and their lives here, others have formed their own opinions about them. Spoiled and pampered though he is, Jit is discerning enough to know what Jason has meant to them. He observes that Jason's marriage will hit them all, particularly Sandy and Jane because both were a little in love with him. "They will be feeling very slighted that he has chosen to marry an Indian girl. Sorry Mama, but all these foreign ladies (not you of course) are really very conscious of being foreign, and therefore superior." (p. 24) The ex-Raja of Dilawar, Vikram Singh, knows precisely what the coffee sessions are for. Of Sandy he enquires, "Is your little club still functioning ? Still acting as a shield against the dirty Indians ?" (p. 51)

Why the five married Indian men is clear, but, in reverse, why did the men choose them ? What has marriage meant to the husbands ? For George Das, it has been an achievement, something to boast about. "My wife is English," he would say to total strangers as though the fact gave him some special standing. (p. 21) To an astonished Michelle, the General confesses how much of an asset she has been to him in his career. "All my senior officers fell over themselves trying to get an invitation for one of your famous little French dinners. They began to feel somehow, that there must be something special about me to have engaged the attentions of so charming a foreigner. We Indians, as you know by now, have a complex about foreigners. If you had changed immediately into a good Indian wife, deferring to me on every point, wearing your hair down your back in a long greasy plait and opening your mouth only to eat, I should have felt very let down indeed." (p. 99)

When Sandy asks Dilip for a divorce (which she has wanted since the first week of marriage), he is brutally frank. She can have it on condition that she goes back to America. She will get no alimony but she can keep all the considerable amount of jewellery he has given her, and he will pay her airfare back. But if she stays on in India, then there will be no divorce. Resentfully, Sandy asks if he is satisfied to go on in the same way, day after day: "I don't see why not. I am an Indian remember ? I don't have any romantic illusions about marriage. So this one has failed partially. So what ?" To a still puzzled Sandy who wonders what he can gain by the arrangement, Dilip is quite explicit: " I shall list the gains if you are so dense that you haven't realised yet what they are." He mentions the efficient way she runs the house, the excellent parties which delight his business colleagues and friends. The house is done up beautifully and they have what is perhaps the best garden in Dehra Dun. Sandy takes care of all petty details and he is not bothered by them. " That fact," Dilip concludes, "that somehow we don't click sexually is not necessarily the absolute end of everything." (pp. 144-145) Earlier, Dilip has spoken of Mataji liking Sandy and their being able to get along so well as one more plus point in her favour. On his own, Jason has recognized why Dilip wants to continue the marriage. "Dilip is very old fashioned in many ways but he likes being married to a foreigner for the status he thinks it gives him. Marriage with a foreigner transcends class, carries a particular social stamp and keeps the wife an outsider." (pp. 42-43)

For the 'girls from overseas,' marriage to Indian men offered an escape route with all the attendant glamour of going to a faraway and exotic land. Disillusionment coupled with shock at the reality set in swiftly. Louise has told Jason that being in India "was like going back a hundred years in time." Jason thinks all of them have the same sense of time displacement. "Children working ten hours a day, little girls getting married off before they are out of the school room—animals roaming the streets with no one to care for them, and beggars, lepers and mutilated people begging for alms, like in medieval times. And this constant sense of fatality—kismet—which makes them accept everything with listlessness." (pp. 43-44)

Once Sandy ponders over the difference between the temperate and tropical zones. Like night and day, it is equal to the impact on the mind of day-to-day life. Climate is not merely a physical thing. It goes much further, and "what happened in the mind was inextricably bound up with one's physical surroundings and the mental climate of a place could be as foreign as the physical terrain." Coming as they do from a totally different geographical milieu, the women cannot fathom the country of their adoption. At every level in this ancient land, the past casts its shadow over the present and on the future. To the five, its centuries of history, its culture in its deeper sense is quite incomprehensible. Sandy feels "If she lived here a hundred years she would still not understand it." (pp. 56-57) Louise recalls Margaret Mead's advice—"separate cultures should remain separate. Although human beings have their own personal lives they are yet in some measure the victims and promoters of a collective spirit, whose years, according to Jung, are counted in centuries." (p. 90)

Jit has told his mother about the foreigners's sense of superiority. Mataji echoes the very thought. Speaking to Michelle about her daughter-in-law, Sandy, of whom she is very fond, Mataji says,"But you know it is a curious thing. Although she too has a genuine liking, a sympathy for me, yet this white, western feeling of superiority is always there, inherent in everything she says or does, as much a part of you too as the colour of your skin or your hair." Distressed, Michelle denies it at once and demands a concrete example. Mataji narrates an incident. A couple of highly intelligent articulate girls from Delhi who happened to be Dilip's cousins were sitting with all of them in the garden one evening. Sandy was holding forth on Indian women—how bored they were with their lives, how they had no individuality at all. Performing those ritual fasts and pujas for the welfare of their husbands, they had no idea of their own potential, being aware of their identity at the most superficial levels. Sandy spoke of their having 'only partial minds.' One of the girls picked up the phrase at once, and quoted from Yeats:

When a man is fighting mad
Something drops from eyes long blind
He completes his partial mind,
For an instant stands at ease,
Laughs aloud, his heart at peace.

Sandy could not conceal her astonishment. Mataji adds, "That an Indian should catch the allusion and that she should actually be able to quote the relevant verse—to her it was simply unbelievable. As though a pet dog or cat had suddenly opened its mouth and spoken to her." (pp. 113-114) Seeing how upset Michelle is over the charge of superiority, Mataji asks a single pertinent question, "My dear, have you ever asked yourself, who are your friends ? You feel most at home, able to communicate most easily with the other girls like you—foreigners married to Indians. I am not blaming you. I am merely stating a fact." (p. 114)

Perhaps the 'girls' would be taken aback by the charge, but the attitude is there. It is not that they have not tried to be friendly with Indians, but as Jane concluded after the Holi episode, they are barbarians who under their civilizead surface are violent savages. There is also the sad fact that in spite of the coffee hour, each one is alone. "Although all five were together in the same room each of them remained isolated. Loneliness is the most central and most inescapable fact of all human existence." (p. 11)

It is Louise who puts her finger on a vitally important factor. "Do you think we are not sufficiently involved with life here ? Perhaps we need to identify a little more with the people. After all we are planning to spend the rest of our lives here." (p. 88) Notwithstanding their expertise in kitchen and garden, and at interior decoration, there is the fact that their capabilities are not being put to full use. Maya's advent into their circle makes them deeply aware of this. Sandy remarks, "You know, it's kind of funny. Here we are, liberated foreigners—people in our own right—which Indian women seldom are—and we seem to be doing nothing but frittering away our lives, while this Indian girl is a dedicated careerist and famous as well. It's unsettling." (p. 82)

Why then do they stay in India ? Why not give up all and return home ? The answer is that there is nothing to go back to, neither status nor financial security. In a very real sense, they have burnt their bridges behind them. They came to India to get away from the situations at home, and it would hardly be in order for them to return to what they ran away from in the first instance. Take Sandy for example. Discussing the divorce she wants, Dilip taunts her about the small one-house town in Louisiana from where she comes. He knows only too well about the small house there, her grocer father, her mother who helps in the shop and goes home to scrub and cook, whereas she is virtually a princess with a retinue of servants and all the luxuries which he as a very successful jeweller can give her.

For the 'girls' the fact of their being from overseas gives them special privileges. Dalal observes, 'Foreigners and especially white foreigners in India are so spoilt, sought after, fussed over and made to feel important, that they begin to have very inflated ideas of their own worth. In their own countries they would have been nobodies—insignificant and totally unremarkable. Here, in India they at once become excessively important." (p. 24)

And finally what it boils down to is a sense of survival. At all costs, no matter how bleakly the future stretches ahead, with nothing to transform their lives in the long vista of the years to come, they must cling to the status and security that marriage to Indians has brought them.

In Ruth Prawer Jhabvala's *A Backward Place* (1965), as in *The Girls from Overseas*, the tone of the novel is set from the very first page. In the latter, the story begins with Louise in the middle of her bath, smothered in soap and suddenly in trouble because the water has been shut off. "Oh God! This bloody country," she yells. (p. 5) In Jhabvala's novel, Etta resumes her efforts to wean Judy away from her Indian husband. "Marriages, my dear, are made to be broken, that's one of the rules of modern civilization. Just because we happen to have landed ourselves in this primitive society, that's no reason why we should submit to their primitive morality." (p. 5)[3] The backward place is, of course, India. The three women here are all foreigners, Clarissa and Judy from England, and Etta from Hungary. Of them, Clarissa is single, Judy is wedded to Bal, while Etta is divorced from no less than three Indian husbands. Each woman has a totally different perspective on India.

No one quite knows how Etta makes a living. It is supposed that her marriages must have yielded substantial compensation, but actually not one of her former husbands, handsome educated young Indians though they were, had been even moderately affluent. Still, her life style is luxurious, and she is satisfied with nothing but the best.

Blonde, green-eyed and sophisticated, always elegantly dressed, she sometimes takes on very high class jobs. Without quite seeming to go after these, they come her way. They include teaching German to an important industrialist with business interests in Germany, or English to a maharani wishing to make an entrée into society. She escorts American tourists around New Delhi, and acts as interpreter to some visiting Hungarian judges. Accepting a substantial fee for services rendered, she is very nonchalant, as if she really does not want to take it. And then there are her admirers. Mostly elderly Europeans in the past when she was younger, these have now been replaced by Indians who cannot resist her. True, in her mid-forties now, she attracts fewer admirers, and they are older and fatter. "She made them feel as if they were not in dull, homely backward Delhi at all, but in places they dreamed of—Paris, Vienna, Berlin, where the women were all beautiful and accessible and knowledgeable, and one drank wine out of long stemmed glasses and made husky conversation against a background of waltzes played on the violin." (p. 42) As she teaches them what to wear, how a gentleman behaves with ladies, all the while holding forth on India and Indian men, they try eagerly to show her how they are not like other countrymen, and hold finer values of which she is the embodiment.

Of late, her admirer is Mr. Gupta, a rich hotel owner, fifty years old and a self-made man. Having settled all his children, and established his business on a sound footing, he looks for relaxation and finds it in Etta. "She was feminine, sprightly, spoiled and kittenish for him, and he indulged her with the good humour of one playing a game that he had not played before." (p. 43) She has given him a name—Guppy, to rhyme with puppy—which he finds novel and funny.

As a white woman in India, Etta can be very imperious. She makes a tremendous fuss in a restaurant over the coffee she is served with, demanding to see the manager and succeeding in obtaining a freshly made cup of the beverage. Incensed at her behaviour, Clarissa wonders aloud if Etta has no feelings for the poor waiter who is surely in trouble. She tells Etta she does not seem to have any sense of human dignity. "How terribly wrong you are," Etta retorts. "It's because I've got so much sense of human dignity that I refuse, but absolutely and entirely refuse, to drink bad coffee. . . . Let alone pay for it," and she takes out her compact and powders her face. (p. 22)

Etta always professes to be sick of India. "India, India, India, all the time, as if there was anything interesting to be said ! One has the misfortune to be here, well all right, let's leave it at that, but why do we have to keep on torturing ourselves by talking about it ?"(p. 34) When Clarissa tells her "people like you shouldn't be in this country. You don't belong," Etta responds, "No, thank God." (p. 24) There are times when India seems to overwhelm her. A band made up of lusty young Goans sets up a terrific racket causing Etta to hold her head and groan. Over the noise, Clarissa shouts, "One either merges with Hindu civilization or is drowned by it !" Her companion, still holding her head, admits, "Oh I'm one of the drowned ones, most definitely one of the drowned ones." (pp 24-25)

To Etta, Europe is still the ideal, the most desirable of all places on earth. Dr. Hochstadt, a visiting German professor, compliments her on having lived in cosmopolitan capitals and known the best of cultures. "She felt depressingly aware of how far away and long ago those capitals were. The larger part of her life had been spent in hot, dusty Delhi, where memories of opera, ballet, theatre quickly faded—or perhaps receded so far into the distance that they retained nothing but a vague outline which, for want of anything more real, one had to fill in with as glittering colours as one's imagination could still furnish." (p. 106) When had India ever given anyone anything, Etta thinks, except germs and disease? "What had it given Etta, after all these years, after taking her youth, her looks, her buoyancy and charm ?" (p. 107) It gives her a feeling of excitement to visit Guppy's international hotel where piles of expensive pigskin and calf leather luggage are plastered with international labels. She strolls by posters of Paris and Venice, flicks through folders about Mediterranean cruises and holidays in Spain with a casual, almost bored air, all her being longing to be a part of this different world once again. She sits turning the pages of a magazine and sipping iced coffee, cigarette in hand, but her eyes are avidly taking in two superbly dressed European ladies, filing away details in her mind."She was never too proud to learn, and these transient passengers, these brief emissaries of a Europe she had left over twenty-five years ago but still looked to for everything that was valuable to her, were her only mentors." (p. 82)

Much of Etta's resentment towards India is directed against Judy's husband. She continually undermines Judy's marriage, lecturing, scolding, urging her to leave Bal. "I hate to see you going on and on like this. Married to that awful—well, he *is* awful, don't expect me to mince words." (p. 8) It disgusts her to see Judy wearing a sari. "You're just rotting here. Look at you in that *thing*—" (p. 6) About Judy's complexion she asks, "Did you go out in the sun ? That's of course the best way of ruining one's complexion. Don't you know that the Indian sun has been put expressly in to the sky to ruin our complexions ?" (p. 7)

When Judy does not accompany him on a picnic, even the normally sweet-tempered Bal erupts at Etta's taunts. She sneers and calls Judy 'a good Hindu wife,' accusing him of bringing her here to "treat her as if she were one of *your* women . . . my sense of humour, somehow, in this particular case . . . it absolutely fails me." Not satisfied with having said so much, she goes on, "Of course, no one can accuse you of being a reactionary husband. You don't keep her locked up at home—oh no, you're a modern man with advanced ideas. You send her out to work." (pp. 171-172)

Ironically, it is Etta who has had three Indian husbands and a series of Indian lovers. Her ire is aroused against Clarissa because she sponges off a rich family, the Kapurs, although in a far less obvious way, Etta herself does exactly that. She tries every persuasion to get Guppy to take her to Europe when he goes on business but fails as Guppy appears to have found another woman as a relaxation. Etta is plunged into gloom. She emerges only when Jimmy Jumperwala, bore though he is, looks like becoming Guppy's successor.

Of the three foreign women in Jhabvala's novel, Etta most resembles Dalal's 'girls' in her attitude towards India. Like them, she enunciates her views in no uncertain terms. She came to India as they did, following a romantic dream, found marriage with Indians hard to take. While they stay married to one man, she attempted marriage thrice, and divorced all three spouses. She met the first one in Vienna the "handsomest, most cultured, charming boy one could imagine." The rest of that particular story has a familiar ring. "Who would ever have thought that, once back in India, he would turn out to be so very much attached to his most uncultured family and, moreover, altogether so different from the gay youth with whom she had gone dancing in all the nicest cafes ?" (p. 25) India might have made her the centre of much admiration and attention, given her a status she might never have achieved in Europe, because she is a foreigner, but in her mind all Etta has found is heat, flies and, what is to her, a bizarre uncouth culture. Her sense of superiority is akin to that of the 'girls'. And yet, as they discover, going back, if at all that is possible, will not be the paradise one expects. For one, where is the security or family she can fall back on ? Besides, the world has moved on in twenty five years. Etta may dream of Europe, but she is no fool. "It was infinitely distant and infinitely desirable. But she was afraid of it too. Here at least she had her personality: she was Etta, whom people knew and admired for being blonde and vivacious and smart. In Europe there were many blondes, and there they might more easily notice that she was not so young or as vivacious as she once had been; and they might not think her smart at all. She no longer knew the way they dressed there, or the way they talked, or the fashionable foods they ate and drinks they drank, the books they had read, the conversations they had held with one another, while she was out here." (pp. 212-213)

As Gertrude Das has done, Etta has spent much thought on decorating her room, giving it as continental an atmosphere as possible. Judy loves its elegance, its good taste, the white rug, raw silk lampshades and sophisticated black and white prints on the walls. Here amidst a delicious blend of fragrances from bath oil, perfumes and expensive soaps, Etta listens to Piaf and Sablon, reads French magazines, and drifts away for a time from this backward place. Interestingly, Jhabvala speaks of her own room: "So I am back again alone in my room with the blinds drawn and the air conditioner on. Sometimes, when I think of my life, it seems to be contracted to this one point and to be concentrated in this one room." She says the *oppression* of very hot long afternoons is indescribable: "heat pressing down on me and pressing in the walls and the ceiling and congealing together with time which has stood still and will never move again. And it is not only those two—heat and time—that are laying their weight on me but behind them, or held within them, there is something more which I can only describe as the whole of India."[4]

How far do Etta's opinions echo those of Jhabvala, herself a foreigner married to an Indian ? The novelist puts it thus: "The most salient fact about India is that it is very poor and backward. There are so many other things to be said about it but this remains the basis of all of them. We may praise Indian democracy, go into raptures over Indian music, admire Indian intellectuals—but whatever we say, not for a moment should we lose sight of the fact that a very great number of Indians never get enough to eat . . . can one lose sight of the fact ? God knows I've tried."[5]

For Jhabvala, the undermining of her first feelings for India was a gradual process. An interview by Ramlal Agarwal is revealing:

R.A. The third novel *Esmond in India* shows a sudden change in your attitude and there has been an unmistakable note of bitterness in your work since then. What has brought this change in your attitude ?

R.J. I suppose it could be put down to my change of attitude towards India. I love everything during my first years here—I really loved it and was wildly excited by it and never wanted to go away from here. But later that changed. I saw a lot I didn't like. I'll go further: a lot that horrified me.[6]

That feeling of bitterness and horror spills over quite clearly into *A Backward Place*. Significantly, Jhabvala no longer resides in India, but has moved to the United States. "She still spends three months a year at her home in Delhi, but she's become an American citizen." Connie Hayball explains the move: "It is not surprising that Mrs. Jhabvala has found it impossible to live permanently in India. Her spirit shrank and trembled from the impact of Indian society, like naked flesh touched by knives."[8] Jhabvala found the escape that Etta and the 'girls' crave.

Odd though she is, Clarissa presents a refreshing change from Etta. Of the eight foreign women we are concerned with here, she alone is not married to an Indian. Indeed, she is not married at all. Years ago in England, she had read Romain Rolland's *Life of Vivekananda.* " I can remember so well the first time I read it. Something in me just—oh, I don't know, just snapped, I suppose, and I knew—that's where I belong." (p. 115) She congratulates Judy on how lucky she is to be in a typical Indian family. "Really I do, do so envy you, Judy. To live here among these simple people and speak their language and be just like them, I think it's wonderful." At this moment, the rag-merchant passes by shouting for old bottles and old papers. Clarissa adds, "You're part of India here ! You're right where its heart beats !" (pp. 158-159) Warmly approving of Judy, she passes judgment on Etta. "A person like Etta has no right to be here at all. She simply doesn't grasp that India calls for spiritual adjustments. She carries on as if this were Europe all over again—thinking of nothing but dressing herself up and strolling down Chandni Chowk as if it were the Champs Elysees." When Judy disagrees, Clarissa says firmly, "She's frivolous. Spiritually frivolous." (p. 159)

Of herself, Clarissa claims to be trying her utmost to shed "Western sophistication, to be simple again and in touch with the deep truths. It's not easy." (p. 159) As an artist, she claims to find inspiration in simple earthy types. Displaying the sketch of an old man that she has done, she says to an unappreciative Etta, "Doesn't he remind you of one of those Russian peasants you get in Tolstoy ? The same strength and earthiness. Only of course the Indian peasant has a sort of spiritual quality about him, a divine yearning which raises him—don't you feel that ?—above his own earthiness." (p. 23) Etta finds such talk hypocritical. "You may have noticed that she takes good care to get in with people who don't live in villages and who aren't in the least bit humble. She likes her comforts, does our Clarissa." (p. 34) And Etta speaks the truth. Clarissa enjoys every moment of the lush comfort in the home of the Kapurs who are not really her friends at all. During a meeting at the luxurious home of Mrs. Kaul, a rich pseudo-intellectual, having eaten heartily of the refreshments, and after a minor argument with Etta, Clarissa slips away to soothe herself with the comforts of a hot bath in Mrs. Kaul's beautiful primrose bathroom.

Clarissa may be more than a little foolish and her undiluted gushing over all things Indian need not be taken too seriously, however sincere she thinks she is. As she says herself, "Of course I'm mad, anyone'll tell you I'm completely crackers." (p. 117) Still, after the outpourings of Dalal's 'girls' and Etta, she offers an interesting contrast. But there is something quite pathetic about this aging English woman. Sudhir, a young Indian, thinks she is "intent on a quest in which notions of soul and God played a prominent, if vague, part; and how valiantly she had kept up this quest, or at least the pretence of it, though she was getting older year by year, and lonelier, and more ridiculous, and soul and God perhaps no nearer." (p. 117)

And finally there is Judy, the best-adjusted of all the women from overseas, though she is far from enjoying a comfortable life as most of the others do, free of financial worries. For all that, she has maintained her individuality as a person. She is not given to constant whining or carping about India, though in the material sense, she has the least. Judy and Bal with their two children live in a double-storeyed house in a side street, surrounded by shops. The courtyard which anyone can see from outside has a few old string cots and clothes drying on a line. One bedroom accommodates all four, and the other room is a kind of sitting room. The store has been given to the old aunt Bhuaji. The upper storey is occupied by Bal's brother and his family. A cooking shed and a very small bathroom complete the picture. Coming back from Etta's elegant place, Judy often rearranges the two cane chairs they possess, or strips the cover off the mattress concealing their trunks which constitutes their sofa. She is not unduly disturbed. Some day they will have nice furniture, " 'a sofa—and curtains—and new pictures—and a coffee table with an ashtray on it.' But even while she was saying it, she was losing interest. She was lying face down on what was now their sofa, and found it really quite comfortable; what more should one want ?" (p. 11)

Unlike the other foreign wives, Judy has no yearnings about England. Rather "Judy never cared to think much of home nowadays (whenever memories of it came up, she did her best to think of something else)." (p. 12) Her recollections of England are far from romantic. It was not that her childhood had been unhappy. But neither had she been very happy. Her father had worked in a factory making precision instruments. Her mother "cooked and cleaned and kept Judy away from strangers. Her mother didn't trust strangers; these included the neighbours. You were safest if you kept yourself to yourself. So they did, just the three of them, in that tight little house, with the doors and curtains firmly shut to keep the cold and the strangers out." (p. 39) Judy finds it painful to speak of her parents. Her father died of lung cancer after Judy came to India, and her mother committed suicide. Such memories were hardly pleasant. "She was vague about everything to do with England. Perhaps she had forgotten, or perhaps she only didn't want to remember." (p. 38)

Judy and Bal met in London at an International Youth social. She had collided with him and a splash of lemonade from his glass had fallen on her dress. Hardly worth mentioning, it had been enough to give them both an excuse to talk. Bal was just over twenty with a beautiful profile, white teeth, black eyes and thick black hair. He was full of dreams which he described to a wide-eyed seventeen year old Judy with her fair hair and bright blue eyes. Now ten years later and after two children, he is still dreaming, first about a theatre, and then about a cinema star he knows in Bombay, and becoming famous. His words are only too familiar to his wife. "It will be my big chance. It is everything we have always been waiting for Judy, just think, what an opportunity !" (p. 67) Far from being sarcastic or irritated by these recurrent enthusiasms, Judy loves them. Adoring Bal, she excuses his inability to hold down a steady job, for he is always chasing rainbows, while she works to support the family, actually enjoying her job.

No one knows Bal's weaknesses better than Judy. She worries about the future and makes a determined effort to save, fending off Bal's efforts to blow up her hoard on some lame-brain new scheme. She is no docile wife and sometimes even her patience is sorely tried. Once when her little son, Prithvi, is sick, Judy having nursed him all that hot day, lies exhausted on her string cot. Bal comes in, speaks very sweetly to the child, then announces he has to go out. "How I would love to stay with you, but you see how it is, poor Papa has to go and earn lots of money so he can buy his children nice food and toys and clothes, and medicines too when the poor darlings are sick." (pp. 26-27) Bal who likes to call himself an artiste, is actually a small time actor. Just now he is off to see the film star, Kishan Kumar, in the hope that he will put something big in Bal's way. When Prithvi asks for ice water, Judy asks Bal to get some ice. Pretending he has not heard, he goes out quickly. Judy catches up with him on the street, and holds his kurta sleeve. Her face is pink and the blue eyes are angry. Bal tries feebly to explain how important it is for him to keep his contacts, but looking at his wife, thinks better of it, and goes off to bring ice. Judy feels no satisfaction over her victory. In fact, she feels mean for the rest of the evening.

In Dalal's novel, Louise and Jane find the presence of their in-laws infuriating. Judy, however, has established a fine rapport with her sister-in-law Shanti, and the old lady, Bhuaji. To entertain Shanti who is confined to the house, she tells little stories about the many things that have happened that day, delighting that individual. Judy enjoys sitting with them in the courtyard late at night in pleasant companionable silence when all the children are asleep. The other two love Bal and so Judy does not resent Shanti saying she wishes Bal would earn something, especially in view of the children's future. "God provides," Bhuaji says, and Judy agrees, although she does not share the old lady's deep belief in God's goodness. But she has "a kind of easy faith that someone—and she didn't much care who—would provide, and that, when the time came, everything always worked out." (p. 79) From her father, she has inherited a distrust of the pious—"bloody hypocrites, the lot of them," he would say, (pp. 79-80) but her visits to the river with the good Bhuaji make her feel that perhaps the aged aunt is right.

In a significant episode, Judy gets cross with Bal. She and a few others have been working hard on plans for the theatre of Bal's dreams, only to find he has almost forgotten it, and is now busy with other rosy dreams about Kishan Kumar. Bursting into tears, leaving behind an anxious Bal, Judy goes out to join Bhuaji who is just leaving the temple, and walks with her to the river. It is full of people sitting in a relaxed way in the cool of the evening. Bhuaji soon gets engrossed in the talk of a holy man, but Judy understands only snatches of it. "Suddenly and for no particular reason she could mention she remembered evenings at home in England: how they sat hunched round the fire muffled in their woollies in their little parlour in their little house with the windows and curtains shut tight against the rain.. But that was far away, long ago, and now here she was where all was boundless and open in the warm air, the river and the sky and the sand, everything wrapped in a veil of pearl-grey evening light faintly tinged with pink, through which gleamed only the golden clouds and the black bridge with red buses on it." (pp. 111-112) The peace of the atmosphere touches her. She forgets why she ran away and her anger. "She only remembered Bal sitting so sweetly on the string cot and looking after her surprised and sad, and she felt full of love for him and wanted to go home." (p. 112)

Yet Judy's love for Bal is sorely taxed with his latest most exasperating dream. He wants to go to Bombay. In his mind, he is already a film star. "You don't believe in me, but when you see me acclaimed by millions, then you will know !" (p. 223) It is rare for them to quarrel, but on this issue there are long frequent arguments. Bal is fully confident about his future, whereas Judy clings to what security she has. Still, what is she giving up ? Their furniture is mostly fit for the junk heap. "These too seemed a trivial cause to tie one down in a world which was so wide, encompassed by a sky out of which perhaps someone spoke." (p. 223) Ultimately she capitulates. She could always get a job. "She had done it before, she could do it again." (p. 223) It would be a happy thing to be able to feel that at last applause and bouquets await Bal. But if they do not, with a wife like Judy, loving and loyal, they will manage.

Both *The Girls from Overseas* and *A Backward Place* probe deeply into East-West relationships, more specifically, East-West marriage. With the exception of Judy, no single wife has accepted her situation with equanimity. For them, the cons have far outweighed the pros. In one case, that of Gertrude Das, the individual's very sanity is affected. India has shaken to the core values they grew up with, has set them adrift on an endless, often stormy, sea. Yet all of them must resign themselves to a lifetime in India because there are no alternatives, because survival becomes the prime concern. The culture will remain alien, the Indians to them impossible 'barbarians,' the heat and flies ever-present, and the in-laws forever underfoot, but they must stay on.

NOTES

1. Nergis Dalal, *The Girls from Overseas* (Hind Pocket Books, Delhi, 1979).

2. D.R. Sharma, "The Creative Art of Nergis Dalal," *The Journal of Indian Writing in English*, January 1977, p. 23.

3. Ruth Prawer Jhabvala, *A Backward Place* (Hind Pocket Books, Delhi, 1965).

4. *London Magazine*, September, 1970, quoted by Vasant Shahane in *Ruth Prawer Jhabvala* (Arnold-Heinemann, New Delhi, 1976), p. 22.

5. "Myself in India" in *An Experience of India* (John Murray, London, 1967), p. 8.

6. Ramlal Agarwal, "An Interview with Ruth Prawer Jhabvala," *Quest* (Bombay), September-October, 1974, p. 34.

7. Laura Shapiro, "When East Meets West," *Newsweek*, August 31, 1987, p. 48.

8. Connie Hayball, "Ruth Prawer Jhabvala's India," *The Journal of Indian Writing in English*, July 1981, p. 54.

The Art and Achievement of Jhabvala

R. G. AGARWAL

Jhabvala's novels and stories were written during her stay in India. As such, her work belongs to the literary scene in the country. Her achievements too have to be studied in relation to the achievements of the best of contemporary writers in India. Raja Rao and Jhabvala write with diametrically opposed visions and styles. In *The Serpent and the Rope* Raja Rao deals with India as an idea of the Absolute, an idea of eternity. As Meenakshi Mukherjee says in her book *The Twice Born Fiction:*

> It is India, Brahminical India, which represents the quintessence of *advait* philosophy. India at all other levels is excluded.[1]

Jhabvala, in contrast, deals with India at the social, cultural and intellectual levels. She is more concerned with the social realities than with abstract philosophies. In this respect Jhabvala is in tune with the Western concept of the novel.

Jhabvala's work is closer to R.K. Narayan's. Both writers view their worlds ironically and with detachment. Both of them do not make radical experiments in the use of English but stick to the standard prose. But they differ from each other in their approach and vision. R.K. Narayan observes petty villainies and follies with amusement. 'India will go on,' said Narayan to Naipaul. In an article in the *New York Review of Books* dated April 29, 1976, Naipaul says that the conviction that India is eternal leads to indifference. He points out how the hero of *Mr. Sampath* has withdrawn into a world of non-doing—'Life and the world and all this is passing—why bother about anything ? The perfect and the imperfect are all the same. Why really bother ?' The theme of *The Man-eater of Malgudi* is that evil destroys itself. It is this kind of religious conviction in Narayan which provokes Naipaul to comment:

> For all their delight in human oddity, Narayan's novels are less the purely social comedies I had once taken them to be than religious

books, at times, religious fables and intensely Hindu.[2]

Jhabvala is totally unaffected by religion. She is not concerned with ideological interpretations. Her only concern is with the presentation of a graphic picture of the society around her. She writes about the furious social scuffling in present-day India, and describes the head-on collision between the traditional and the modern, the East and the West and the confusion that follows in the wake of these collisions. She is not a practitioner of the psychological novel. In each of her novels, she writes about the corporate life of two or three families. Her novels are singularly devoid of accidents, coincidences and sudden shifts of fortunes. On the contrary, they are full of the drab routine of daily life, so much that they tend to be tritely repetitive. It is for this reason that she has been able to describe the domestic and social life of Indians as no other writer writing in English has ever done. In her work to date, Jhabvala has handled a variety of themes. In her earlier work she deals with the stronghold of tradition and traditional wisdom and how in present-day India tradition and modernity go hand in hand. She also takes up the theme of East-West encounter and its disastrous effects. In her later work she is engaged in writing about *gurus* and the fate of Europeans who come to India, the country of vast stretches of dry, parched land and white, monotonous landscape smouldering with heat and boredom, and its debilitating effect upon people. Jhabvala's art is the art of portraiture and each one of her novels is a portrait of some aspects of India, larger than life by design.

II

Jhabvala's novels and stories are about Indians and Westerners in India. In her first five novels about Indians Jhabvala has mainly dealt with marriage, money, the Indian wife, the Indian householder and the Indian social reformer. The titles of these novels, except *Esmond in India*, indicate Jhabvala's approach. She presents Indians in terms of Indian codes of conduct for businessmen, wives, householders and social reformers. Indian society, for all its progress in science and technology, is traditional to the core. It still works according to the ethical and moral stipulations as expressed in sacred books. Therefore, the Indian girls are to be married in a class and caste to which they belong, the Indian businessman need have no pangs of uneasy conscience as it is his nature to make more and more money, the Indian wife has to put up with the tyrannies of her husband, the Indian householder must live up to the duties expected of him and a social reformer must continue to work, treating alike gain and loss. Indians accept these codes almost instinctively. Hari in *To Whom She Will* accepts the dominion of tradition; Lalaji in *The Nature of Passion* accepts his selfish nature because he thinks it is his fate; Gulab in *Esmond in India* accepts the duties and obligations of a wife as they are defined by tradition; Prem in *The Householder* tries to live up to the traditional role of a householder; and Sarla Devi in *Get Ready for Battle* accepts the philosophy of 'treating alike pleasure and pain, gain and loss, victory and defeat, then get ready for battle.'

Jhabvala's depiction of the working of these codes in modern times is in terms of the major concerns of the novel like appearance and reality, snobbery, uneasiness, illusions, fantasy and other effects of money and the dangers of passions which tend to be wilful, imperious and impatient.

All through her work Jhabvala shows a concern for reality. Her characters, on the other hand, are reduced by mere appearance. Amrita feels drawn towards Hari because he seems to be unsullied by the vulgarity of opulence. Nimmi is attracted towards Phiroz because he seems to her to be the quintessence of modern man. Esmond married Gulab because he thought that her eyes were deep, sad and full of the wisdom of the East. Jhabvala describes her characters's fascination for mere appearance, and their slow disillusionment.

Her novels about Westerners in India show the Western involvement in post-Independence India. In these novels Jhabvala deals with the various reasons for which Westerners come out to India and how their attitudes towards India are conditioned by the nature of their stay in the country and by their native sensibilities. In her novels about Westerners in India Jhabvala emphasizes the fact that Westerners are no longer here as conquerors but as the conquered ones.

In her novels about Indians as well as in her novels about Westerners in India, Jhabvala presents vivid portraits of certain aspects of Indian society. Her area of exploration is the social world and the material of her analysis, manners. To Jhabvala, reality is whatever is external and hard, though it could be gross and unpleasant. She writes the novels of character which are concerned with expressing the modes of existence rather than the images of experience. Her work is devoid of thrills, violence and esoteric elements. Jhabvala is never a mere casual observer of the Indian scene. She writes mainly about the middle class because this is the class she knows best. She shows a characteristically Western awareness of social problems.

III

Indian critics have said that Jhabvala deals with surfacial life, that her characters are static and that her fiction is monstrous distortion. In fact the very titles of her novels about Indians show that she is concerned with Indian wisdom and philosophy. Though she writes about the middle class society and about Westerners in India, she shows an admirable awareness of Indian problems by and large. She is aware of Indian poverty and of the indifference, callousness and moral squalor that afflict the middle class. She succeeds in presenting the will-less, wavering and drifting lives of Indian youth, the bickering and possessive Indian mothers and the raising callous and unscrupulous middle class in post-Independence India. The charge about 'static' characters is not wholly untrue. Her characters are definitely static and there is certainly some exaggeration in her depiction of characters and situations. All her characters have exaggerated traits which creates an impression that they are meant to be caricatures. But static characters and exaggerations are necessary for the kind of novel Jhabvala writes. She writes about anti-heroes who are terribly conditioned by their religious, social and economic traditions and oppressed by sweltering heat. Small wonder if they lead false and empty lives. It is not Indians alone who are depicted in this manner but also the English and the Americans who abandon themselves to the weird charm of the East. She takes a group of men and women and describes them as they move from day to day. The boredom or routine life and desperate attempts to run away from it by taking refuge in *ashrams*, which promise peace but make life more complicated, form the bulk of her fiction. Jhabvala adjusts her prose to suit her purpose. Not for nothing is her prose so slow and devoid of poetic embellishments. It is the slow, dull, false lives of her characters described in slow, simple, economical prose which creates a cumulative effect of total futility and aimlessness. Jhabvala has an eye for the ridiculous but she is also aware that what is ludicrous on the surface is tragic underneath. Jhabvala's characters are given just enough definite traits to carry on. Their deeds and adventures, their tragic predicaments, or the rowdy pranks in which they deport themselves are not mere episodes in a literary farrago: these are, unmistakable, pages torn from the daily register of life as it goes on.

A kind of puerility marks the entire behaviour of Amrita and Nimmi, two of Jhabvala's heroines. A kind of looseness or will-lessness is the hallmark of Hari and Viddi. Greed is the driving passion of Lalaji. Sloth and sloppiness rule the world of Gulab. Sarla Devi is a little too unworldly and Kusum is a little too coquettish. In an article on Dickens, George Orwell says: "His (Tolstoy's) characters are struggling to make their souls, whereas Dickens's people are present far more often and far more vividly than Tolstoy's, but always in a single unchangeable attitude, like pictures or places of furniture."[3] Perhaps unchangeability is the cause of the popularity of Dickens's characters. And so it is with Jhabvala's. Hari, Viddi, Inder Lal are characters, who in spite of their 'flatness' leave a lasting impression. 'India always changes,' Jhabvala has said time and again. It certainly changes Westerners, though they do not grow. On the contrary, there is a marked diminution in them. Etta, Clarissa and Judy from *A Backward Place* and Margaret, Evie and Lee from *A New Dominion* might have lived a full life in their countries but here in India they sink to the bottom of degradation and sloth. Moreover, India changes them much in the same way. So there is always a static pattern of action in Jhabvala's novels.

Jhabvala's fictional strategy in creating her fictional world is to take a central character and build around him or her a set of incidents which are so arranged as to reinforce the validity of the kind of world she creates. Jhabvala's art consists in recreating a typical social context by slow, patient, careful accumulation of details. The details include small actions, dress, decorations, gestures, the words that are used with a special frequency, the choice of food etc. The massive accumulation of detail leads to the establishment of a cultural identity of the people she writes about. As an outsider, Jhabvala's first business is to know and then to impart all she knows in terms that would make her readers see and hear and feel a lively sense of actuality. Jhabvala fastens herself instinctively on to the truly revealing aspects of life in India. In her first five novels

Jhabvala is mainly concerned with the presentation of Indian codes of conduct. In order to do so she plays up certain character-traits and introduces extreme situations. The situations are so arranged as to highlight the character-traits. They are continuously reshuffled and redistributed to suggest a mode of existence. This strategy suits Jhabvala's purpose because she is not interested in individuals or their psychology. She is interested in social life. A part of her fictional strategy is her art of juxtaposition of highly incongruous characters. In her novels about Westerners in India, Jhabvala is concerned with various attitudes the Westerners in India adopt towards this country. So she takes up characters that represent these attitudes and brings them together in situations that would highlight their attitudes. But while her characters are busy reaffirming and reinforcing their various points of views Jhabvala is busy showing how the overall reality of India affects them. In *A New Dominion* and *Heat and Dust* Jhabvala employs more sophisticated techniques. *A New Dominion* uses the combined technique of direct narration, epistolary form and autobiography to present its characters. In *Heat and Dust* Jhabvala employs the strategy of two parallel stories to distinguish between the temporal and the timeless aspects of life in India.

IV

Jhabvala's distinctive achievement as a novelist lies in the fact that, while Indian writers writing about Indian mores tend to deviate from the British tradition of the novel and evolve a more indigenous form especially suited to Indian life, but not universally acceptable to the Western readers, she works within the British tradition and presents Indian life in terms that would be acceptable to the Western readers. Though an outsider, Jhabvala shows an unusual insight into Indian mores. She sees India with a Western perspective. Radha and Uma, the two anxious mothers in *To Whom She Will* and *Esmond in India*, for example, are presented ironically rather than sentimentally as they would be by Indian writers. What is sentimental for Indian writers is comic to her. The material that would get melodramatic treatment from Indian writers gets ironical treatment from her. She never allows her Western sensibility to be overwhelmed by the Indian scene. Writers like Kipling and Forster were highly fascinated by Indian mysticism but not so Jhabvala. So her fictional presentation of Indian life with a strictly Western perspective is unique. A theme through her novels about Indians in post-Independence India is the frustrations of people who fought for Independence. It is fully treated in her first three novels. Few novelists writing about India have dealt with it more poignantly. Running parallel to this theme is the theme of moral squalor among the newly rich. The intensity and technical excellence with which it is dealt is rarely met in writings about India. In her novels about Westerners in India, Jhabvala is perhaps the only writer who has dealt with the nature of Western involvement in post-Independence India, on a large scale.

For over a quarter of a century Jhabvala's novels and stories have been the Westerners's window on India. Her technical skill, her unusual insights, her cool and controlled brilliance and her sustained work have carved for her a place in the front rank of the writers of the world.

NOTES

1. Meenakshi Mukherjee, *The Twice Born Fiction* (New Delhi: Arnold Heinemann, 1971), p. 91.

2. V.S. Naipaul, "India: The End of a Civilization," *New York Review of Books*, April 29, 1976, p. 20.

3. George Orwell, "Charles Dickens," *The Dickens Critics*, ed. Fort and Lane (New York: Cornell University Press, 1961), p. 166.

Anita Desai and Arun Joshi: A Comparative Study

LAL UDAI BHAN PANDEY

The mechanized industrialization has come down very heavily on the nerves of modern man. It has injected into man terrific speed and has thrown him to "sick hurry and divided aims." It has instilled in him enervating sense of competitiveness. Modern fiction has made bold attempts to trace out the fundamental crux of the social crisis in the pervading gloom of human affliction. It has shifted its focus from the outer space of social phenomena to inner atmosphere of individual's predicament. Leslie Paul observes: "If there is one constant theme in the works of modern novelists and playwrights, it is the depth and persistence of human affliction, and indeed that this affliction scourges most heavily the sensitive, the loving, the compassionate, so that not to be afflicted is to be less than human."[1]

Arun Joshi and Anita Desai faithfully record contemporary man's tortures and traumas. Chief protagonists of their novels are abject outsiders and stark strangers. They are unable to communicate with the world at large and relate themselves with the surroundings. In *Cry, the Peacock*, the protagonist Maya experiences stifling alienation from her husband, so does Bimal Biswas from his wife in *The Strange Case of Billy Biswas*. For them the house itself becomes a cage, where their souls groan and grumble and struggle to untie the chains around them. Existential predicament is the *Zeit quist* of all the major characters of their novels. They are tormented, tortured introverts, non-conformists and stranded wanderers. Nirode and Sindi Oberoi are rootless drifters devoid of love and affection; Monisha and Sita are highly sensitive and lonely women pitted against upper and middle class philistinism. Experiencing disgusting absurdity of the world, they discover meaning only in self-immolation. John Cruickshank writes: "If the world is irremediably absurd, and if one is a stranger to oneself as well as to other people and to material things, then to commit suicide is to behave as though such action itself could have value or meaning in a meaningless existence."[2]

Major characters of these two novelists come closer to Kafka's heroes or Camus's outsiders. Billy Biswas, Deven, Maya, Monisha, Sita persistently endeavour to unravel the hidden meaning of life. They are enamoured of a primaeval, pagan life lived in a close communion with Nature. Billy Biswas is like Arnold's Scholar Gipsy wandering to listen to the silent whispers of the unseen and behold the spark from heaven.

Arun Joshi's *The Strange Case of Billy Biswas* is a harsh indictment of engrossing materialistic pursuits of civilized world. To Billy, materialism deadens the sparkle of life and dehumanizes the being. He is astounded to note mad rush of civilization after the getting and spending of fortunes. Billy believes that civilization can't be imagined without money and fortunes. He exclaims: "I sometimes wonder whether civilization is anything more than the making and spending of money. What else does the civilized man do ? And if there are those who are not busy earning and spending—the so called thinkers and philosophers and men like that—they are merely hired to find solution, throw light, as they say, on complications caused by this making and spending of money. What need would there be of psychiatrists, research foundations, learned societies, great scholars, scientists, ministerial advisers, ambassadors, generals, had the world not initially been hung on this peg of money." [3]

In Anita Desai's *Voices in the City*, Monisha too feels the agonizing disgust ensuing from the loss of ethics in the urban houses of Calcutta. She is overtaken by nausea: "Here they dwell, in these houses of cut-throat, eye-for-eye rapacity, of money greed and money ruthlessness, to bless those who fatten upon it."[4] (p. 117) *In Cry, the Peacock*, Maya is vexed at the way people get farther and farther from the radiance of real and sublime vision of life and pained at the blind pursuit of people for the meaningless trivialities of life. Her depression limelights the modern existential predicament: "It is because they are so engroosed in—in all that's gross and useless, that they don't see what really matters." (p. 91)

Arun Joshi and Anita Desai behold something mysterious and magical in the fabulous bounty of Nature. Both are captivated by the charms of Nature. Both believe that man's true elements are traceable and revealed in the Nature's benign presence. Sublimating impressions of Nature are discernible in the hero of *The Strange Case of Billy Biswas:* "He stood on a rock and saw in the night sky a reality that blinded him with its elemental ferocity. It was as though his life had been reduced to those elements with which we all begin when we are born. 'Come' they cried. 'It is with us that you begin and with us that you will end.' " (p. 141)

The heroine of Anita Desai's *Where Shall We Go This Summer ?* considers the Island as the only 'alternative' amidst the torments of her city life. Moreover it will have rejuvenating effect upon the personality of her children. Their true elemental grandeur would unfold in the graceful environs of Island, since "the tides would lull the children, too, into smoother, softer beings. The grove of trees would shade them and protect them." (p. 101)

Both these Indian-English writers have a sombre vision of human existence. Both have tried to invent a new world based on justice, continuity and coherence as Camus in his concerted and life-long endeavour tried to transcend the merciless, discontinuous and unjust climate. They have "kept watch o'er man's mortality" and human suffering and have tried to evolve "faith that looks through death."[4]

NOTES

1. Leslie Paul, "*The Writer and the Human Condition,*" *Kenyon Review*, No. 1, XXIV (Jan. 1967), p. 37.

2. John Cruickshank, *Albert Camus and the Literature of Revolt.* (New York: O.U.P., 1960), pp. 60-61.

3. Arun Joshi, *The Strange Case of Billy Biswas* (New Delhi: Hind Pocket Books, 1971), pp. 96-97.

4. Wordsworth, "Ode on Intimations of Immortality."

The Image of India in Anita Desai's *Clear Light of Day*

VRINDA NABAR

My students commonly respond to *Clear Light of Day* with misgivings about what they call "its real Indianness." According to them, (1) its ethos is too Westernized; (2) Bim is not "typically Indian"; (3) the koels at the beginning of the novel, like the other Indian images in it, are too strident to be more than obvious attempts at introducing local colour.

These doubts could equally appropriately be applied to the study of Ms. Desai's fiction as a whole. They are partly related to the Indianness or alleged lack of it in Anita Desai's work. More precisely, however, they are responses to the very select section of Indian society which she writes about. It is, obviously, a largely Westernized section. But Westernization, as seen in the novels, is a definite aspect of Indian urban reality.

It should be said of Anita Desai that she presents this aspect more convincingly, more authentically too, than any other contemporary Indian English writer of fiction. The authenticity is strengthened by the fact that she is also the most skilled of the Indian English novelists from the point of view of pure craftsmanship. Whatever one's differences with her in terms of the attitudes/stances taken in the novels, it cannot in all fairness be denied that her work is characterised by her awareness of the formal needs of the novel as a genre. Nor are these Aspects of the Novel used as mere appurtenances. They are intrinsic to the story and are handled with an instinctive and imaginative understanding of their potential in fiction.

This is clearly seen in the present novel. Anita Desai is reported to have described it as an attempt to write "a four-dimensional piece on how a family's life moves backwards and forwards in a period of time."[1] The fourth dimension, she has further clarified, is the dimension of Time.[2] The novei is in four chapters, effectively four parts. Each of these deals with distinct periods in the lives of the principal characters, the first and the last of them being set in the present.

The "four-dimensional" reality is used by Ms. Desai to make the intervening sections more than just a conventional trip down memory-lane. While she retains control of the narrative, the scenes from the past are made to unmistakably relate to the present consciousness of the characters. Tara's homecoming triggers off in Bim memories of a past that has lost much of its enchantment in the drab framework of the present. The past is suppressed by Bim in an attempt to put the lid on unpleasant pointers to the truth about her situation. At the beginning of the novel, we see her largely in relation to the myth she has allowed to develop around her. In Chapter 4, Tara wonders how this myth had grown, seeing little to support it in the Bim she now encounters:

> She had always thought Bim so competent, so capable. Everyone had thought that—Aunt Mira, the teachers at school, even Raja. But Bim seemed to stampede through the house like a dishevelled storm, creating more havoc than order. Tara would be ashamed to run a house like this. Bakul would have been horrified if she did. Then how had Bim acquired her fine reputation ? Or had her old capability, her old competence begun to crumble now and go to seed ? Tara saw how little she had really observed—either as a child or as a grown woman.

Tara's return home, her tactless blundering into the past, her naive responses to the present, force Bim to face up to the real emptiness of her life. It is not as if she was actually unaware of it, merely that she had tried to suppress the awareness. The journey into the past could thus be seen as a journey into the subconscious. Ms. Desai gives it just that degree of distortion, of formlessness, while adhering to the sequential pattern, to create the impression of a "psychoanalytic" process at work. Tara's presence and the undercurrents she generates form a kind of figurative psychiatrist's couch on which Bim as it were finds herself.

Just before Bim comes to terms with her real situation, she is shown as dangerously close to neurosis. Tara says she talks to herself. Almost paranoid, Bim begins to see Tara as a mean, prying person. She resents the unspoken opinion that spinsterhood was making her queer. When her anger erupts, it finds an easy target in Baba, whom she has never consciously admitted as a brake on her freedom to choose.

Bim's loss of control is followed by a mood of introspection in which she sees "as well as by the clear light of day" that she is inextricably bound to her siblings, as dependent on their love and approval as they are on hers. Whether such a denouement is wholly satisfying or not, the direction it takes is significant for two reasons. First, it gives us evidence of an organic growth in character. Bim, like most of Ms. Desai's other characters, is not the "same" at the end of the novel. Ms. Desai uses the various events, incidents etc. in the plot to affect her characters substantially. In this way she prevents the characters from becoming static and the novel from degenerating into little more than an anecdotal narrative. Secondly, the kind of reconciliation with the self that Bim achieves, inseparable as it is from her family set up, emphasizes that *Clear Light of Day* cannot be anything other than an "Indian" novel. This not merely because it is set in Delhi, or because its characters are all Indian, but because its situations, images, as well as its central conflicts can only be satisfactorily explained in an Indian context.

Bim's entire dilemma is born out of this context. Approaching middle age, Bim is fairly representative of a certain type of contemporary Indian urban woman—single, independent, self-assured. On a superficial level, such a woman may be seen as "westernized." After all, Bim even smokes !

Further, she clearly belongs to a class easily identifiable in Ms. Desai's novels, a class which is comfortably off, anglicized, even neo-colonial. However, like Ms. Desai's other female characters, like most of the Indian women whom she recognizably resembles, Bim is also conditioned by her Indian environment. It is *this* environment which positions her as the moral and physical caretaker of the Das household after her parents die. Their deaths unhinge timid Mira-*masi* who had functioned capably enough as long as they pulled the strings and gave the orders. As she disintegrates into alcoholism, Tara marries Bakul, largely to "escape" as she admits later. Bim, saddled with her alcoholic aunt and retarded brother, accommodates them into her scheme of things. Her Western counterpart in similar circumstances would have most likely dumped them both into appropriate homes in order to preserve her existential freedom. Even Raja leaves for Hyderabad as soon as he is physically fit enough to do so.

Bim's continued solitude is likewise a reflection of her environment. Except for the unfortunate trespasses of Dr. Biswas, she remains singularly devoid of any male companionship. Nor does this singleness appear to produce any visible tensions or conflicts. In another, Western, context it is easy to imagine Bim having some kind of a compulsive relationship with a man—sexual, of course, even if not necessarily harmonious or secure—if only as an emotional release.

The Das household, seen at different periods of time, follows a recognizable pattern. The endless games of bridge the parents play, punctuated by their visits to the Club, the self-contained world in which they move, throw the children closer together. Raja is the characteristic older son, spoilt, self-centred, largely irresponsible. Tara, timid and insecure, generally withdrawn from the games Bim and Raja play, draws comfort and warmth from the presence of Mira-*masi*. Mira-*masi* is true to type, a widowed aunt, a financial dependent and therefore *persona non grata* in the household. At the same time, she provides the only affection and caring the children know. Ms. Desai effectively sums up her presence as associated, for Tara, with her smell.

> . . . she was solid as a bed, she smelt of cooking and was made of knitting. Tara could wrap herself up in her as in an old soft shawl. This Tara needed for she had lost most at Baba's birth and the turning of the entire family from her to the new baby. Wrapped in the folds of Aunt Mira's white cotton sari, or into her loosely knitted grey shawl, or the plump billows of the plum-coloured quilt in winter, she became baby again, breathing in her aunt's smell, finding in it a deep, musty comfort.

In the Indian context, Ms. Desai could not have picked a more effective image. The role of an elderly aunt, of an *ayah* as the children's most constant companion was and is an all-too-familiar feature of Indian family life. This presence is usually bound up with a sense of the person's smell. In later years, it is this smell that remains as a memory, not so much the way a person looked or dressed.

Having "escaped" from home, the two siblings are not wholly "free." Guilt becomes a major emotion in the novel. While there is nothing specifically Indian about such guilt it supports the basic ambience of Indianness. Faced with Raja's letter in the first chapter the reader responds principally to its insensitive tone. In Chapter 4, the letter, seen retrospectively, becomes a symbol of Raja's sense of guilt. That guilt is evident at the end of chapter 2 when Raja leaves, promising to return and look after Bim and Baba. It is evident in his angry justification of his action, provoked by Bim's silence which is more effective than any reproof:

> She kept calm while Raja packed his bags, put away all his things, telling her that now he would go to Hyderabad. Looking up at her as she watched silently, he shouted 'I have to go. Now I can go. I have to begin my life some time, don't I ? You don't want me to spend all my life down in this hotel, do you ? You don't want me to spend all my life down in this hole, do you ? You don't think I can go on living just to keep my brother and sister company, do you ?
>
> 'I never said a word,' said Bim coldly.
>
> 'You don't have to. It's written all over your face. Just go, go, take your face away. Don't sit there staring. Don't stop me.'

Had Bim reacted otherwise, a bitter confrontation might have provided Raja with a framework to rationalize his leaving. When he goes, he is unable to help himself but he continues to feel uneasy about this assertion of his choice. His letter is a means to prove to Bim that he still cares for her, that he wishes to help. It is characteristic of his ego-ridden temperament that he can only make reparations in this clumsy, hurtful way.

Tara's marriage, seen as an escape, liberates her in several superficial ways. When she returns she is socially poised, more confident, less nervy. Yet, coming back, she slips into the old grooves in a manner which irritates her pompous diplomat husband. He can't understand her wanting to spend her time with her sister and brother instead of romping around New Delhi with him. The reason for Tara's confused inertia is that her homecoming shows her sharply and unmistakably what she had left Bim to cope with.

As Tara reluctantly confronts the reality of life in her childhood home Ms. Desai uses an incident from adolescence as a symbol of her guilt. As young girls, Bim and Tara had accompanied some neighbours on a picnic to the Lodhi Gardens. Bim had been attacked by a swarm of bees. Tara recalls abandoning Bim and fleeing away to the others—to safety. Bim's matter-of-fact explanation—Tara had to get help—is not acceptable to Tara. She continues to beat her breast, metaphorically speaking, at having escaped and abandoned Bim. It is easy to see a parallel between this somewhat superficial incident and the real abandoning of Bim by her sister and brother.

Like Raja and Tara, Bim too is subject to a kind of guilt. At one level it is apparent that her staying back was a matter of compulsion, not of choice. At another level, however, one suspects that, even given the choice, Bim would have found it extremely difficult to go away voluntarily as Raja and Tara had done. Having stayed, however, she sees her action as a kind of sacrifice. Naturally, too, she feels hemmed-in. A sort of defensive mechanism makes her project herself as self-sufficient and satisfied with her mode of living. This is why her attack on Baba produces the turmoil in her. It makes her guilt surface, and forces her to recognise the ambivalent feelings in herself.

The handling of these characters makes it apparent that an exclusive concentration on the narrow boundaries of class-experience need not in itself be limiting. It becomes so only if the writer allows such exclusion to become a fetish. And Ms. Desai appears dangerously close to doing so. Her novels, understandably, deal with the class she knows best, but they do so at the expense of shuttering out the much more complex Indian reality. She admits as much in reply to Ramesh Srivastava's observation that vast areas of the Indian experience cannot be within her easy reach: "Lack of experience may be a handicap but lack of sensitivity, thought, intelligence or memory would be far greater ones. I do restrict myself to writing about people and situations I know or can understand."[3]

In the novels such a stand tends to black out the kind of intermingling of classes which is inevitable in the Indian context. Where presented, the method is far from satisfactory. Its limitations can be seen in the depiction of servants who are commonly described as being either sullen and inefficient (like Janaki) or cringing and false (like Bhakta, Hyder Ali's driver). At a more serious level, such exclusion raises doubts about the creative development of a writer. It is, after all, a writer's business to expand his or her experience, not to justify a fictional ivory tower based on a limited class-experience. The drawbacks in Ms. Desai's refusal to transcend her class-conditioning are apparent in at least two major instances in this novel, both of which effect the authenticity of the Indian experience.

The first relates to Mira-*masi*. We have already noted how Ms. Desai brings out the essence of Mira-*masi*'s presence—her smell. It must be added that this picture, though convincing, is still somewhat amorphous since it does not really individualise Mira—*masi*, but merely puts her into a recognisable slot. All the same it emerges as authentic, especially in contrast to the attempt to shade in Mira-*masi*'s past, obviously done in order to give her depth:

> Aunt Mira was younger than their mother although she looked so much older. She had been twelve years old when she married and was a virgin when she was widowed—her young student husband, having left to study in England immediately after their wedding, caught a cold in the rain one winter night, and died. She was left stranded with his family and they blamed her bitterly for his death: it was her unfortunate horoscope that had brought it about, they said. She should be made to pay for her guilt. Guiltily, she scrubbed and washed and cooked for them. At night she massaged her mother-in-law's legs and nursed wakeful babies and stitched trousseaux for her sisters-in-law. Of course she aged. Not only was her hair white but she was nearly bald. At least that saved her from being used by her brothers-in-law who would have put the widow to a different use had she been more appetising. Since she was not, they eyed her unpleasing person sullenly and made jokes loudly enough for her to overhear. There was laughter, till they grew bored. She stayed with them so long that she became boring. They suspected her of being a parasite. It was time she was turned out. She was turned out. Another household could find some use for her: cracked pot, torn rag, picked bone.

That is Mira-*masi*'s history, dismissed in just one paragraph. The details are Indian alright, but too pat. They sound suspect, a little too reeled-off. They almost add up to The Life of the Typical Indian Widow. One might argue that Mira-*masi* was too lifeless to be individualised in any distinctive way, but such a view does not support the evidence of the final drama—her alcoholism and insanity, both consequent upon the death of Bim's parents.

As a psychological outcome to these deaths, Mira-*masi*'s collapse is an example of imaginative versatility. But Ms. Desai flounders because the imaginative world, not sustained by the reality of experience, produces weird pictures of Mira-*masi*'s madness. She projects an

Ophelia-like lewdness and this sense of her is borne out by Bim's own recollection of her aunt as a drowned Ophelia. While the form Ophelia's madness takes is logically accountable within the dramatic framework of *Hamlet* there are no corresponding logical connections in the instance of Mira-*masi*. In her the transformation from self-effacing aunt to dipsomaniac slattern comes across as bizarre and inappropriate, an unhappy consequence thrust upon her by the novelist.

Almost as ludicrous is the description of the Misra household in Chapter 3. In it, the Misras are contrasted with the Das household to the partial detriment of the latter. There is an ironic reference to the paraphernalia which constituted the hallmark of respectability to Tara's parents: "curtains at the windows, carpets on the floors, solid pieces of furniture placed at regular intervals, plates that matched each other on the table, white uniforms for the house servants."

The Misras are meant to provide a healthy contrast, but even so a fastidious reserve on the novelist's part converts informality into sloppiness and chaos. The picture painted is moreover so inaccurate in parts as to underscore the writer's remoteness from her subject. For instance we are told that "Meals were ordered in a haphazard way and when the family smelt something good cooking, they dipped impatiently into the cooking pots as soon as it was ready instead of waiting for the clock hands to move to the appointed hour."

One can't really conceive of a conventional Indian household operating in this way. The plates may not match, the servants stay bare-chested, the furniture appear irregular and unfashionable, but routine there will most certainly be. It will, besides, be a routine that will not permit of whimsical dipping into cooking-pots since, to the traditional Hindu, such an act would make the food "unclean."

But even these cameos are not wholly unacceptable. They may appear partly limited but a basic sense of wanting to do the right thing is apparent. Not so when certain other experiences are presented. In this novel, the most obvious example is the tea-party at the Biswas's. Before it, we see Dr. Biswas, an earnest, pathetic figure whose love of Mozart is a subject of immense amusement to Raja and Bim. Already an attitude which becomes obtrusively neo-colonial is beginning to assert itself. Not being "one of us," Dr. Biswas has of course no right to admire Mozart. In response to the knowledge that he does, Raja can only clutch at his heart and theatrically murmur "Ach so Mozart !"

One might concede here that it is Raja and Bim whose responses are depicted, that the novelist may be using them to show us an aspect of Indian life which is real if not desirable—the existence of the brown sahib and memsahib. It is less easy to approach the tea-party in a similar manner:

> The tea party was of course a mistake and Bim scowled and cursed herself for having softened and let herself in for what was a humiliation and a disaster for everyone concerned.
>
> Had Mrs. Biswas dressed for it ? Bim had never seen anyone so dressed. So bathed, so powdered. She seemed to be dusted all over with flour. Perhaps she had fallen into a flour bin, like a large bun. But she smelt so powerfully of synthetic flowers, it must be powder after all. And her white sari crackled with starch, like a biscuit. And her hair gleamed with coconut oil, and flecks of gold glinted at the lobes of her ears and in the ringed folds of her neck. Altogether a piece of confectionery, thought Bim.
>
> She was given a platter with all the goodies already heaped on it—neatly counted out, so many biscuits, so many pieces of mithai, so many fritters and a spoonful of chutney. Similar plates with exactly the same number of goodies were handed to Dr. Biswas, one kept by her. They ate.
>
> A china cabinet against the wall watched them. It stood on four legs and housed little plaster figures from Germany—a miniature beer mug, Hansel and Gretel skipping in a meadow, a squirrel dressed in a daisy chain. There were Indian dolls, less travelled but more worn, tinsel garlands flaking off onto red organdie saris and gold turbans. There were clay toys in cane baskets—yellow bananas, green chillies. A parrot. A cow. A plastic baby. And they all stared at Bim munching her way through the goodies. Dr. Biswas stared at his brown shoes, so highly polished. He ate nothing.

Sniggers and loud laughter have been, in my experience, the commonest responses to this passage. One needs to examine these responses, to try to understand what provokes them. Essentially, what is being depicted is a middle-class drawing-room which is more representative of urban Indian than the Das household could ever be. Mrs. Biswas, powdered and bedecked with jewellery is likewise a "typical" middleclass Indian housewife. The plate of goodies, the china cabinet with its odd mixture of curios, its plastic baby and clay fruit, are similarly redolent of middle-class India. What moves us to laughter is the slight distortion in context which makes of all these images obvious objects of satire.

The tea-party is to prove decisively the incompatibility of Dr. Biswas and Bim as marriage-partners. Further, it will do so in a way which somehow discredits Dr. Biswas rather than Bim. As Bim scurries away she significantly notes "How much his mother's son he was . . . he had inherited her gift for loading the weight of his self-sacrifices onto others." It is with conscious design that Dr. Biswas and his mother are presented in an unattractive comical light and there is no evidence to support the stand that it is Bim alone who looks at them in this way. On the contrary, the novelist appears a firm ally, since our response is to the mother and son comedy rather than to any irony in the depiction of Bim's reactions.

A neo-colonial attitude is at work here,[4] a class-consciousness which is sufficiently present in the Indian Context to become recognisable as an upper middle-class characteristic. It is neo-colonial because it is a take-on, a caricature, of the old colonial stance which (a) was convinced of the superiority of its own life-style (b) mocked attempts by the natives to "ape" the manners of the masters. Such class-superiority is blatantly evident in urban India. It is unfortunate that Anita Desai herself is not always above a supercilious wrinkling of the nostrils when she is on such territory.

NOTES

1. In an interview with Sunil Sethi, Ramesh Srivastava refers to this interview in "Anita Desai at Work," *Perspectives on Anita Desai*, ed. Ramesh Srivastava (Vimal Prakashan, Ghaziabad, 1984).

2. *Ibid.*

3. *Ibid.*

4. I use the phrase "neo-colonial" in the absence of one which best approximates the stance taken.

Anita Desai's Search for Roots in *Baumgartner's Bombay*

SURESH C. SAXENA

Baumgartner's Bombay is Anita Desai's second successive novel where the spotlight is no more on the solitude and interior landscape of the sensitive women. This shift in her thematic content had its germs in *Clear Light of Day* and some stories included in *Games at Twilight*. Anita Desai changed the direction of her writing in *In Custody* when she viewed Deven's situation from a different angle. In a way it was inevitable because Desai had been "conscious of the need to write outside oneself, to be able to feel oneself into completely different personalities from one's own."[1] In her latest novel, she deftly telescopes different segments of time and places and in the process poses some disturbing questions about the world of exiles. *Baumgartner's Bombay* extends Desai's horizon of human concern. The novel is a significant milestone in the long journey of creative writing by one of India's foremost writers in English.

Baumgartner's Bombay makes a complete departure from her earlier writing. Here, Desai makes an attempt, rather tenuously, to explore her roots and family backgrounds. As she revealed in a recent interview, "All these years I've been searching for a way to return to that German part of my background. . . ."[2] The Indo-German aspect of Desai's background is the centerpiece of all her writings and no worthwhile study of her work can be made without taking notice of her parents's past and their influence on Desai's sensibility.

Anita Desai's father, Dhiren Mazumdar was an engineer. He met a German woman with a strange name Antionette Nime there and married her in the 1920s as the Nazi period was knocking at the doors of Germany. Anita Desai's mother "very dark, not in the least Teutonic" was brought up a Christian but Anita Desai now seriously thinks "about the possibility of her having had Jewish blood." And this possible Jewish 'connection' of Anita Desai gives *Baumgartner's Bombay* a cutting edge and thrust.

The seeds of this chilly novel had been lying at the back of her mind since the time she was in Bombay. She knew an Austrian Jew there who "used to walk around in the back streets looking for scraps to feed his cats."[3] He was not as poor as he appeared to be. In fact, he was quite rich. In course of time, he died. A friend of Desai knew him. The friend handed Desai a bunch of letters in German left by the old man. She found nothing unusual in the letters except the stamp number on each of them. The letters came from the Nazi regime in Germany and were the muted testimony of the Nazi concentration Camps and signified the utter depravity of the period. The blank spaces in letters told a story of their own. And "because they had been so empty, they teased my mind; I had to supply the missing history to them." So much was in her mind when Desai finished *In Custody* in 1984 and was toying with an idea to start her next project. While going for a stroll in her favourite Lodi Gardens, the title of the novel came to her mind. Like a magic word, it brought everything to life again. "Like seeds that had been buried deep in the soil and stirred to life on feeling a shower of rain and the coming of the right season,"[4] the memories of the Austrian Jew in Bombay "became living experience once again." Desai imparted the missing history to the empty letters of the Jew and *Baumgartner's Bombay* began to take shape as a living entity. Desai's work was made somewhat easier as she went down the memory lane and her mother's "experience of India from the late 1920s onwards and her memories of pre-war Germany she'd talked a lot about, and the memories of her German friends who'd actually been in internment camps during the war,"[5] served an important purpose. In 1986, Anita Desai had moved to England and by that time *Baumgartner's Bombay* was already in rough draft. "It was a perfect book to work on in England since it allowed me to look on India from a distance, just like the Character does."[6] The novel took final shape in the early 1988 and has recently been released.

A good novelist creates a self-enclosed world, "a totalized fiction" where the novelist is the master of the show. He uses a strange amalgam of memories, experiences, instinct and imagination to make his work a living experience. In *Baumgartner's Bombay*, Anita Desai paints a wide canvas of different segments of time-past and present. The past is projected through a prism of vivid memories. She deals peripherally with reality in the novel by juggling events and places. A streak of ever present violence and cruelty provides a poignant touch to the narrative. Anita Desai's focus is on Baumgartner but at the same time she penetrates the dark areas enveloping her protagonist and comes out with a truth which is artistic and psychological at the same time.

The scenario changes in the novel frequently but the focus is on the problems and predicament of Baumgartner all the time. He is always the prototype outsider on the run through milieu changes around him. "In Germany he had been dark—his darkness had marked him the Jew, 'der jude.' In India he was fair—and that marked him the 'firanghi.' In both lands, the unacceptable."[7]

The East-West interface is a recurring motif in Indo-Anglian fiction. In one of her novels, *Bye-Bye, Blackbird*, Desai, too, touched on this aspect though rather briefly. But in *Baumgartner's Bombay* she fuses the two strands in an artistic fashion. Her Indo-German parentage provides the novel a transparent sincerity. Desai's in-built Indo-European sensibility filtered through her parents, in fact, has "created for her a synthesis that is the base of all my work and that I didn't have to strive for, was not even conscious of ever but quite naturally inherited from them."[8] Baumgartner views India through Desai's mother's eyes, as an outsider. In fact, the entire narrative of the novel is structured on Anita Desai's tinted view of her mother's past, her memories, experiences and old associations. This meeting of the East and West is a tenuous affair and as a reviewer puts it: "Desai has penetrated that heart of darkness in which the two do unhappily meet."[9]

Baumgartner is the protagonist of this deeply disturbing novel. He closely resembles Job—the central personage in "The Book of Job." Like him, Baumgartner also suffers a lot with no fault of his own. He runs for refuge from nowhere to nowhere. His predicament is universal. Anita Desai has created a memorable character in Baumgartner. The life story of this German Jew follows a text book pattern of an ancient Greek classic with all its trappings of suffering through several vicissitudes in life.

Baumgartner's escape from the Nazi regime in Germany to India in search of a safe refuge leaves him bitter and frustrated. It was a jump from one hell into another. If in Germany, Hitler termed the Jews as 'Subhuman races," in India they were labelled 'hostile aliens.' In the traumatic war years, the Jews had not much to choose between Germany and India. If in Germany, Hitler made them the target of his reckless actions and imprisoned them in the concentration camps, in India, the situation was not much better either. Here, in a central internment camp, they "had to stand in a line and sing 'Deutschland, Deutschland uber alles' and as the German flag flew "the order rang out: Raise your right arm, say 'Heil Hitler !" The locales were different but the humiliation heaped on the Jews was identical.

Baumgartner's arrival in Calcutta of pre-war years unveils the other face of this metropolis. Anita Desai is superb in sketching an environment. The Calcutta she profiles in the novel may not be "the most wicked place in universe" as Robert Clive called it, but it is also not the 'city of joy' as Lapierre would like us to believe. In Baumgartner's Calcutta there are the Marwari businessmen who are awash with money. There are also glittering hotels where cabaret goes on and the dancers with exotic names, display their flesh. It is the frivolous city of bars, restaurants, racehorses, cabaret dancers and "the black, back streets" of downtown. As the dark clouds of war gather in the horizon, Baumgartner passes through the painful ordeal of being a Jew in an alien territory with the Nazis and British guards collaborating to harass and humiliate the 'hostile aliens'.

As the communal cauldron simmers, Calcutta becomes, to quote the poet Rudyard Kipling "City of dreadful night." It witnesses a flurry or riots with the criminals dominating the scene. If in *Clear Light of Day* Raja expressed his apprehensions by prophesying "there'll be more riots—killing—they'll slaughter every Muslim they can find—anywhere,"[10] in *Baumgartner's Bombay* it is the protagonist's friend, Habibullah who stoically comments, "Every night they set some Muslim house on fire, stab some Muslim in the street, rob him too. . . ." I have a sneaking suspicion that the bloody communal riots after Mrs. Gandhi's assassination in Delhi and other towns left a deep imprint on Anita Desai's sensitive mind and this is reflected in the graphic manner she creates the scene in a few crisp well-chosen words. The shadow lines of communal riots as sketched in the novel shift the novel to the contemporary scene where communalism in a new 'avtar' stalks the streets of towns in the country.

Baumgartner meets his nemesis in Bombay which to quote Anita Desai is an "abrasive city with its unrelieved ugliness, squalor and noise."[11] Anita Desai's portrayal of this phase of Baumgartner's existence is modelled on a real character, "a decrepit old man" who lived in the slum area of Bombay with his pet cats and looked for bits of left-over food in nearby eating places to feed cats. People in the neighbourhood mockingly called him 'Billewallah Pagal.' It is a poignant commentary on the degradation of human life and cruelty and callousness of the environment that a man caring for his pets is made a butt of silly jokes. Baumgartner's life comes to a full circle rather dramatically when he meets the German "a certain type that Baumgartner's had escaped, forgotten. Then why had this boy to come after him, in lederhorsen, in marching boots striding over the mountains to the sound of the wander-vogels lied ? The Lieder and the campfire. The campfire and the beer. The beer and the yodelling. The yodelling and the marching. The marching and the shooting. The shooting and the killing. The killing and the killing and the killing."

In *Baumgartner's Bombay* Anita Desai profiles a city which is nauseating with its squalor, violence and oppressiveness. In her last novel *In Custody,* too, Desai prominently projected the oppressiveness of the city scene. It is of some significance that a perceptible change is gradually emerging in her writing lately. It has something to do with the overall change in the milieu around her protagonists. In *In Custody,* Delhi's gloomy and disgusting environment matched perfectly with the interior landscape of Desai. In *Baumgartner's Bombay* Desai looks at the city from her protagonist's angle. Anita Desai asserts that the disgustive picture of Bombay she has presented in the novel is without any motive. She "was just trying to create Baumgartner's experience of Bombay, which wasn't the glittering side."[12] Anita Desai's last two novels have a darker edge though "it's unintentional" and beyond her control. Last six years or so, during which Desai's two novels have been written, have witnessed a lot of upheaval in the social, cultural and political realms. There is a lot of change in the people's attitudes and social mores and the environment reeks of violence and cruelty. A writer lives in society and can't remain immune to the changes taking place around him. In this fast-changing disturbing environment, it is not surprising that Anita Desai is haunted by an 'Indian guilt.' She is appalled at the rising graph of cruelty and violence in the country and doesn't think she "could again write a romantic or gentle book about India."[13]

Baumgartner's Bombay marks a turning point in Anita Desai's growth as a novelist. There is a perceptible change of direction as far as thematic aspect of her fiction is concerned. Desai's early novels from *Cry, the Peacock* to *Clear Light of Day* "seem to be rooted in that world of childhood, old Delhi, of pre-independent India which was very quiet and sober and regular."[14] Now, she is "beginning to experience India in a different way as the comparatively tranquil, protective, supportive world of childhood is beginning to fall away, really crumble away . . . ."[15] It appears Desai has emerged out of her cocooned existence with this novel. And it is of some significance that in her last two books Desai's protagonists are men.

Baumgartner's Bombay is a cruel book laced with her fine prose and keen observation of objects around her. "That was the evening when the breeze came up with the tide, and the sun fell headlong into the waves . . . and people strolled . . . one was not conscious if one loitered too." [16] Anita Desai is superb in evoking sharp images which go deep in the mind and provide a visual intensity to her writing. In *Baumgartner's Bombay*, she describes the coming of the Jews into the camp like "ants from a closed fist into a bowl of dust, and swarmed there in . . . frenzy."[17]

Anita Desai's latest novel raises some pertinent and pointed questions regarding the status of an exile in a different milieu. Baumgartner's struggle for survival and the formidable forces operating around him provide this novel a deeper meaning. The novel may not be having depth, dimensions and complexity of E.M. Forster's celebrated *A Passage to India.* But for its sweep and appeal and feel of the exile and his milieu, *Baumgartner's Bombay* may easily be handpicked as the best novel written recently in Indo-Anglian literature.

Dr. Meenakshi Mukherjee in a review of Anita Desai's *In Custody* perceived a thematic shift in her writing. According to her the change was "towards a widening out of human concerns and a willingness to integrate concrete historical and specific cultural dimensions in the creation of interior landscapes."[18] Anita Desai's latest novel confirms this anatomy of her writing. In *Baumgartner's Bombay*, Anita Desai extends her milieu. The novel, according to her, has "too many shortcomings" and is a sketch "not really the full history of a man, not a full portrait." This brilliant but rather chilly novel may simply be a silhouette of a man at a particular moment in history but it is a tell-tale commentary on the times we live in. The persecution of the Jews and people's attitude towards them in the Nazi period could well apply to the minority communities in India, the Tamils in Sri Lanka, the Arabs in Israel and the Jews in Lebanon or may be even the Blacks in America. As Anita Desai pointed out to Andrew Robinson, "There's just as much violence and cruelty going on in India. Baumgartner had left Germany and gone far away but never really left crime and violence." F. Scott Fitzgerald once said, "Begin with an individual, and before you know it you have created a type." In her novel Anita Desai starts with Baumgartner and before we know it 'Billewallah Pagal' becomes a part of our psyche, our consciousness. Herein lies the true significance and achievement of Anita Desai's art as a novelist.

NOTES

1. Ketaki Sheth's interview with Anita Desai, *Imprint*, June 84.

2. Andrew Robinson's interview with Anita Desai, *The Saturday Statesman*, August 13, 1988.

3. *Ibid.*

4. "Flight of Forms" by Anita Desai, *India International Centre Quarterly*, Vol. 10, Number 4, 1983.

5. Andrew Robinson's interview with Anita Desai.

6. *Ibid.*

7. *Baumgartner's Bombay* by Anita Desai (Heinemann, London).

8. Andrew Robinson's interview with Anita Desai.

9. *Baumgartner's Bombay* by Anita Desai: A Review by Madhu Jain, *India Today*, August 15, 1988.

10. *Clear Light of Day* by Anita Desai (Allied Publishers, 1980), pp. 93-94.

11. *"Flight of Forms"*

12. Andrew Robinson's interview with Anita Desai.

13. *Ibid.*

14. *Ibid.*

15. *Ibid.*

16. *Baumgartner's Bombay*

17. *Ibid.*

18. *In Custody* by Anita Desai: A review by Meenakshi Mukherjee, *Express Magazine*, October 7, 1984.

19. Andrew Robinson's interview with Anita Desai.

20. *Ibid.*

Rama Mehta's *Inside the Haveli:* The Winds of Change

SARALA BARNABAS

Capturing an era which is fast-vanishing, if not already gone, is a novel to which regrettably little scholarly attention has been given. Yet this recipient of the Sahitya Akademi award (1979) presents an intimate picture of a system which existed since feudal times and is a revelation of attitudes towards women and their status in a certain section of Indian society. As such it makes a fascinating study. As a presentation of life behind purdah in Udaipur, it focuses particular attention on Geeta, the young modern educated girl whose marriage is arranged to the scion of one of the most orthodox families of Udaipur and what happens to her in the haveli, as well as the metamorphosis brought to it by her advent.

In *Inside the Haveli*, the role of women is sharply defined. Faces veiled at all times, seldom leaving the haveli, and then only under escort, subject to the unwritten but rigid rule that young daugthers-in-law must be docile and obedient, silent unless spoken to, they are never expected to voice an opinion, and must unquestioningly follow every instruction of the older women, particularly the mother-in-law, and even privileged senior maids. "Within the Haveli, all is traditon-bound, and while this means strength and security, it also means isolation and stagnation," Srinivasa Iyengar observes.[1]

The novel covers a period of fifteen years, the three sections spanning five years each, starting in the closing years of Sangram Singhji's lifetime, continuing into Bhagwat Singhji's and concluding with Ajay Singh becoming the new head of the family. Before embarking on a closer examination of *Inside the Haveli*, perhaps it would be in order to pause a little at this point to refer briefly to the findings of Mrs. Mehta's research into the life of a community in which the system of purdah was an integral part. With such a background, the novel becomes more meaningful, besides throwing light on the inspiration behind its writing.

As a sociologist, Rama Mehta published *The Western Educated Hindu Woman* and *The Hindu Divorced Woman*. During the International

Women's Year, under the auspices of the Nehru Memorial Museum and Library, a volume *Indian Women: From Purdah to Modernity* (1976) was published which includes an article by Rama Mehta entitled "From Purdah to Modernity."[2] The article presents an in-depth study of the Oswal community of the former state of Mewar. Twenty-five families and their way of life were studied, with special emphasis on women of the community, and how their position was determined by the social environment.

Tracing the history of the Oswals of Mewar (Udaipur), Mrs. Mehta reveals that they were hardly touched by the liberal or modern influences which prevailed in the rest of India during pre-Independence days. The court of the Maharana set the pace which had been followed since Mughal times. The strict restrictions placed upon women were imposed by both governmental and social norms. For example, upper and middle class women could go out only in curtained vehicles or covered by a large sheet. The men too had to cover their heads on the streets and wear the prescribed *achkans* over their *dhotis* or *churidar pyjamas*. By accepting such tradition-bound etiquette, it being almost obligatory to follow the example set by the court, the Oswals were assured of protection and economic security from the "Durbar." Because of its economic means, the State of Mewar supplied employment to its subjects. The Oswal community could thus function for more than three centuries as an endogamous unit, formulating its own patterns and practices of domestic ethics. One such practice was that of strict purdah within the havelis.

From the age of seven, little girls were conditioned to playing within the *zananah*. As they grew, they absorbed the training which would befit them for carrying out duties and obligations in the future. Even amongst the women the lines were rigidly drawn. Faces must be covered in front of the elder women of the family and community. In the family hierarchy, the mother-in-law occupied the highest position, the daughter-in-law the lowest. The latter could speak to the former only through the daughters of the house or the maid servants, although after about seven years the practice was eroded. Mrs. Mehta cites the instance of some women in the 65-80 year bracket from whom she learnt that though they had lived in the same house for two or three decades, they had not seen the faces of their sons's wives. The daughter-in-law was expected to show courtesy to the old maid servants in her husband's family, even touching their feet. The Oswal woman might be ignorant of the metaphysics of Hinduism, but her whole life revolved around the discharge of the sacred family rituals in which she had implicit faith. A widow's position was pathetic. Head shorn, minus all jewellery, she had to sit confined in a room for a year to receive condolences. If she had ruled the house, she now became a shadow, all authority removed from her hands.

Warning against outright condemnation of the customs described above, Mrs. Mehta points out that the historical perspective needs to be examined carefully. The need for economic stability as well as the socio-economic conditions of feudal Udaipur were responsible for their evolution. Dissent could have had catastrophic repercussions. The Udaipur Oswals were isolated from Oswals elsewhere in India. If at all a marriage was arranged with a girl from outside, it was considered second best. The girl had no alternative but to become an integral part of the haveli.

After 1948, when the State of Mewar merged with the Union of India, the Maharana's power being eclipsed, a restructuring of an age-old way of life was indicated for the community. Young sons needed to opt for higher studies, to leave ancestral homes and seek employment. The haveli too very slowly but inexorably felt the change. Girls were sent to school and eventually, larger and larger numbers were sent to college, a dramatic break from the historic past.

No world-shaking events are recorded in *Inside the Haveli* (1977), published a year after Mrs. Mehta's in-depth study appeared. The novel contains no intricate plot, no deep character study, nor does it have as its background a canvas of epic proportions. Indeed the story revolves around a very small isolated world—that of a haveli in Udaipur in which dwells a single family, that of the highly-respected Sangram Singhji, oldest living descendant of an ancient and noble lineage. Yet small though it is in comparative terms, the haveli encompasses a microcosm of traditional values, customs and a way of life that have existed for many centuries. That Rama Mehta writes from personal and first-hand knowledge becomes clear from the dedication which reads: "To Mohan Kaka and Bhabhi, who gave me of their affections, and made for me a home in Udaipur."[3]

Inside the Haveli retains the impression that it is a fictional work written by a sociologist. At times, the effect is that of a documentary, particularly the first chapter of Section I where it outlines a colourful historical panorama of Udaipur as it was in bygone days, and how it is today. "In the city wall there are four gateways to the city. These gates are huge with metal spikes on each panel. In the days when the kings of Udaipur were ever ready to meet the invading armies of the Mughal rulers they were shut during the night. Now there is no danger, so they are never shut. All traffic flows through them in and out of the city." (p. 1) Underlying this highly evocative description is a distinct feeling of nostalgia as well as of lingering regret for what has gone forever: "The white granite place in which the Ranas held court for four hundred years stands on the crest of a ridge that overlooks Lake Pichola . . . the people . . . looked at the lights and heard the grunts of elephants and were content. Their king the Rana was there to look after them. It was only twenty-five years ago that the palace lights were dimmed and the flag of Mewar came down. . . . But the people in the Old City remember the days when everything was bright and gay, when the Rana sat on his throne and received his people, rich and poor alike. No one in the city can forget those days when Udaipur belonged to the people." (p. 2)

Newcomers to the town, puzzled by the havelis, find it impossible to see what is hidden behind the walls. Like so many others, Sangram Singhji's haveli is placed in a gully. When it was built three hundred years ago, it only had a courtyard and three rooms but "like a banyan tree, once it had taken root it spread." (p. 3) Haphazard in structure, having been expanded without any plan, the strong three-storeyed building cannot be shaken by the hot winds of summer or the monsoon rains. Inside, since the days when women began to observe purdah, the quarters for men and women are completely separate.

The story proper begins one stormy night. Two births are imminent. One young girl in the throes of childbirth is the maid Laxmi, wife of Gangaram, one of the men servants. The other is Geeta, granddaughter-in-law of Sangram Singhji, wife of Ajay Singh. It is here that the novelist introduces the first hint about the attitude towards women in the reaction to the arrival of Laxmi's child. Gangaram sighs after the birth. He knows it is a girl because the midwife, Sarju, has not braved the rain and thunder to shout, "It is a boy; it is a boy. Give me money." (p. 5) Khyali, an older maid, tries to comfort him, "God takes care of all those He sends into the world. Girls are a burden, I admit, but what can one do once they are born. So far I have been lucky. But who can tell of the future ?" (p. 5) Of the young mistress, Gangaram says bitterly, "Of course, she will get a boy. The rich always get what they want; it is the poor who have all the bad luck." (p. 5) However, the young mistress has a daughter.

The news is brought by Pari who has served the family for forty-five years, and therefore is specially privileged as the senior-most maid. She pauses a moment to commiserate over Laxmi. The birth of a daughter is no cause for rejoicing. "The poor girl must already be worrying about the dowry which will have to be given, especially if the child looks like the father." (p. 6) Sitting down for a brief rest, Pari thinks of the infant she has just left. "So what if it is a girl ? After all it is the first time in sixty years that there are four generations under the roof of the haveli. This birth must be celebrated as if a boy had been born to the family." (p. 7) Upstairs, the exhausted young mother drops off to sleep amidst the chatter of the maids.

Coming to the haveli as a young bride, Geeta has had to face innumerable problems. Growing up in Bombay, in the atmosphere of that metropolis, she had developed a lively spontaneous nature. Her parents had always encouraged her to speak her mind, not to hold back in giving affection or to conceal her feelings. The thought that marriage meant going to different surroundings had not alarmed her. She was quite sure that with love, anyone could be won over. Much of that youthful exuberance has gone after two years at Jeewan Niwas, though with her younger in-laws, she still talks frankly. But she has learnt that in "the haveli no one really expressed their feelings. They covered their emotions in an elaborate exchange of formal gestures and words. Even her husband talked to his parents as if they were dignitaries with whom he could take no liberties. . . . In the two years Geeta had never heard any really unpleasant exchange of words between different members of the family." (p. 28) Even when greatly disliked relatives come to the haveli, her mother-in-law, Kanwarani Sa, greets them as if overjoyed. Every word must be weighed before utterance. Even a reprimand to a servant must be couched in polite if cutting words. Geeta finds it stifling to endure such an elaborate deliberate curbing of one's natural feelings.

Kanwarani Sa is a tiny lady with a deceptively fragile appearance. She holds herself erect, has a firm thin-lipped mouth. For all her size, she "walked with indescribable self-confidence and exuded strength and dignity as if she were naturally born to command." (p. 26) Over her nineteen year-old daughter-in-law, she establishes firm control. "She had her own way of prevailing over others, a blend of craft and tenacity." (p. 27) Contradicting her, or even expressing a different point of view is almost impossible. In preparation for the celebration of the birth of Geeta's daughter, Vijay, Kanwarani issues gentle but firm instructions: "Binniji, keep your face covered; by now you should be able to move around without uncovering your face. Do not talk too much to your young cousins-in-law, it's not becoming. You know, the women are critical because you are still clumsy. I want to show them that even an educated girl can be moulded. That I was not wrong in selecting you as the wife of my only son." (p. 26) Thus does the lady try to re-fashion the young girl into a model daughter-in-law. Geeta is overcome with bitter humiliation. Even after two years, there are fears that she might bring shame to the family by a wrong word or deed.

Geeta's parents had worried about her furture-in-laws. Their daughter was leaving behind a way of life in which men and women mingled freely. At college, she had studied with boys. But in Udaipur, upper class women were still in purdah. How would Geeta adjust to such a restricted atmosphere, they asked themselves. The thought of Ajay brought some comfort. Rare for the scion of such an aristocratic family, he was highly educated and a Science professor. To the disappointment of his parents, he had rejected some more prestigious careers. Geeta hardly had time to take a good look at him when he came to her home with a group of her brother's friends. Asked by her parents if she had liked the man in the grey suit, she had said, "Yes." Ajay belonged to a new forward-looking generation, the parents thought, and he would accept Geeta as she was. Still, Geeta's mother gave her advice: "Keep your head covered; never argue with your elders; respect your mother-in-law and do as she tells you. Don't talk too much." (p. 14) The mother had not mentioned purdah. Perhaps she had not guessed her daughter would be subjected to it at Jeewan Niwas.

Geeta's ordeal begins upon arrival at Udaipur railway station. Extremely homesick, married to a man she hardly knows, she is at once surrounded by a singing group of women with faces covered. Her bewilderment and fright grow when one of the women pulls her sari over her face, and says horrified, "Where do you come from that you show your face to the world ?" (p. 14) On the way, in the tightly packed car, surrounded only by women, Pari points out various sights to the bride, but when Geeta lifts her sari aside to look, Pari pulls it back and snaps, "No, no, you cannot do that. In Udaipur we keep purdah. Strange eyes must not see your beautiful face." (p. 15) As she alights, inquisitive women crowd around her, trying to peep at her face. Their opinion of her looks differs from Pari's: "She has good strong features but she is dark. Let us see how she adjusts. After all she is educated and on top of that she is not from Udaipur. What a risk to get an outsider, especially when there is only one son." (p. 15) Geeta is awkward as she bends to touch the feet of what seem to her a hundred women's feet. Even here she comes in for criticism. "Look at her," the older women say disapprovingly, "she does not even know how to touch the feet properly." (p. 16)

Geeta learns quickly about the way of life in a haveli. It is a woman's world she lives in. The maids are constantly around her wherever she is. They chatter continuously as they work or simply sit on the floor between tasks. They gossip freely, making frank personal observations, all of them very much a part of the family. Dhapu is the maid specially assigned to Geeta who, in the first months of marriage, suffers from a terrible loneliness, without a single friend, no woman of her intellectual level to talk to, and certainly none she can trust. Only Dhapu is her close advisor. But the other maids are frequently in the bedroom. There is little privacy possible. Everyone knows what goes on in these confined quarters. "There are no secrets; there could be none in the haveli. It is one household, all the courtyards are connected." (p. 4) The only men she meets are Ajay and the few men servants. She must touch the feet of Sangram Singhji and Bhagwat Singhji, keep her face completely covered, and never venture to utter one word.

The one bright spot in her life is the presence of Ajay, whom she calls by name, a fact which, if it became known, would bring down upon her head the strongest condemnation and censure. Although she does not meet him during the day time, their three-room apartment in the women's section is a comparatively private place. Here Ajay has a desk where he reads. There are book shelves lining the walls of the sitting room. Geeta has hung paintings and the rooms are comfortable and cheerful. She has every cause to be grateful that Ajay is an educated man to whom she can express her views fully. Having no opportunity to go out and buy books for herself, Ajay purchases them for her. Even this becomes known and the maids speak to her about extravagance, echoing, as Geeta knows very well, her mother-in-law's sentiments. Nor is her buying of old statues and brass objects from dealers who come to the haveli appreciated.

Ajay realizes how difficult it is for his wife to live at Jeewan Niwas, and that she is not meant for purdah. Geeta reminds him of his assurance that they would be here only for a short time, and almost three years have passed. Although she says it is his career she is thinking about, Ajay is not deceived. He is quite happy at the University and likes both his subject and students, he tells her, but he has not given up the idea of going to Delhi University some day. At present he cannot leave, with his father growing old and needing him. Geeta can no longer conceal her anger, "I know the men have no problems in this world of Udaipur; you are all pampered. You lead your lives and think women are mere chattels. In fact, I don't even see any point in being here. I may as well go and stay with my parents. You won't miss me; there are hundreds of people to take care of you." (p. 45) Ajay does not deny that the men are spoilt "but surely, you know how important you are to me. Do you know, Geeta, I could never have been content in Udaipur had you not adjusted to the ways of the haveli. I would then have really run away from here." In a controlled voice, he adds, "I am really proud of you, but that's little consolation to you." (p. 45) In Geeta's heart a dream dies. She knows now how deep are Ajay's roots here, and how impossible it is for him to go when his father needs him. In a strange way, she is also relieved that the uncertainty is over, that she must accept the haveli as a permanent part of her life.

For Ajay, after his marriage, the familiar haveli has become oppressive. Geeta is not merely a wife, but an intelligent well-informed companion. Together they discuss many topics not related to Udaipur. Ajay has to maintain certain forms of behaviour. The men can enter the women's apartments when they wish, but it is not generally done. Soon after they were married, knowing Geeta yearned to know what was happening beyond these walls, Ajay would find a pretext to go upstairs, but the visits were brief and hurried for the "maids laughed as if they understood why he came so often to the women's apartments." (p. 18) So now after bathing and dressing, Ajay went to his own section to study and receive friends.

Rama Mehta stresses the fact that as a Bombayite, Geeta is regarded as an outsider. Worse, as an educated girl, she is considered a liability. Choosing her as a bride for Bhagwat Singhji's heir was a matter for commiseration, not congratulation, and for criticism. Kanwarani and the maids constantly try to "mould" her into the set pattern of a model daughter-in-law. Although outwardly Geeta is docile and obedient, at heart she is still the product of a liberal upbringing. Behind her veil, she can think her own thoughts, see but not be seen. Injustices rankle within her, but she must remain silent. When she takes a stand for the first time, she precipitates a crisis for the haveli is resistant to any change.

The little girl, Sita, has been abandoned in infancy by her mother, Laxmi, who left the haveli, incensed over the accusation that she was being unfaithful to Gangaram because one of the other men servants gave her small gifts. The child is raised by the maids, and becomes the special friend of Geeta's daughter, Vijay, who was born on the same night. Vijay starts going to school. One morning she says, "Come to school with me, Sita. It would be such fun if you too went to school at least with me to the car." (p. 77) Dhapu scolds her sharply and drags Sita away. Such a thought is too ridiculous even to contemplate. But Geeta who has heard this exchange observes to Pari that if Vijay can go to school, the other little girl should too. Pari is horrified at the very idea. She speaks bluntly: "Vijay Bai Sa, God bless her, is the daughter of this haveli. How dare anyone point a finger at her. She has the protection of wealth and family. What does Sita have ? She must be protected from the outside world. Binniji, you do not yet know Udaipur and its customs. Sita has to marry. Leave her to us, the servants. We know what is best for her." (p. 79) Geeta is furiously angry and upset until Dhapu suggests a plan: "Binniji, your father-in-law is a big man with a big heart. Suggest it to him. he is afraid of no one. You are fortunate that Kanwarani Sa is not here." (p. 81) When Bhagwat Singhji is eating his meal, Dhapu sits in the doorway, Geeta in the adjoining room. Dhapu says in a supplicating voice, "Hukkum, Binniji wants to ask your advice." (p. 83) She then broaches the matter of Sita's schooling as Pari sits woodenly. Bhagwant Singhji ponders for a moment. Then he speaks: "Education is a good thing. I know it is not the custom in Udaipur to send girls to school. People are afraid of marrying educated girls. But times are changing, Pari." He gives Pari an intent look. "After all, it is better to be in school than play in the streets." But he adds, "We must think this out carefully. It is an important decision to take. We must not do anything in haste. Sita is our responsibility." (p. 84)

One person gives her whole hearted approval to the plan. She is a woman in her sixties, a cousin of Bhagwat Singhji, Manji Bua Sa, dignified with a beautiful, still smooth and unlined face. She is known for her tenderness and compassion. She draws Geeta to the terrace where they can speak privately. Manji was widowed at fourteen, she tells Geeta, but fortunately she had wonderful in-laws. She took great pleasure in bringing up the two children of her brother-in-law who was a widower. But as a young girl it hurt her when she was forbidden to wear coloured saris and jewellery like other women, or not allowed to attend festivities and religious occasions because the presence of a widow was considered inauspicious. "But later on I understood. No one was to blame for that, it was the custom in Udaipur. It was my fate to be a widow . . . I had to learn to accept that. All of us have to pay for our past actions. Who knows what sins I must have committed to have lost my husband." The children she brought up would be leaving some day and then time would hang heavily on her hands."If I could read and write, I would not feel so lonely. . . . No, you must send Sita to school, even if it means a little inconvenience to you." (p. 95) The final outcome of this incident is that Sita begins school. Bhagwat Singhji has given his approval. No one dares to challenge it. Ajay, returning from Delhi, tells his wife he is proud of her. New ideas are long overdue in the haveli. "I am now back and will support you in every way possible. . . . My mother's generation will die and with it the traditional way of life and purdah too." (p. 112)

Geeta is not reprimanded by her mother-in-law over this incident. Lately, Kanwarani admits how much her daughter-in-law has tried to conform, "I should be grateful. An educated girl like her could so easily have been a total misfit here. What could we have done, Pari, if she were insolent, or worse, indifferent. No, she has never raised her voice to me, and in her own way she is proud of the haveli." (p. 118)

It is not Geeta's intention to create problems yet unwittingly, in her concern for the unlettered children and women around her, a second, more serious crisis occurs. A small orphan boy comes to live with his uncle Gokul, one of the men servants. Geeta notices him and learns that before his mother died she had promised to send him to school. Her heart touched by his sad vacant eyes, Geeta begins to teach him how to read and write. Other children come with him to listen to stories and practise the alphabet. "News of the classes spread like monsoon floods and the young maids from the havelis came and joined the children." (p. 130) Soon, they are able to recognize and understand words. They express a desire to go faster. In her turn, talking after classes with the women, Geeta acquires a deeper understanding of poverty. To her, the challenge of keeping alive their interest and enthusiasm in their lessons is something to look forward to. Even the older maids who joke about the haveli being turned into a school, find excuses to come upstairs, one with potatoes for peeling, another with her sewing.

The mistress takes a tolerant view. "Let Binniji amuse herself. Her enthusiasm won't last long; she will soon get tired of the women. Then let us see what she starts next." (p. 131) A group of women visit her to complain about the ill effects of the classes. In one case, a husband is incensed because he has to eat cold *rotis* left for him while his wife is here listening to stories; in another, a young girl's engagement is broken off because "who wants a girl who is already defiant ? Now her poor mother weeps; she should have locked up the girl and starved her rather than allow her to join these classes." (pp. 131-132) Another woman warns that soon all the men will desert their wives and this haveli will have to shelter them. Kanwarani is not unduly disturbed. She listens, but is quite certain that once the monsoon comes, the classes will stop. She says nothing to Geeta.

Three months later, far from stopping, the classes have become even more popular. Kanwarani is visited by her sister-in-law, Nandu Bua Sa, a thin stern looking woman whose face always wears an expression of chronic disapproval, accompanied by Manji. Without pausing for the usual courtesies, Nandu goes straight to the point. She has come to find out more about Binniji's classes. Kanwarani tries to be lighthearted about it. The children are occupied and no longer raid the fruit trees. So for a few hours each morning it is a blessing to have peace. Nandu tells her sharply, "There may be peace in your haveli, Hukkum, but there is confusion in ours." (p. 133) All the maids have been disappearing for the whole morning. Who is to do their work while they waste time listening to stories ? How will Pari feel if Ganga and the others disappear, leaving all the household tasks undone ? Even Manji who still approves of Sita's schooling agrees that the girls are simply using the excuse to shirk work. Maliciously, Nandu adds, "Kaki Sa, let me tell you also that all the havelis are criticising you. They may not say anything to you, but behind your back they are saying that Jeewan Niwas always tried to maintain the dignity of our way of life—now this very haveli is undermining our authority and making rebels out of our servants. Because you are rich and have many servants and your son is well placed is no reason why you should disrupt the havelis of the less fortunate ones." (p. 134)

Proud as she is, Kanwarani almost breaks down for the first time over such criticism at this juncture of her life. When her husband became the Prime Minister of Udaipur and the Maharana bestowed a title on him, thus honouring this haveli, no one thought of her as being arrogant, but now even her own relatives are accusing her of undermining the traditions and dignity of the havelis. Obviously it is time to for her to step aside. The maids and the visitors are greatly upset over the reaction of this proud woman. Even Nandu is ashamed of herself, but it is Geeta who is truly enraged. To her Manji's attitude is that of a traitor. Most of all, she bitterly castigates herself for her own impetuous impulsive behaviour in starting the classes. The last thing she intended was to hurt her in-laws or to have them at the centre of unkind gossip.

She is astonished, gratified and touched to the heart by two points her mother-in-law makes sometime later. The first is that Binniji is not to let Nandu disturb her. The classes for the maids are not to be discontinued. Once Bhagwat Singhji has given his approval, she is not afraid of what the world will say. The second is that she knows Ajay Bapu has been offered a big job in Delhi. She knows he has not mentioned this to his father because he would rather sacrifice his happiness than give his parents a single moment of pain. Gravely she continues, "Binniji, listen to me. I want to tell you that Bapu should not think of us this time. We are old and our work in the world is over. But you both are young and the future is open to you. Bapu should not let an opportunity like this pass. I am a mother. I want to see my children happy and fulfilled. You alone can make him see this, you must not let him give up something that will bring him respect and satisfaction. There are times when you must not think of the haveli." (p. 140) Overwhelmed, Geeta puts her head in her mother-in-law's lap and sobs helplessly like a child.

Years pass and the family is faced with two vital decisions in which Geeta is once again deeply involved. The first is the marriage offer which comes for Sita. In fact, surprisingly, there are two offers, the better of which is a gratifyingly good one. Shivram's family won five acres with a well, two bullocks and a brick house. More than that Shivram is studying in the tenth class, the first boy in the village who has gone beyond primary school. For him, they want a girl who can read and write. Reassured by the cooks's information that Shivram's father is the headman of the village, that they have not asked one word about the dowry the haveli will give the bride, as well as by her meeting with the well-behaved courteous women of the party, Kanwarani is ready to accept the offer. Looking at Geeta fondly, she speaks humbly, "Binniji, you will be blessed. It is all your doing. I am glad you did not listen to us ignorant women. We could never have arranged a match like this for Sita." (p. 149) Geeta is embarrassed, but a moment later her ire is aroused by the one condition the would-be groom's family makes, that Sita should discontinue school at once. Years ago, Geeta would never have spoken up, but in her changed position, she demands to know what right they have over the girl even before marriage. Do they not realize once she has passed the tenth class, she will be capable of earning a hundred rupees a month ? Speaking as if to a child, Pari points out gently that sending a daughter-in-law to earn a wage should be an intolerable disgrace which even a poor family would not wish to face. To them, family customs would matter more than money. Sadly, Kanwarani agrees. Binniji proved them wrong and made Sita's life. Now there is no alternative but to yield to the condition.

The second decision is heralded by the totally unexpected visit of the women from Daulat Singhji's haveli, the most prestigious one in the city. The visit throws everyone into a flutter, no one being able even remotely to guess the reason for it. Indeed, Daulat Singhji, though head of the richest family in Udaipur, has had much cause to hate the household of Sangram Singhji. At one time the ministers of Udaipur had been chosen from the former's family, then the honour had gone to Sangram Singhji's father and passed on to the son and grandson. Therefore, an amazed Kanwarani listening to fulsome compliments about Jeewan Niwas couched in extravagant terms from the lips of Daulat Singhji's wife, an arrogant forbidding woman whom she has no cause to like, and how the names of Kanwar Sa and his forefathers were written in the annals of Rajasthan, is more than a little alarmed. Ultimately, the true cause for the visit is revealed. Vir Singh, her son, has just passed his B.A. with a first class and would soon be going abroad for higher studies. "Bai Sa, I have come today to ask you to give us Vijay Bai Sa. One day I want to hand her the keys of the haveli's safe; if I knew she were coming into our family, my happiness would be complete." (p. 162)

In former years, the acceptance or refusal of this offer would have rested entirely with Vijay's grandparents and father. It is a measure of Geeta's position in the household now that her outrage over the thought of her thirteen-year old daughter being given in marriage postpones the decision. Yet Geeta is disturbed by one undeniable fact. Had not her own mother been on the lookout for good marriages for herself and her sisters since they entered their teens? When they selected Ajay Singh, her parents hoped their judgment of him was right. She is further disturbed when on the return visit to the other haveli, Daulat Singhji's wife does not bring up the marriage issue at all, but the youthful Vir Singh comes in, ostensibly to ask Kanwarani's blessing. It is not possible to remain unimpressed by the tall handsome young man who, despite the awkwardness of youth, possesses dignity, and is extremely respectful and courteous. The encounter upsets Geeta. Even she cannot deny how fine he is.

From the beginning it has been made clear that in the haveli, males are looked upon as gods. Giving their blessing to younger women, the older ones will say, "May you have eight sons." Pari's words to Geeta when she touches her feet, "May you live in your husband's shadow for a hundred years" (p. 86) are not intended as a curse but as a heartfelt benediction. It would appear that Rama Mehta has no derogatory observations to make about the menfolk of the haveli. Indeed, she makes a point of emphasizing that it is not male chauvinism that imposes the restrictions on women, but they have come out of a system, and that it is the senior women who are the stern guardians of its traditions. Seen mostly through Geeta's eyes, the men at no time are shown to be overbearing or domineering in spite of the status they have enjoyed in the state, and the fact that in the haveli they are the undisputed masters around whom the entire household revolves. An almost worshipful reverence is accorded to them from all the women. In their presence the chattering of women and maids is stilled. When Bhagwat Singhji comes into the women's courtyard, for example, the maids bend low with folded hands and touch the ground at his feet. Geeta standing behind them does likewise. The most vital decisions are taken by the men who are looked upon as the fount of all wisdom and authority, though ones of lesser import are left to the mistress of the household.

For all that Geeta has had no direct conversation with her husband's grandfather and father, and has lived isolated from the men, with the exception of Ajay, much of her growing awareness of and a slow but unmistakable pride in the past is based on the outstanding qualities of these descendants of Rajput nobles who had brought great honour and glory to the history of Rajasthan. Unknown to the men both long-gone and living, they are responsible for much of the change in Geeta's attitude towards Udaipur and the haveli itself. In early days of her marriage, in her great curiosity she had stolen to the men's section, strictly out of bounds for women. Later of course, Pari scolded her soundly, and told her that daughters-in-law of the haveli did not behave like this. Still Geeta had managed to study the portraits of Ajay's ancestors lining the walls of the audience hall. In richly jewelled attire, with strong determined faces, they looked out of the frames, evoking in Geeta the proud feeling that men like these had won battles against the Mughals. Another time, Dhapu had smuggled her up a narrow flight of stairs. Peering through a lattice window at the quietly dignified elegant guests in silk brocade coats and turbans, she saw Sangram Singhji, frail but erect on a mattress, clearly a man of strength and determination. "Geeta stared at the scene below as if hypnotized. Even though Udaipur was no longer a feudal state the traditions of Mewar seemed safe in the hands of these stern looking men, all of whom seemed so composed, so determined and so refined. A glow of pride and affection filled Geeta. These were good people, gentle, kind and chivalrous. Looking at the men below she forgot her daily irritations; she felt proud to be the young mistress of the haveli. How could she allow little discomforts to blind her to the great traditions of the family ?" (pp. 34-35)

It is Bhagwat Singhji who always stands out in splendour. Once the Prime Minister of Udaipur, he stands tall and erect. "There was a natural simple elegance in the man that commanded respect. A wonderful calm seemed to radiate from his reserved personality. In his presence people were subdued. There was an aloof reticence in his bearing that did not permit frivolity." (p. 82) This is the man whom his dying mother called an ideal son and over whose generosity the shopkeepers said he was a noble son of a noble father. More than once Geeta has cause to feel profound admiration and appreciation for him. With the passing of years she can talk directly with him and 'the more she saw him the more she admired him. He saw more than the ordinary eye and felt more than the normal heart." (p. 143) Warmly encouraging over her efforts to help unlettered women, he has instructed his accountant to pay all expenses for the classes from his own accounts, even giving her two sewing machines for the use of those women who find it impossible to learn the alphabet. He defers to Geeta over the issue of Vijay's marriage for she has won his esteem and affection. Only in his final illness does he ask her to think again for it seems like an ideal match. Even so, if Geeta agrees to it, he will still want Vijay to continue her schooling. As a final act, typical of the large-heartedness of this great man, he tells his accountant to pay all the debts Gangaram incurred for Sita's wedding. Geeta is wonder-struck. "All of a sudden, she realized what real greatness meant. He was like a towering tree under which the family sheltered. It was from him that everyone got their nourishment. Now that the tree had fallen, the saplings growing up at its base were exposed. The haveli might never again be as strong. Something already seemed to be shaking its foundations." (p. 207) With the passing of Bhagwat Singhji, comes the greatest change for with tradition decreeing that Kanwarani must step aside, Geeta becomes the new mistress of the ancient haveli.

Inside the Haveli portrays the ebb and flow of life behind purdah. The central figure, Geeta, is introduced as a bride faced with the mind-jarring impact of having to undergo humiliation in this suffocating alien world where age-old traditions are inviolate. Whether bride, widow or maid, every woman is subject to them. But the vast world beyond the haveli walls is taking giant strides. Very gradually but surely some of this seeps in. Geeta is introduced to purdah, but in her turn, she introdces new concepts, bringing into the narrow isolated confines of the haveli the winds of change. Because of it, she faces censure from the older generation of women who are unable to comprehend the need for education and progress for women at all, and certainly not for the maids. In time, Geeta wins accolades from two of her sternest teacher-critics, Pari and Kanwarani. It is Pari who tells Bhagwat Singhji in deeply emotional, almost reverent tones that Binniji is spending hours each day teaching the poor children from the neighbourhood. Who else would do this for them, she asks, thereby causing that distinguished personage to leave the room in haste to hide the fact that he is greatly moved. For Kanwarani too it has been a slow progression in attitude towards her daughter-in-law. She has gone from dissatisfaction to acceptance, from tolerance to generosity, and finally to magnanimity.

But it is not the haveli alone which is transformed. Geeta herself has not remained untouched. In the beginning this way of life had "frightened and fascinated her at the same time." (p. 27) Once alienated, she had then been drawn to it, until now finally she has accepted it as a part of herself. She reaches a point when she says to herself, "I don't want to leave Udaipur now. The haveli has made me a willing prisoner within its walls. How stupid I was not to see all that it holds. Where else in the world would I get this kind of love and concern ? The children must grow up here. They must learn to love and respect this ancient house." (p. 137) Warmth floods her heart as she hears her little son, Vikram, gurgling with delight as Dhapu bathes him. "Where else in the world could children be enveloped in such affection ? This kind of devotion is almost superhuman. The servants go hungry if the children haven't eaten, they go without sleep if a child has a slight headache." (p. 137) Tradition which she rejected as an anachronism in this day and age becomes meaningful and precious to her. Through her exposure to the history of Rajasthan, and particularly to the annals of her husband's noble ancestors, she has come to realize that in the process of moving forward, one has to draw one's inspiration and strength for what has gone before, "feeling a pride in what is best in the family tradition and trying in other respects to make the Haveli community of relatives and dependants move with the times, making sure of each forward step,"[4] as Srinivasa Iyengar says. It will be upto Geeta to strike a delicate balance while guiding the haveli into the future without breaking the link with the past.

It becomes apparent from her novel that Mrs. Mehta in writing about a world she knows well, is deeply aware of the implications of life within the haveli. Although the drawbacks in the form of outright injustice and a terrible denial of the rights of a woman to have her own identity, are brought out into the open, she takes care to underline the feeling of security in this secluded world. In its timelessness there is continuity, a precious commodity for those born under the haveli roof. Yet through Geeta, the novelist makes it clear that the time has come to rid the haveli of some of its outworn practices, allow the outmoded concepts to die. Through Geeta she shows how this can be done.

NOTES

1. K.R. Srinivasa Iyengar, *Indian Writiing in English* (New Delhi: Sterling Publishers, 1984), p. 753.

2. Rama Mehta, "From Purdah to Modernity," *Indian Women: From Purdah to Modernity*, ed. B.R. Nanda (New Delhi: Vikas Publishing House, 1976), pp. 113-128.

3. Rama Mehta, *Inside the Haveli* (New Delhi: Arnold-Heinemann, 1981).

4. Iyengar, p. 754.